The Forgotten Castles of Wales

by
Paul R. Davis

Logaston Press

LOGASTON PRESS
Little Logaston Woonton Almeley
Herefordshire HR3 6QH
logastonpress.co.uk

First published by Logaston Press 20011
Copyright © Paul R. Davis 20011

All rights reserved. No part of this publication
may be reproduced, stored in a retrieval system,
or transmitted, in any form or by any means,
electronic, mechanical, photocopying, recording
or otherwise, without the prior permission,
in writing, of the publisher

ISBN 978 1 906663 55 1

Typeset by Logaston Press
and printed in Great Britain by
Berforts, Stevenage

Contents

Acknowledgements　　*vi*

Introduction　　1

North Wales
Castell Carndochan　　41
Castell Prysor　　43
Deganwy　　44
Dyserth　　45
Gerald's castles　　52
Holt　　54

West Wales
The fortified houses of Pembrokeshire　　59
Eastington　　64
Newhouse　　66

Mid Wales & the Marches
Aberedw　　71
Aberyscir　　74
Blaencamlais　　76
Blaenllynfi　　78
Castell Coch (Mellte)　　81
Castell Dinas　　82
Castell Du　　86
Castell Tinboeth　　88
Cefnllys　　90
Hen Gastell (Llangattock)　　93
Painscastle　　95
Pencelli　　97

Glamorgan
Castles of the Vale   101
Candleston   108
Dinas Powys   110
Kenfig   112
Landimôr   117
Llangynwyd   119
Morgraig   121
Morlais   125
Penlle'r Castell   132
Penrice   134
Plas Baglan   140
Sully   142

Monmouthshire
Castell Meredydd (Machen)   146
Castell Taliorum   149
Castell Troggy   151
Dinham   156
Llanfair Discoed   157
Llangybi   161
Pencoed   170

Appendix: Lesser Sites
Aberlleiniog   173
Cardigan   173
Hawarden   174
Hay-on-Wye   174
Knucklas   174
Llanddew   175
Newport   175
Nevern   175
Ruthin   176
Usk   176

Bibliography & References   177

Index   181

For Martin Davies and the good ship Barbary,
long may she sail

Acknowledgements

Many thanks are due to a number of people who have helped with the research for this book over the last two years and patiently answered my various queries, including the staff of the National Monument Record at RCAHMW (Aberystwyth), Will Davies (CADW), Neil Maylan (Glamorgan-Gwent Archaeological Trust), Neil Phillips (APAC), Rob Scourfield (Pembrokeshire Coast National Park) and in particular Rick Turner (CADW). Grateful appreciation goes to the various landowners up and down the country who allowed me access to survey their ancestral ruins, including David Addams-Williams and Liz Wheedon; and to those whose land I tramped across (inadvertently or otherwise) in the pursuit of knowledge, a retrospective thank you.

All the illustrations belong to the author, apart from the following for which permission to reproduce is gratefully acknowledged: for that on page 83, Logaston Press; for those on pages 88, 91 and 96 ,Crown Copyright: Royal Commission on the Ancient and Historical Monuments of Wales (RCAHMW); for that on page 97, The National Library of Wales.

Introduction

There is something in ancient ruins that fills the mind with contemplative melancholy ... they point out to us the striking proof of the vanity of those who think their works will last for ever.

From the 1744 edition of the complete works of
Samuel and Nathaniel Buck

Of all the ruined buildings and monuments of the past that lie scattered throughout this land, it is arguably the castle that provokes the most fascination. The thrill of crossing the drawbridge, exploring the dark dungeons and 'secret passages', climbing interminable winding stairs to the dizzying tops of the towers, recalls our childhood games and the memory of innumerable Hollywood films, as well as satisfying the most adventurous ego – to be 'king of the castle' holds a far greater attraction than exploring the contemplative environs of a ruined monastery. For centuries these imposing relics have drawn artists, writers, travellers, and inquisitive passers-by, while academics and archaeologists have sought to unravel their histories with pen and spade and preserve what remains of their shattered walls for posterity. Perhaps it is, as the above quote suggests, the inherent melancholy of fallen splendour that intrigues and attracts us. Would the castles have the same ambience if they were still intact and occupied, or had been rebuilt in make-believe splendour like many a continental chateau? Surely it is their very ruined state that makes them so interesting, half-hidden by creeping greenery, devoid of floors, roofs, windows, furniture, decorations and – most importantly – people, to make the buildings live and breathe. These stark walls and stony foundations dare us to imagine what they once looked like, to know the history behind the bare masonry, the fate of the people who built them and the purpose they served.

Wales has an astonishing legacy of castle sites. Five hundred is a conservative estimate, and of that figure some two hundred are major stone edifices whose longevity is a tribute to the skills of the original builders. The strongholds of Beaumaris, Carreg Cennen, Caernarfon, Harlech, Kidwelly and Pembroke (to name but a few) yearly draw thousands of visitors to marvel at their imposing structures and cunningly designed military features. These vast fortifications once symbolised the armed might of a brutal and oppressive class system, and from this safe and distant vantage point that aspect, too, may be part of their attraction. But what of the less well-known sites – the neglected and uncared-for ruins that have avoided wider notice for various reasons, and are located away from busy towns and villages, hidden from the public gaze? These are the 'forgotten' castles surveyed here.

An apology is perhaps warranted at this stage for the slightly misleading title of this book. None of the castles included here are really forgotten in the true sense of the word; they have not been obliterated from the face of the earth or wiped from all records and memory, and in almost all cases there is still something left to see. They are generally marked on Ordnance Survey maps and will have some documented history of varying degrees preserved in libraries and national archives. Furthermore, anyone with an interest in the history of their locality will surely be aware of them. This book explores the castles that have neither been resurrected as stately homes nor saved for the nation as visitor-friendly ruins complete with car parks, ticket offices and audio guides. These neglected strongholds are rarely visited and may not be fully accessible to the public, yet they have a story to tell about the turbulent history of this country and the often ruthless men who ruled it with a grip of iron. The castles range from minor strongholds like Aberedw, Morgraig and Plas Baglan, to relatively large fortresses such as Dinas Powys, Llangybi, Morlais and Penrice.

The definition of a castle will be looked at in greater detail below, but the term basically covers the fortified dwellings of the upper classes built between the end of the eleventh century and the end of the fifteenth century. Defensive sites from earlier eras and mock-military structures raised afterwards are often misleadingly termed 'castles', but are not included here. Nor too are the hundreds of earth and timber forts established in the immediate wake of the Norman invasion, even though the majority of these are truly forgotten and linger in overgrown obscurity. The castles examined here are their successors, the masonry buildings that have left more tangible remains in the landscape than grassy mounds and silted-up ditches. This book explores those forgotten fortresses, the reasons why they were built, the story of the people who ordered their construction, the architectural development of the buildings and the causes of their subsequent decay. Reconstruction drawings are used throughout to help the reader visualise the original appearance of these neglected castles, though any such illustration is bound to be a personal interpretation and very much a 'work in progress', subject to revision should any new features come to light in future excavations.

What is a castle?

A castle was in the nature of things a most important part of its lord's property, often his residence, or one of his residences, by its strength enabling him to hold his position in the world, to enforce his rights and perform his duties.
David Cathcart King (*Castellarium Anglicanum* 1983)

Thus one of the greatest students of medieval military architecture broadly summed up the definition of a castle. Fortified residences had been used on the continent from at least the ninth century, but the appearance and proliferation of the castle throughout the British countryside was a direct result of the invasion of Duke William of Normandy in 1066. The penultimate Anglo-Saxon king of England, Edward the Confessor, had allowed some Normans to set up camp during the closing years of his reign and it is possible that a few castles were built before that iconic date; but to all intents and purposes the castle was introduced here by the Conqueror and, along with the mounted knight, proved to be a major factor in the rapid subjugation of Anglo-Saxon England.

The castle primarily fulfilled the role of an aristocratic fortified residence, but it had other uses and functions and these changed as society itself changed during the course of the Middle Ages. Most of the first generation castles were short-lived forts solely designed to gain a foothold in an invaded land and to act as springboards for further advance. Behind the front line larger and more substantial castles would be built to provide security to the owners and their retinue, and also to protect settlements established in an effort to bring economic as well as military stability to a conquered territory. A purely military base rarely survived for long once the immediate threat had been subdued.

During outbreaks of unrest the castle was a fortress and refuge for the owner, his family and supporters, and a place where soldiers prepared for a siege or gathered for armed conflict in the field. In the longer spells of peace it was a residence and an administrative centre to run the surrounding estate, a place where rents were collected, courts were held and wrongdoers punished. The medieval aristocracy were highly mobile, travelling on horseback from one manor to another to consume locally produced goods *in situ*. A rich lord might own several castles, but he and his retinue could only be in one place at any given time, and so his other properties would be run by an appointed constable with a nominal garrison. When danger threatened, the call went out to the neighbouring vassals to perform their feudal duties and boost the size of the garrison.

But aside from all these practical functions, a castle had a very important symbolic purpose as well – it represented the power and domination of an invader in a conquered territory. By erecting a castle the invader was saying 'I'm here to stay' and therefore it was essential to capture that castle in order to oust the enemy and remove his symbol of lordship. Once taken, the castle might be retained and garrisoned by the victor or else destroyed to prevent its reuse by the opposition. Thus a long chain of taking and re-taking might begin, as fortresses changed hands through the vicissitudes of war.

The exact number of castle sites in the Principality has long been a matter of debate, and any definitive list is bedevilled by the inevitable categorisation into *probable, possible* or *uncertain* sites. Some earthworks which look like medieval castles may actually be Iron Age forts, prehistoric burial mounds, or even natural geographical features. Many late-medieval buildings have such vestigial defences that they can hardly be deemed castles at all, but must instead be classified as tower houses, fortified manors or strong houses, according to individual interpretation of their architectural features. Other sites have disappeared altogether so that the researcher is forced to rely on antiquarian accounts of sometimes doubtful veracity. Cathcart King wrote an amusing chapter in his magnum opus *Castellarium Anglicanum* detailing the many attempts to play the numbers game. His own total of existing sites in Wales was 427, but more recent studies have shown this to be an underestimate. For instance, King lists 67 in the county of Glamorgan, but a detailed survey subsequently carried out by the Royal Commission on Ancient and Historical Monuments in Wales has pushed this up to 81 extant sites (plus a further 19 vanished or possible castles, and an astonishing 71 rejected entries that were once thought to be castles but almost certainly are not!). Some internet sites suggest the total for Wales may be in excess of 700.

Why were castles needed?

> *To meet the danger the king rode to all the remote parts of his kingdom and fortified strategic sites against enemy attacks. For the fortifications called castles by the Normans were scarcely known in the English provinces.*
>
> Oderic Vitalis (1075-c.1142)

The Norman Conquest was an act of piracy on a colossal scale. William of Normandy had only a flimsy claim to the throne – Edward the Confessor had once promised him the crown and Harold Godwinson, the foremost magnate of the realm, had sworn allegiance to William whilst staying as his guest in Normandy. There was an equally tenuous link to Edward's bloodline. These vague promises and half-hearted oaths may have been forgotten by the English aristocracy when Harold was enthroned in January 1066, but not by William. When no crown was forthcoming, he took direct action. After the bloodbath of Hastings, William redistributed vast tracts of confiscated Anglo-Saxon territories among his followers as reward for their services on the battlefield. He also refined a system of land ownership based on the bonds between the ruler and his vassals, which has since become known as feudalism.

Simply put, the king would reward a nobleman for services rendered by granting possession of a piece of land (thereafter termed a *fief*) in return for loyalty, homage and certain obligations. The nobleman might subdivide his land among his vassals and expect the same loyalty and services in return. The most important of these feudal obligations was to provide armed support when the need arose. The vassal also had to perform a fixed period of military service every year at his lord's castle, an onerous duty known as *castle guard* (although in time this responsibility could be avoided by paying a small fine). A fief was valued on the basis of a *knight's fee*, which is the amount of money or services that would be expected to support one knight. A knight had to be self-sufficient and provide for his family, run a castle, supply his own arms and armour, and pay any taxes out of the income produced from his estate.

The value of fiefs varied considerably depending on the size and resources of the land; thus Penmark in the Vale of Glamorgan was considered to be worth four knight's fees, while neighbouring Llantrithyd was just a half-fee. Another example from the Vale shows how complicated the procedure could become; thirteenth-century documents record that the lordship of St Nicholas was held by William Corbet from the chief lord at Cardiff, and was valued at three knight's fees. Evidently this was a burden for one family to maintain, and two sub-fees were created and granted to vassals who stamped their authority on the land by building their own castles. Today, there are three small earthworks within a kilometre of St Nicholas village; the larger mound near the parish church probably represents the main Corbet seat, while the outlying sites belonged to his sub-tenants. Although simple in theory, the feudal system could result in complex interconnected relationships amongst the nobility, particularly if a vassal possessed several estates and therefore owed allegiance to more than one magnate.

Soon after his victory King William I (1066-87) created three of his most trusted warriors earls of Chester, Shrewsbury and Hereford, and allowed the establishment of the March as a buffer zone between Norman England and the independent kingdoms of Wales. This frontier territory was not a single unit but a diverse group of lordships ruled by Marcher lords rather than the king or native princes. Within their own territories they could act in kingly fashion, dispensing justice and waging war, establishing castles, towns and markets, giving and taking further territory as reward or punishment. From these three capitals the Marcher lords looked west and saw opportunities to bring more lands and revenues under their sway. The subjugation of Anglo-Saxon England may have been accomplished relatively quickly, but it was to take more than two centuries before an English king would rule over the whole of Wales.

At the time of the Norman invasion Wales

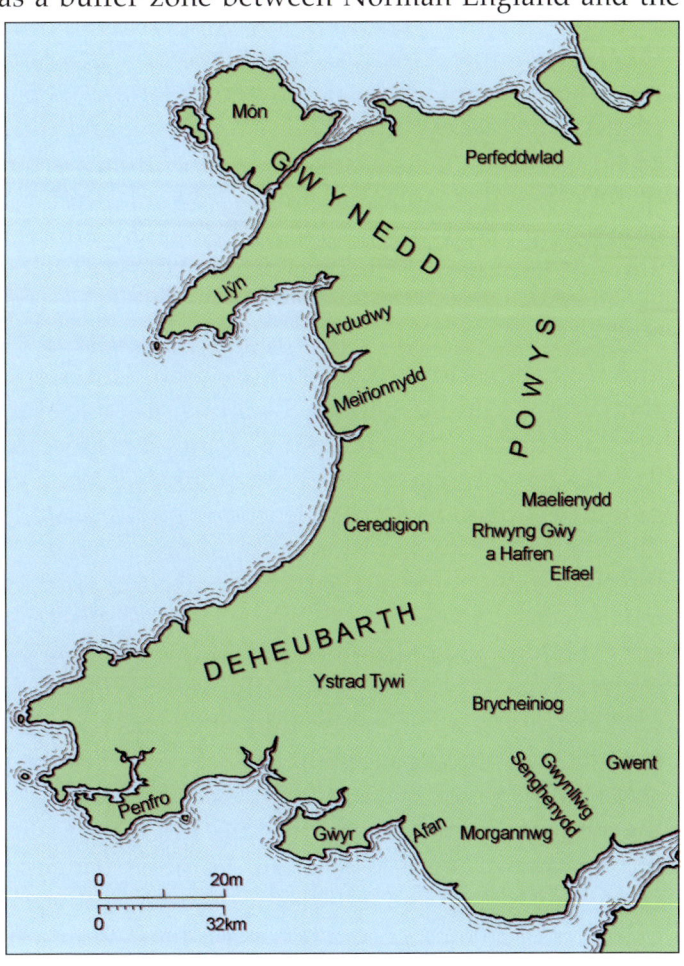

The main native territories of Wales at the start of the Norman invasion

was not a unified country but rather a patchwork of petty kingdoms based on the traditional territorial division of a *cantref* and its smaller constituent *commote*. There were three major princely houses – Gwynedd in the north, Powys in the midlands and Deheubarth in the south-west – along with a number of lesser dynasties; but it was these three realms that dominated the political scene. For over two centuries that struggle continued, alternating years of enforced peace with vicious uprisings as invader embarked on campaigns of conquest and the defender lashed out with fire and sword. The fluctuating fortunes of war changed the map of Wales, territories were lost and gained, borders enlarged under aggressive rulers and dwindled during power vacuums. The Welsh princes were hardly paragons of nationalistic chivalry, and they were quite happy to employ Norman aid in getting rid of an opponent or seizing the territory of a neighbouring ruler if the occasion presented itself.

The early castles

With a few rare exceptions, the first castles built by the Marcher lords were relatively simple structures that relied on earth ramparts and wooden buildings for defence, quite unlike the towering strongholds now familiarly thought of as castles. They were certainly less imposing and durable than what was to come, but it would be misleading to think of them as nothing more than a collection of little wooden huts and flimsy towers. Timber was the cheapest and most convenient material available in the heavily afforested lands of medieval Britain and was used to construct buildings at almost all levels of society. Evidence from excavated sites, and timber-framed buildings surviving from later periods, would suggest these were quite formidable structures in their day, strongly constructed and well suited to the needs of the time. The deep outer ditches and high inner ramparts would have formed serious obstacles for any attacker to cross, while the thick timber palisades and watchtowers gave the defenders height and cover to retaliate with spear and bow. A simple fort could be erected in a matter of months (William brought at least one prefabricated castle with him in 1066) and, despite the obvious vulnerability to fire, such earth and timber castles became the commonest type of fortification used in war zones for the next century and a half.

The Normans introduced a completely new type of fortification to Britain, the *motte and bailey*, of which the most characteristic and unique constituent was the motte, a conical mound of earth crowned with a timber tower, which functioned as the strongpoint and last resort of the garrison in case of siege. The size and height of the motte varied considerably depending on several factors: the strategic importance of the site, the wealth and standing of the owner, and the number of locals who could be press-ganged into building it. The largest motte in Wales is at Cardiff; it measures almost 11 metres high with a summit diameter of 33 metres, and it was probably built on the orders of the Conqueror himself in 1081. Most are far less ambitious than this.

Beyond the encircling ditch at the foot of the mound lay an enclosed courtyard, the bailey, which served as an outer line of defence and a protective enclave for ancillary buildings. These would include workshops, garrison quarters, stables and stores, the sort of buildings essential to the running of the castle and its surrounding estate. Kitchens were usually free-standing structures positioned a short distance away from the main buildings to reduce the risk of fire. Chapels, too, were commonly found within the castle walls since religion played a vital role in everyday life at the time. But the most important building within the defensive perimeter was the great hall, a symbol of lordly status and hospitality, where the owner could reside in greater comfort than would be possible in the cramped confines of a lofty tower. Within the great space of the hall a fire burned on the central hearth, providing heat and light, and making some cooking possible. After permeating all the furniture and occupants, the smoke from the hearth would eventually drift up and out through a vent in the high roof. At the far end of the hall the high table was positioned, and here the lord of the castle and his immediate family would sit, a highly visible indication of who was in power. Doors beside the table led through into the final element of the hall block, the innermost private chamber or solar. As an added security measure many castle halls were located on the first floor above ground-floor storerooms, and accessible by an external staircase.

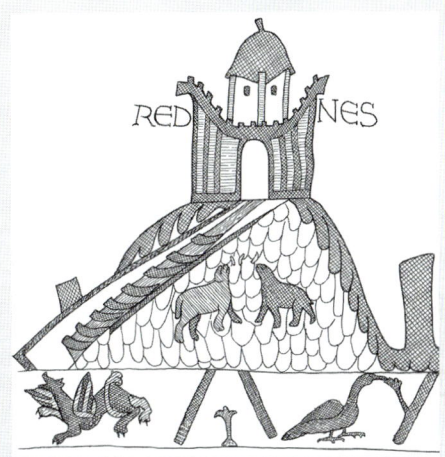

Two examples of the Norman motte from the Bayeux tapestry, the building work underway at Hastings and a completed hall at Rennes, Normandy, with a photograph of the remains at Aberlleniog, Anglesey

> The Normans also used another type of wooden castle known as a ringwork, which consists of a massive rampart and ditch encircling the main buildings, with no motte or keep present. Although there is often no obvious strongpoint, some excavated ringworks have produced evidence of timber towers on, or close to, the gateway.
>
> Wherever possible the builders saved time and labour by constructing the castle earthworks out of natural features like ridges and hillocks, scarping the slopes and piling up the surplus earth from the ditches to create suitable mottes. Nor did they ignore the advantages of pre-existing fortifications – the mottes at Cardiff, Caerwent, and Loughor were built within derelict Roman forts, while the enormous baileys of Llanrhystud, Twmbarlwm and Wiston must surely be reused Iron Age hillforts.

The Anglo-Norman consolidation

> *Gerald, the steward of Pembroke, founded the castle of Cenarth Bychan where he settled and there deposited all his riches, his wife, his heirs, and all dear to him; and he fortified it with a ditch and a wall and a gateway with a lock on it.*
> Brut y Tywysogion (trans. John Williams 1860)

From Chester, Hereford and Shrewsbury, the Normans pushed into Wales and established a series of key military bases from Chepstow in the south to Rhuddlan in the north, which served as springboards for further advances. As if oblivious to the growing threat, the native princes carried on fighting amongst themselves, even using Norman mercenaries to bolster their own forces on occasion. After a particularly bloody civil war, Rhys ap Tewdwr emerged as the main leader of the south, while Gruffudd ap Cynan ruled the north.[1] King William progressed through south Wales in 1081 and met Rhys at St Davids Cathedral to receive homage and tribute in return for acknowledging the Welshman's position. The king also took the opportunity to establish a castle and mint at Cardiff, at that time the most westerly Norman foothold in the south. When Rhys was killed in battle in 1093 the last obstacle to a full-scale invasion was removed and Morgannwg, Deheubarth and Brycheiniog were swiftly overrun. This sudden onslaught provoked a series of violent counterattacks the following year, and the invaders were driven out of Gwynedd and Deheubarth. Yet despite a further series of uprisings the Norman grip proved too tenacious to be shaken off, and areas like Pembrokeshire and south Glamorgan were to remain more or less firmly under foreign control.

Henry I (1100-35) adopted a less confrontational approach to ruling Wales than his predecessors, installing trusted Welshmen to control certain territories as vassals under the king's terms, rather than relying on the driving force of the Marcher lords. Warring dynasties were left to weaken themselves by infighting; lands were given or taken away as rewards or punishments; occasional shows of military might were used to frighten any overbearing prince into submission.

Inroads were made in Ceredigion by Gilbert fitz Richard of the House of Clare in Suffolk, Henry de Beaumont was allowed to seize Gower, while Ralph de Mortimer and Philip de Braose began to consolidate lands around Radnor and Builth. This slow, steady encroachment was reversed during the troubled reign of King Stephen (1135-54), and not for the last time did the Welsh take advantage of a temporary weakness in the English Crown and the preoccupation of Anglo-Norman lords with dynastic rivalries elsewhere in the country. The accession of the Plantagenet King Henry II (1154-89) ended the anarchy of Stephen's reign and brought about a measure of stability to the Marches. Henry quickly set about restoring authority and putting the princes in their places. In 1157 an invading army wrested homage and obedience from Owain Gwynedd, prince of north Wales, and the following year another show of force humbled Rhys ap Gruffudd of Deheubarth. But an even larger expedition to curb the wayward leaders in 1165 ended in dismal failure due to the appalling summer weather.

Henry never repeated the attempt to crush the native rulers with force. Because of his subsequent complicity in the murder of Archbishop Becket in 1170 and the disastrous loss of prestige this incurred, the king was more amenable to reach some agreement with the opposition. Owain died in the same year, and the authority of Gwynedd waned as civil war amongst his heirs fragmented the realm. Powys too had weakened since the glory days of the forceful Madog ap Maredudd (d.1160), who had extended his dominions beyond Offa's Dyke as far as Oswestry. With an exposed border facing England, Powys was always vulnerable to Anglo-Norman incursions, and after Madog's death the land was split in two and controlled by separate dynasties.

For the remainder of the twelfth century Rhys was the foremost leader of the native princes and through his alliance with the crown, ruled virtually undisturbed as lord of Deheubarth. Rhys was shrewd enough to realise how much his position depended on the goodwill of the king and made considerable efforts to keep on friendly terms with Henry, supporting him in times of need and fostering an interest in Anglo-Norman culture and society. Welsh literature and arts flourished under the largely benevolent reign of the Lord Rhys, culminating in a celebrated contest between bards and musicians at a Christmas feast in 1176, the first recorded Welsh Eisteddfod. Rhys also took up the practice of castle building with some enthusiasm, rebuilding Cardigan and Dinefwr to enhance his standing within his own lands, and using military bases at Aberdyfi, Nevern and Rhaeadr to secure his territorial conquests.

Castle architecture in the twelfth century
For all the convenience and thrift of building in timber, masonry was a far stronger material and better at withstanding damage from fire and siege machines. A few strategically important castles had been built from stone soon after the Norman invasion (such as Colchester, London and Richmond), but these were the exception rather than the rule, and it was not until the beginning of the twelfth century that the use of masonry fortifications became more widespread.

Building in stone was a costly and time-consuming process. Specialist workers such as miners, diggers, quarrymen and masons had to be employed. The raw materials would be obtained from the nearest quarry but good freestone for shaping into doors, windows and other decorative details might have to be sourced from further afield and brought to the site by cart or boat. Limestone was rendered into powder to produce mortar and to make limewash to cover the walls inside and out, thereby brightening the gloomy rooms immeasurably and creating a striking impression when seen from afar. Blacksmiths had to produce hinges, bolts and nails (43,000 nails were required at one stage during the building of York Castle). Plumbers were needed to fix lead sheets and flashing to ensure the roofs were watertight. Carpenters were still an essential part of the workforce since timber was required in large quantities for scaffolding and temporary defence works, as well as for floor beams, roof trusses, doors, panelling and furnishings for the completed interiors.

Construction could only be carried out during a period of prolonged peace since it would have been necessary to breach the existing defences, and the labourers had to be adequately protected whilst the works progressed. Building generally took place between April and October and the usual estimate is that medieval workers could raise walls up to a height of three metres per season. This average could, however, vary considerably, depending on the size (and enthusiasm) of the workforce. Orford Castle in Suffolk was built by Henry II over an eight-year period from 1165 and cost just over £1,400 (an enormous sum by the standards of the day, when the royal income for an average year was about £18,000). The castle has a three-storey tower 30 metres high, surrounded by an outer wall studded with additional towers and a gateway. Because few building accounts survive from this period the actual progress and cost of constructing a major stone castle are rarely known, but at least with Crown properties there was always an army of clerks on hand to record the king's expenditure with bureaucratic efficiency.

Orford Castle, Suffolk, built over an eight-year period at a cost of just over £1,400

The donjon *or keep at Porchester Castle, Hampshire*

And so within the protection of temporary wooden stockades new stone towers began to rise. Invariably of rectangular plan, these forbidding structures were called great towers or *donjons* (a term that has since been downgraded to mean a basement prison); today they are more familiarly known as a keep. The keep contained several floors of residential accommodation for the lord and his entourage, and were capable of resisting attack even if the rest of the courtyard had been overrun by an enemy. Access into the tower was often through a fortified porch, or forebuilding, which might contain a drawbridge and portcullis to defend the approach to the main apartments. The ground floor was generally used for the storage of food and goods, and often contained a well dug below the foundations in search of water (essential if the garrison was to endure a long siege when no supplies might be obtained from outside).

This room in the keep at Dover Castle, Kent, has recently been restored to its medieval appearance

The principal residential chambers were situated on the upper levels for added security. Originally these rooms were a far cry from the dark echoing stone cells that the long years of decay and disuse have created. The floors were usually timber planks strewn with rushes or furs, but if the rooms had a solid stone surface then decorative ceramic tiles might be used. The rough masonry walls were concealed with smooth plaster and enlivened with painted decorations or fabric hangings. Research has shown that medieval tastes in interior decor bordered on the garish (as can be experienced by any visitor to the keep at Dover, which has recently been restored to its twelfth-century splendour). The main rooms of the keep would be heated by fireplaces in the side walls, but a chamber located on the topmost level might have had an open hearth set on the stone floor, with the smoke escaping through a louvered vent in the roof above. There were few windows in the massively thick walls, just splayed openings secured with metal bars to allow in some light and air. Glass was an expensive luxury few could afford in medieval times (nor was it very practical in a building liable to be attacked) and so wooden shutters were used to control draughts.

As for sanitary arrangements, castles rarely had the luxury of water-flushed systems enjoyed by monasteries, and the method of waste disposal consisted basically of a hole in the floor discharging down a shaft into a cesspit. These latrines were known as garderobes (literally 'mind-your-clothes') a euphemism that is matched by today's use of the work 'cloakroom'. Some claim that the

Dolwyddelan Castle in north Wales dates from the early thirteenth century but was extensively rebuilt around 1850. The protruding stone supports below the battlements for a timber hourd were added by the Victorian restorers

ammonia fumes from the latrines deterred moths, hence the habit of hanging clothes there. Garderobes were located in small rooms within the thick outer walls, reached by dog-leg passageways that helped cut down smells. Sometimes the latrine chamber was built jutting out from the castle wall on stone brackets (corbels) which offered a draughtier, but less odoriferous option for the user.

The thick walls also incorporated passageways, fighting galleries and stone stairs leading to the upper levels. The stairs might be arranged in straight flights, but more usually spiralled up around a central newel post and rose above the battlements within a small turret. The classic design of Norman keep has a turret on each corner and shallow buttresses strengthening the flanking walls. The small square holes often seen dotted about the exterior faces of walls and towers are *putlog holes* where scaffolding poles were inserted during construction. Other holes would have served to drain excess water from the roofs, or else marked the position of vanished timber fighting galleries, known as hourds or brattices. These temporary structures were erected in times of war and jutted out from the battlements so that defenders could oversee the base of the walls and drop missiles on any attacker below.

In England, the keep symbolised the brute power of Norman authority, typified by monumental examples at Corfe, Dover, Hedingham and Rochester. In Wales and the Marches they are slightly smaller, and rarely contain more than two floors. Good examples can be seen at Chepstow, Ogmore, Manorbier, Monmouth and Usk. The restored keep at Dolwyddelan is a particularly fine example of the Welsh following trends, although it actually dates from the early thirteenth century. When compared to the level of comfort enjoyed by today's householders, these medieval buildings seem basic, unhygienic and

The shell-keep at Cardiff on the summit of the motte

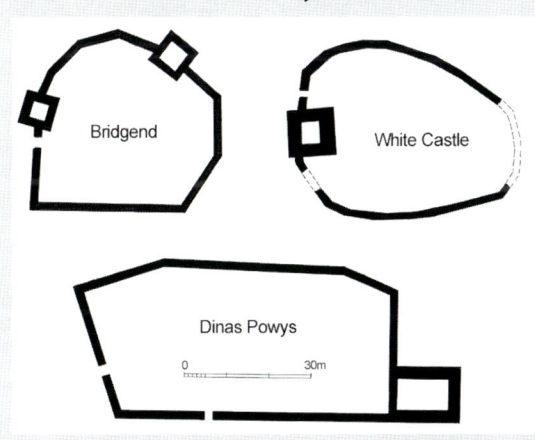

The outline plans of three Welsh castles showing the location of keeps and square towers as part of a circuit of defences

The entrance gateway and adjacent tower at Bridgend

claustrophobic, but by medieval standards they were palatial residences. Although the rectangular keep was the plan most often adopted by the castle builders, on occasion more adventurous designs were attempted. At Cardiff, Wiston, Launceston and Totnes (the latter two both in Devon), the summit of the motte was encircled with a high wall, termed a *shell-keep*, which resulted in a cramped space filled with lean-to buildings. At Chilham (Kent) the keep is octagonal, while the polygonal tower at Orford (Suffolk) has so many sides as to be practically round, although the elevation of the building has been obscured by three massive flanking turrets. Conisbrough (Yorkshire) was truly cylindrical (again with reinforcing turrets) and foreshadows the next generation of keeps to appear after 1200.

Whatever its shape, the keep would not have stood alone. The earthworks and timber stockades of the earlier bailey defences would have been retained, or improved with the addition of stone gates and curtain walls. Twelfth-century castles relied on fairly unsophisticated layouts with straight lengths of walling following the line of the outer ditch or the crest of the natural slopes. A few small square towers improved the defensive strength of the enclosure, such as can be seen at Bridgend, Castell Dinas (p.82), Coity and White Castle. The generally simple military designs of the Anglo-Norman period began to be refined and improved as the century drew to a close.

The enemy that the castle was used against was not exclusively the Welsh – there were episodes of civil war amongst the upper classes and rebellions against the misrule of monarchs – but by and large, castles in Wales and the Marches were there for only one thing: to curb the Welsh. The belligerent nature of the Welsh princes is well attested by contemporary scribes and chronicle histories, none more so than the *Brut y Tywysogion,* the 'Chronicles of the Princes', a year-by-year account of events in Wales from the Dark Ages to the beginning of the fourteenth century. This is one of the main sources of information about the struggle between native rulers and Anglo-Norman interlopers, and it can make pretty grim reading.

Another valuable source is Gerald of Wales (*c.*1145-1223), who was born of mixed Norman and Welsh parentage at Manorbier in west Wales, and pursued a long and often turbulent career in the Church. He was a tireless traveller, writer, raconteur and self-publicist, and his surviving works – particularly *The Journey through Wales* (*c.*1191) and *The Description of Wales* (*c.*1194) – provide us with a unique glimpse of life in late twelfth-century Wales. 'They are fierce rather than strong, and totally dedicated to the practice of arms. Not only are the leaders but the entire nation is trained in war,' wrote Gerald about his own countrymen. 'They are passionately devoted to their freedom and to the defence of their country; for these they fight, for these they suffer hardships, for these they will take up their weapons and willingly sacrifice their lives.' Yet he did not shrink from the less praiseworthy aspects of the Welsh nation: their cowardice in the face of determined, well-organised attackers, greed of land acquisition, and endemic in-fighting. One of the root causes of this unrest was the old law of partible inheritance, whereby the lands and titles of the deceased were split equally between all sons, legitimate or otherwise. The stubborn adherence to this law, fair though it was, could only lead to division and weakness. One might almost hear Gerald sighing as he wrote 'Brothers show more affection to one another when dead, than when living.' He went on to write, 'If the Welsh would only adopt the French way of arming themselves, if they would fight in ordered ranks instead of leaping about, if their princes could ... unite to defend the country – or, better still, if they had only one prince and he a good one – I cannot see how so powerful a people could ever be completely conquered.'

The fragile peace that had lasted for almost twenty years came to an abrupt end when King Henry died and Richard I (1189-99) acceded to the throne. Lord Rhys had no particular regard for the new monarch and broke out in revolt, capturing and destroying an impressive number of Anglo-Norman strongholds. Before his death in 1197 the aged prince had the misfortune to suffer (just as Henry had in his last years) from the treachery and ingratitude of his offspring. He was even briefly incarcerated by one faction of his rebellious kin. The power of Deheubarth waned as the surviving heirs imprisoned, dispossessed or murdered each other, fatally wounding Rhys's hard-won unity. Once again the king and the Marcher lords moved in to encroach on native territory and exploit any weaknesses among the lesser rulers. Yet within a few short years the balance of power swung to the north, and Gerald's plea for a united Wales ruled by an effective leader seemed about to come true.

The rise and fall of Gwynedd

And the King has heard and in part seen that Llywelyn's ancestors and himself had the power within their boundaries to build and construct castles and fortresses and set up markets without prohibition by anyone.
       from a letter by Llywelyn ap Gruffudd to Edward I, July 1273

When Owain Gwynedd died in 1170 civil war had broken out amongst his successors and the realm of Gwynedd was fragmented. One of the dispossessed heirs, Iorwerth, sent his young son Llywelyn to be raised by relatives in Powys away from the bloodbath that inevitably accompanied native power struggles. When Llywelyn came of age he took back his birthright by fire and sword, seizing the lands of one of his deceased uncles and defeating another in battle. From relative obscurity Llywelyn ap Iorwerth (c.1173-1240) rose to become the most powerful and successful Welsh leader, and one of only two in history to earn the designation 'The Great'. The uneasy reign of King John (1199-1216) gave Llywelyn plenty of opportunity to fight back against the shaky royal authority in Wales and bring more native rulers under his sway, whether they liked it or not. He took southern Powys from its rightful ruler, ousted his cousin, and reined in the squabbling princes of Deheubarth. Llywelyn entered into a politically motivated marriage with King John's daughter to help consolidate his position, and formed several alliances with Marcher lords opposed to the king.

The dominions ruled directly by Llywelyn the Great or controlled through his vassals comprised the whole of north Wales, Powys and Deheubarth, while the territories of the Crown and Marcher lords were pushed to the periphery. The bards lauded him as 'Prince of Wales', yet Llywelyn contented himself with the less provocative title of 'Prince of Aberffraw and Lord of Snowdon'.

> **Castle architecture in the thirteenth century**
> By the start of the thirteenth century new trends appeared in British military architecture, probably introduced by knights returning from the Continent, where more advanced buildings had long been used. The keep as a single massively defended strongpoint, which so characterised twelfth-century castles, began to be replaced in favour of larger and less static designs concentrating on the enclosure as an integrated whole. High curtain walls were built in straight sections linking up with rounded towers on the corners and angles, boldly projecting beyond the enceinte. The defensive advantage of a round tower is that it lacks blind corners and has no awkward angles susceptible to undermining. The shape also helps deflect missiles. Inside the towers, strategically placed loop-holes enabled archers and crossbowmen to provide flanking fire along the line of the walls and target anyone approaching the castle, without being exposed to the enemy. The older form of arrow loop with its restrictive deep splay was gradually replaced by a more effective opening set into a rectangular recess, which gave greater freedom for an archer to manoeuvre and take aim.

One of the continental castles that inspired a long line of similar designs was the Louvre at Paris, built by King Philip Augustus around 1190. It was a simple square enclosure with round towers on each corner and additional half-round towers on the intermediary walls. Two of these towers were set close together to guard an entrance between them, and within the central courtyard stood a round keep. In Wales a very similar layout was adopted at Skenfrith in the 1220s by Hubert de Burgh, chief advisor to the young Henry III. Both Hubert and his older contemporary William Marshal, earl of Pembroke, were at the forefront of the new trends in castle design, and these ideas were put into practice at the key strongholds of Chepstow, Grosmont, Montgomery, Pembroke and Usk.

The preserved walls of the Louvre, Paris, built to a square plan with round towers at each corner, which proved to be an influential design

The effigy of William Marshal, earl of Pembroke in the Temple Church, London

The old concept of a single strongpoint was not completely eradicated despite the introduction of more advanced designs; in fact a change of shape gave the donjon a new lease of life in the first half of the century. Again the inspiration probably came from across the Channel, for William Marshal was an active campaigner in France and built one of the earliest (and certainly the largest) cylindrical keeps, at Pembroke around 1200. Round keeps soon became the vogue amongst the Marcher lords, appearing at Bronllys, Caldicot, Skenfrith, Tretower and just over the border at Longtown. Other vanished keeps are believed to have stood at Brecon, Cardigan and Monmouth. The Welsh followed suit at Castell Meredydd (p.146), Dinefwr and Dolbadarn, but on the whole native castle design was far less forward-looking than in England. Probably the comparative lack of resources was a major factor, as well as the inability to employ skilled designers from outside Wales. The rectangular keep remained a firm favourite well into the second half of the century, although the princes of Gwynedd did develop a curiously hybrid form of keep – square, with one rounded face (rather like an elongated letter D in plan); the best preserved example can be seen at Ewloe.

Aside from the increased use of flanking towers, the other notable development of the early thirteenth century was the improvement in gatehouse design. Gates were the most vulnerable part of any castle, since they offered the enemy a way in. Early gateways tended to be fairly simple structures, just

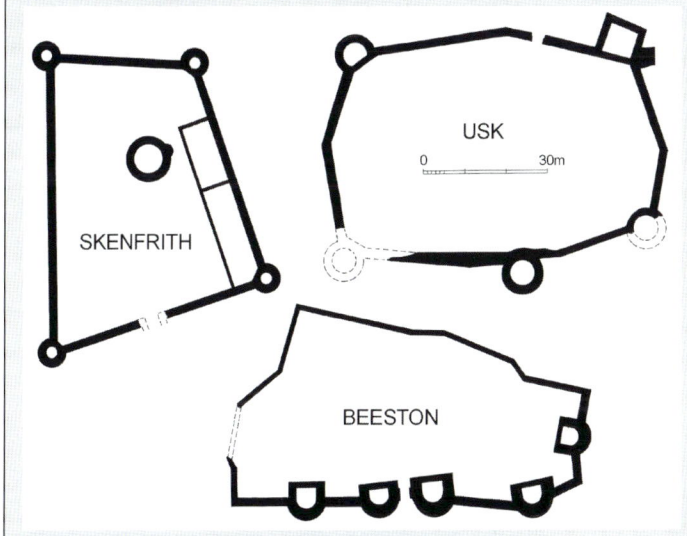

Castle plans of the early-thirteenth century showing the preference for angular enclosures and rounded corner towers. Cylindrical keeps, like the ones at Bronllys (left) and Skenfrith (right), were popular developments at this time

an arched opening through the wall, or a passageway in the ground floor of a small tower. Wooden doors, a portcullis, and perhaps a drawbridge spanning the outer ditch, would be all that stood between the enemy without and the defenders within. As the keep was the most characteristic feature of twelfth-century castles, so it could be said that the great gatehouse was the defining element of the thirteenth century. Recent research has shown that the trail was blazed unexpectedly early by William Marshal at Chepstow, where the outer gate was built in the 1190s as an 'advance guard' of the type of structure that became much more commonplace as the new century progressed.

The square keep with one rounded end at Ewloe, a style adopted by the princes of Gwynedd

The classic form of gatehouse consists of a heavily defended entrance passageway between two round or D-shaped towers boldly projecting out from the walls. Each tower usually contained guardrooms on the ground floor with larger residential chambers above. Montgomery and Beeston (Cheshire) are early

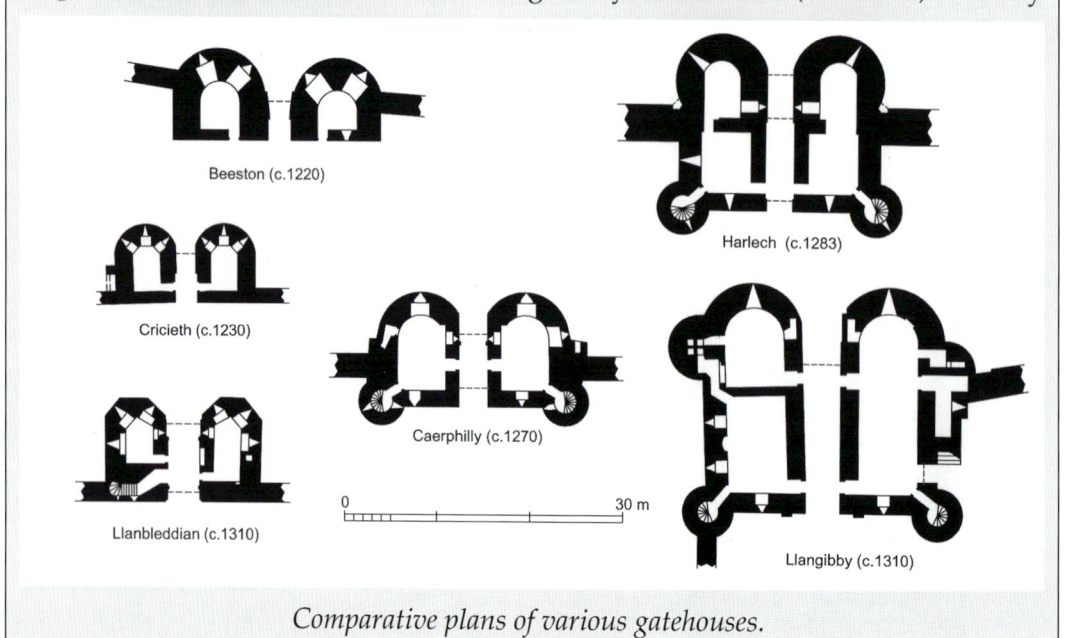

Beeston (c.1220)

Harlech (c.1283)

Cricieth (c.1230)

Caerphilly (c.1270)

Llanbleddian (c.1310)

Llangibby (c.1310)

*Comparative plans of various gatehouses.
The position of portcullises is indicated by broken lines*

18

examples dating from the 1220s, which were imitated by Llywelyn the Great at Criccieth (an unusually advanced type of Welsh castle). The plan was further refined by Richard de Clare at Tonbridge (Kent) and by his son Gilbert at Caerphilly. The latter relies on an imaginative use of water defences to keep enemy siege machines well away from the walls, a concept de Clare surely copied from the huge fortress of Kenilworth he had helped besiege a few years earlier in 1266.

Caerphilly also has a second defensive perimeter surrounding the inner enclosure, effectively creating a castle within a castle. Even if the invaders had managed to break into the outer circuit, they would be exposed to the garrison defending the more massive inner ring. This type of defence in depth is known as a 'concentric castle', and some of the finest examples were later built in north Wales by Edward I and his favoured mason from Savoy, Master James of St George. Edward had returned from the Crusades in 1274 having seen the large and elaborate fortifications in the Middle East, and was no doubt further inspired by his son-in-law's new creation at Caerphilly. Edward decided

An early gatehouse at Beeston, Cheshire (top) and much developed examples at Chepstow (centre) and Caerphilly (bottom)

to subdue the rebellious heartland of Wales by encircling it within an 'iron ring' of fortifications, the most ambitious and costly scheme of castle building ever carried out by the English Crown. A few of his castles, like Conwy and Flint, have a strangely old fashioned layout, but Aberystwyth, Beaumaris, Harlech and Rhuddlan display an almost scientifically precise concentric design.

Caerphilly Castle, showing elements of the extensive outer defensive works

By this time gatehouses had reached quite massive proportions and incorporated a whole host of defensive features aimed at stopping an enemy dead; arrow loops sweeping the approach and passageway, multiple portcullises, thick wooden doors, and 'murder-hole' slots in the roof through which the defenders could drop rocks or pour boiling water on an enemy. The last great gatehouse in Wales was built around 1310 at Llangybi (p.161), a monumental edifice where the carved stone decorations and abundance of garderobes reveal that this was not merely a gate to let people in and out, but one of the principal residential buildings at the castle.

Llywelyn the Great tried to establish a Welsh feudal state united under one ruler, but despite obtaining formal recognition of his legitimate son Dafydd as sole heir and successor, all his efforts were in vain. Once death had removed his forceful presence from the political scene, the princes fell to their usual infighting. Dafydd himself died unexpectedly early in 1246 and the English recovered most of Llywelyn's territorial gains. The struggle for Welsh supremacy was, however, soon rekindled by Dafydd's nephew, Llywelyn ap Gruffudd (d.1282). Like his grandfather and namesake, Llywelyn clawed his way to the top by first defeating his relatives in battle and seizing their lands, and then spreading out from the mountainous heartland of Gwynedd to stamp his authority on the lesser rulers.

King Henry III (1216-72) was a less disliked monarch than his father John, but nevertheless his long reign witnessed a serious uprising headed by the earl of Leicester, Simon de Montfort, with whom Llywelyn became closely allied. Even after Simon's death and the collapse of the revolt, Llywelyn succeeded in forcing King Henry to recognise his title of Prince of Wales and acknowledge his territorial conquests over the native princes and Marcher lords with the signing of the Treaty of Montgomery in 1267. But perhaps because he lacked the shrewd ruthlessness (or the sheer luck) that had gained his grandfather so much, Llywelyn could not deal effectively with the many enemies his progress made.

The accession of Edward I (1272-1307) marked the turning point of Llywelyn's fortunes. In 1274 his own brother Dafydd and Gruffudd of Powys plotted to overthrow the prince and fled to England when the coup failed. Llywelyn persistently refused to pay the expected homage to the new king and feared (perhaps rightly) for his safety should he leave Wales to do so. Relations between the two men continued to deteriorate, and in 1276 Edward finally opted for military action to bring the rebel prince to heel. As the royal army moved against Gwynedd, the usual ploy of retreating into the mountains and launching guerrilla attacks failed, because English ships patrolled the Menai Strait and prevented the Welsh from harvesting the vital Anglesey grain supply. Llywelyn was forced to surrender and make what peace he could. By the terms of the Treaty of Aberconwy (1277) Llywelyn was deprived of much of his former territories except for Gwynedd, although he was allowed to retain the hollow title of Prince of Wales. After finally paying homage to the king, Llywelyn's long-delayed marriage to Eleanor de Montfort, the daughter of his old ally, was allowed to take place.

King Edward safeguarded his position by building a number of major new castles on the edges of native territory and rewarded his allies (including the treacherous Dafydd) with lands confiscated from the prince. With so much pressure from the Marcher lords and royal officials it is hardly surprising that rebellion broke out again after only a few years; what is surprising is that it was Dafydd who sparked it off, fed up perhaps with all the interference from his English overlords, or maybe wanting to be Prince of Wales in place of his brother. Edward swiftly retaliated and used the same military tactics as before. Anglesey was blockaded and Llywelyn was forced to head south to rally troops. In December 1282 he was caught and killed in a skirmish. Dafydd continued the war to its bitter end. He was hunted down and betrayed by his own men, and in October 1283 he was disembowelled alive in the market place at Shrewsbury. Edward was determined to stamp out the princely House of Gwynedd forever; any immediate kin disappeared into prisons and even Llywelyn's little daughter Gwenllian was effectively incarcerated for life in a remote Lincolnshire nunnery.

The king was now free to consolidate his hold on the principality and complete his ambitious scheme of encircling Gwynedd with an iron ring of castles. As the walls went up, so the lands previously seized by the Welsh passed swiftly back into the firm control of the Marcher lords. Restrictive laws were set in place and, as the historian John Davies aptly put it, 'the fate of the Welsh in every part of their country would be to live under a political system in which they and their characteristics would have only a subordinate role'. The title 'Prince of Wales' was used henceforth by the English kings as an hereditary honour reserved for their eldest sons. Edward could be magnanimous to those who had joined the winning side. Llywelyn's brother Rhodri had long since turned his back on the political quagmire and lived out his days as an obscure English squire; Rhys ap Maredudd was allowed to rule in Ystrad Tywi; and Gruffudd of Powys returned in triumph to Welshpool, to all intents and purposes an English baron rather than Welsh prince. His heir Owain even adopted an English surname, de la Pole, after the place-name, Pool (as Welshpool was then known). The native rulers of Afan, once at the forefront of resistance in the south, also bowed to the inevitable and restyled themselves the lords de Avene. A few descendants of once noble dynasties were left in possession of some ancestral lands in Mid Wales.

Yet the destruction of the House of Gwynedd

The territorial divisions of Wales and the Marches around 1300

did not completely eradicate Welsh resistance. Rhys ap Maredudd lost patience with the constant interference of royal officials and struck out in 1287, but his rebellion did not gain much support and hardly spread beyond the west; after several years on the run, he was hunted down and brutally executed. A far more serious and widespread uprising took place in 1294-95, headed in the north by Madog ap Llywelyn, a distant relative of the late prince. The southern insurgents were led by Morgan ap Maredudd, son of the last ruler of Gwynllŵg ousted by Gilbert de Clare. Despite the damage caused to English castles and towns, Edward was surprisingly lenient towards the captured leaders (Madog was imprisoned for life and Morgan released to serve in the royal army); perhaps the king realised that the revolt was just the last flickering of a dying flame. A further uprising in 1316 by Llywelyn Bren was restricted mainly to Glamorgan but thereafter for almost a century the castles of Wales were used only in the wars and petty squabbles of the new ruling classes.

The castle in the later Middle Ages

All Carmarthenshire, Kidwelly, Carnwyllion and Iscennen be sworn to Owain yesterday, and he lay last night in the castle of Dryslwyn ... and there I was and spoke with him upon truce, and prayed of a safe conduct, under his seal, to send home my wife and her mother ... and he would none grant me.
                from a letter written by the constable of Carreg Cennen
                        during the rebellion of Owain Glyndŵr, July 1403

During the early years of the fourteenth century the role of the castle in Wales and southern England changed dramatically, due to the combination of several factors. Most obviously, the defeat of the Welsh princes meant there was no further need for a widespread system of mighty fortifications, and the costly business of castle building slowed to a trickle. Several of the hugely ambitious fortresses started by Edward and his lords in the aftermath of the wars were never completed. Other castles located in remote areas and serving no purpose except as military bases were quickly abandoned once their *raison d'être* had passed, to save on maintenance costs. The long-established feudal system was also beginning to break up, and instead of the old practice of granting land in return for armed support there was a shift toward paid military service and financial contracts.

Within a few generations there was a further change in the need for defence, as the enemy came not from within the kingdom, but from overseas. Edward III (1327-77) started an interminable series of conflicts with France in order to press his claim to that kingdom through his mother's line of descent. Many Welsh warriors found honourable and lucrative employment in the royal armies ransacking French towns and villages. The king built new castles in England and made sure that older fortresses and town defences near the coast were capable of repelling raiding fleets. Robert de Penres earned the wrath of the king by failing properly to garrison and stock his castles at Llansteffan and Penrice (p.134). Increasingly though, any building work at castles was geared towards improving their domestic comforts rather than upgrading their defences. The revenue from a lord's estate that would once have financed the building of strong walls to keep his life and belongings safe, was now being used to make that life as comfortable as possible. There are many records of repairs and alterations to existing structures, but after 1320 virtually no major new castle was built in Wales – there was very little need in truth, since the country had an embarrassing surfeit.

The appearance of a new weapon – gunpowder – on the battlefields of Europe altered the perception of a castle's usefulness in war, and led to a gradual change in military architecture. Small cannons or 'bombards' cast from bronze began to be used from 1320s onwards; but their small size coupled with poorly mixed quantities of powder meant that they were more effective at frightening and demoralising the opposition than inflicting serious harm. As the century progressed, the manufacturing process was refined, and larger, more efficient guns were made from cast iron; the lofty walls and towers that had for so long kept the military aristocracy safe and sound were soon to prove inadequate.

Yet despite the incipient signs of slow decay and changing needs, the medieval castle was far from redundant, and with the start of the new century war once more spread out from the hills and valleys of Wales to threaten the complacent security of English rule. What began as a minor border dispute between two landowners rapidly escalated into a national uprising. Owain ap Gruffudd of Glyndyfrdwy – better known to history as Owain Glyndŵr – was propelled into rebellion by the tactless and underhand actions of his neighbour, Lord Grey of Ruthin. The initial uprising in September 1400 was not an immediate success, but it released the feelings that had been simmering in Welsh hearts for many long years and quickly spread to all parts of the principality. The seemingly invincible royal strongholds of Aberystwyth, Conwy and Harlech fell to the Welsh. By 1404 Owain's dominions extended over the most of the country, and native parliaments were held at Harlech and Machynlleth. Glyndŵr allied himself with powerful and ambitious lords opposed to the Lancastrian regime of King Henry IV (1399-1413) and an unfeasible plan was drawn up dividing England and Wales into three parts, with Owain ruling a vastly enlarged principality. A Welsh army bolstered by French mercenaries even marched into England as far as Worcester. But the momentum of the uprising could not be sustained; support fell away, the successes turned to defeats. By 1409 most of the ringleaders were dead or imprisoned and the last of the captured castles once more in royal control. The revolt was effectively over. Despite a generous offer of a pardon from Henry V (1413-22), the fugitive Glyndŵr disappears from the pages of history into the realms of folklore.

Within a few generations war had broken out again as rival claimants for the throne engaged in a long drawn-out series of bloody conflicts known as the Wars of the Roses. The strife between supporters of the Yorkist and Lancastrian dynasties took place over a thirty-year period, although it is estimated that the actual amount of fighting in all that time totalled no more than three weeks. Many castles were utilised in the struggles (Harlech being the most famous example, captured in 1468 after a seven-year siege), and at least one (Carreg Cennen) was deliberately wrecked to prevent any future use; but by and large the outcome of the wars was decided by pitched battles rather than long sieges, and the main conflicts took place outside Wales.

> **Castle architecture in the fourteenth and fifteenth centuries**
> In the settled years between the sporadic bouts of warfare a slew of new castles were built in England which displayed a far greater emphasis on domesticity rather than defence. They have the moats, gatehouses, towers and battlements of the true castle, but rarely share the scale or structural strength of their predecessors. Though looking like castles, they are in reality grand fortified houses dressed up in the paraphernalia of the recent past. Bodiam in Sussex is probably the best known of these late castles, a magnificently photogenic collection of symmetrical towers reflected in the waters of an encircling moat

for added effect. It was built in 1385 by a veteran of the Hundred Years War, to a design possibly influenced by the more ornamental châteaux of France. Behind the playful military façade of Bodiam lies a compact and lavish suite of apartments for the owner and guests. Old Wardour in Wiltshire (*c*.1393) has a similar level of luxury, although here the rooms are contained within a hexagonal tower-like structure. Within a few generations more of these large 'show castles' were being built across England, in some cases utilising the newly fashionable building material of brick (neglected since Roman times). Herstmonceux (*c*.1440) and Kirby Muxloe (*c*.1480) have residential suites of rooms grouped around a central rectangular courtyard. Castle-like on the outside, a country house within, these are fortified manor houses rather than the feudal strongholds of the previous centuries. The antiquated concept of the donjon was revived with enthusiasm too, not so much as a gloomy bolt hole but rather as a lavishly appointed private tower, containing suites of comfortable chambers with spacious windows and ample garderobes. Nunney (*c*.1373), Tattershall (*c*.1434) and Ashby de la Zouch (*c*.1474) are just three examples of architectural one-upmanship.

Nunney Castle, Somerset, built c.1373

Wales has a single (but exceptionally fine) monument to this late flowering of castle design – Raglan, built between 1435 and 1469 for the ascendant Herbert family. The fortress-like exterior complete with louring octagonal keep, shelters an extensive and complex group of residential apartments within. The walls have narrow loops for archers and cross-bowmen, but the designers of Raglan found it prudent to provide gunports as well (even though some

Raglan Castle, Monmouthshire, built between 1435 and 1469, included gunports and contained an extensive residential complex

were probably for display rather than practical use). Relatives of the Herberts, the Vaughans of Tretower, abandoned their twelfth-century stronghold for a spacious manor house close by, which was undefended apart from a token gatehouse and a battlemented wall to spice up the façade. And perhaps the most forceful image of the declining importance of the medieval castle is provided by Cefnllys (p.90), where on a hilltop between two crumbling thirteenth-century forts Ieuan ap Philip built a fine new timber hall as the seat of the lordship.

However, the situation in other parts of Britain was very different to Wales. In the northern counties of England, border raiders from the independent kingdom of Scotland remained an ever-present danger for several centuries to come. In this region a distinctive type of fortified dwelling appeared, consisting of a suite of rooms stacked up vertically in the form of a tower. Called tower-houses or pele-towers, these miniature keeps offered a flexible and cheap alternative for those not of the castle-owning class. There was a basement store (usually vaulted in stone to safeguard against fire), several upper floors of cramped living quarters, and a battlemented wall-walk from where the inhabitants could mount an effective defence against any minor attack. All the different levels were connected by spiral stairs within a projecting turret, and there was usually another turret for the essential garderobes. This basic layout was subject to a surprising variety of design, with additional rooms and chambers housed in jutting wings that could result in some very odd-looking buildings. The tower-house sometimes stood alone, but was more often associated with a walled courtyard containing ancillary buildings.

A tower-house or pele-tower near Edinburgh, a common design in the Scottish borders, but also in Pembrokeshire

For homeowners further down the social scale then protection might just be a stone-walled farmhouse with a first-floor hall accessible only by a removable ladder. This type of simple defensible building is termed a *bastle*. In the event of trouble all the occupants could do was round up their valuable livestock for safekeeping in the undercroft, retire to the passive security of the upper chamber, and sit things out. Such awkward and inconvenient dwellings were considered a necessary feature of everyday life in the north; and so too it would seem, in parts of Wales, where a number of such buildings appeared for no very clear reason.

A lingering end – the castle in post-Reformation times

> *In England there is no great reckoning made of castles and fortresses, for they do willingly let them go to ruin and instead thereof build them stately pleasant houses and palaces.*
>
> Sir Thomas Wilson (*The State of England*, 1600)

By the early years of the sixteenth century the stable centralised government of the Tudor dynasty had ensured that there was no longer a need for the aristocracy of southern England and Wales to rely on private armies and personal fortifications. King Henry VIII (1509-47) continued his father's policy of sweeping away overmighty subjects and potential rivals to the throne with ruthless efficiency. The power and prerogatives of the Marcher lords was abolished. Wales was united with England and then divided up for administrative purposes into thirteen shires, an arrangement that survived almost to the present day.[2] The more peaceable conditions enjoyed by most was in marked contrast to the Continent, where warfare was endemic and fortifications remained an essential aspect of life for many years to come. Writing in 1644, the Parliamentarian commander Sir John Meldrum observed that 'France, Italy and the Low Countries have found by experience during these three hundred years what losses are entailed by places being fortified, while the subjects of the Isle of Britain, through absence thereof, have lived in more tranquillity'.

The widespread use of gunpowder had rendered the medieval castle largely ineffective in warfare, and to beat the enemy one had constantly to adapt and improve. To protect against a possible French invasion, Henry ordered the construction of up-to-date artillery forts at key positions along the south coast. The forts initially resembled dumpy round keeps with massively thick walls to withstand the impact of missiles, but within a generation startlingly different types of fortifications were being designed, comprising geometrically precise enclosures with long, low ramparts laid out in straight sections. Vulnerable corners were capped by angular bastions where gunners could provide enfilade firepower along the walls and keep practically every line of attack under observation.

Cannons (such as this restored Tudor example at Mount Orgueil, Jersey) were now the deciding factors in siege warfare

Most of the old castles proved too cumbersome and costly to maintain, and those that had outlived their purpose and could not be adapted for residential use were left to decay. Strongly mortared walls could last undamaged for many long years, but once the slates or lead sheets were stripped from the roofs, rain and damp would quickly crumble the interior plasterwork and rot the beams and floorboards. Within a few generations a more or less intact building could be reduced by natural decay into a gutted shell. Add to this stone robbing for building materials or even deliberate demolition, and a once mighty stronghold could disappear completely within a relatively short period of time. The accelerating redundancy of the castle during the early Tudor period finds a surprising parallel in the present-day decline in church buildings. Few would say that religion now has the same place in society and daily life that it had just fifty years ago, and the dwindling congregations would have seemed unthinkable at the start of the twentieth century. Yet the end result of centuries of enthusiastic church construction is a surplus of buildings when the need for such establishments wanes. About thirty Church of England properties become redundant every year. The upkeep proves too much of a strain on local communities, and empty buildings are sold off and converted into houses, offices or workshops. Others are demolished. Although responsibility for castles rested with the Crown and aristocracy rather than parishioners, there was still the same basic problem of what to do with an unwieldy building once it has become surplus to requirements.

The best picture we have of the state of castles at the close of the Middle Ages comes from the work of one man, the remarkable John Leland. Leland was born in London around 1506 of Lancastrian descent, and was fortunate to receive a good education at Cambridge and Oxford. He was a scholar of Latin and Greek and gained a privileged position as tutor to the son of the Duke of Norfolk, one of the most influential men at Henry VIII's court. After returning from studies in Paris in 1528 he managed to secure the patronage of the king's ambitious minister Thomas Cromwell, receiving various ecclesiastical benefices, and used his literary skill to pen flattering verses in praise of Anne Boleyn. In 1533 the king rewarded Leland with 'a most gracious commission' to record the historical documents and books that were held in the monastic houses of England. This was on the eve of Henry's religious reforms, and most of the books ended up in the royal collection when the abbeys were dissolved a few years later. As the 'King's Antiquary' Leland now began to pursue an interest in topography and local history, and between 1539 and 1545 he travelled around a country wracked by the upheavals of the Reformation, inspecting any building or monument that drew his attention. His observations are frequently quoted in the following pages, though for ease of reading, Leland's quaintly archaic spellings have been modernised. The results of his epic trek were presented to Henry as a New Year's gift, and the material was subsequently edited and published in 1549; but sadly by that time Leland was unable to benefit from any success his researches had garnered. He had suffered a nervous breakdown two years earlier (due perhaps to the sheer scale of his task, if not to some underlying physiological cause) and spent his remaining years confined to his brother's care. He died, still insane, in 1552. His copious notes ended up in the Bodleian Library at Oxford, where they were collated and published in nine volumes as 'The Itinerary of John Leland the Antiquary' in 1710.

Given the distances travelled and number of places visited, it is inevitable that Leland's notes tend to be on the lean side, and it is not always possible to interpret the condition of a building from his sparse comments. His description of Castell Dinas (p.82) is comparatively detailed, but more often his observations are restricted to a few brief words or throwaway comments like 'a little pretty pile' (Narberth); 'all in ruin, no big thing but high' (Castell Coch); 'part of it yet standeth' (St Fagans). In a few cases he seems to have relied on second-hand information, and he missed out some places altogether; but despite the brevity of his notes the overall picture that emerges is of a countryside filled with ruined or decaying castles.

Leland noted a small number occupied in a residential capacity, patched up and altered as needs dictated. Carew had not long before been 'repaired or magnificently rebuilded by Sir Rhys ap Thomas', and Newcastle Emlyn had been spruced up by the same Tudor magnate. Cardiff, Chirk, Coity, Holt, Montgomery and Powis were still lived in at the time, and a few other castles lingered on as administrative centres or local prisons. When it was not possible to make do and mend, wholesale reconstructions had to be carried out, even complete demolition and rebuilding anew. Oxwich Castle on the Gower peninsula had been the seat of the Penres and Mansel families from at least the fourteenth century, but was completely rebuilt as a lavish mansion more suited to the complexities of life in Tudor times. An equally ambitious scheme was undertaken by the Morgans at Pencoed (p.170), although here at least a bit more of the old fortress was retained.

Lulworth Castle, Dorset, is a typically grand Elizabethan mansion that clearly derives its appearance from medieval castle architecture. Ruperra, near Caerphilly, is almost identical, but now in a ruinous state

Many of the grand new houses appearing during the Tudor and Elizabethan ages had their roots in the not too distant past. The mock towers and battlements that graced many a mansion proudly recalled the feudal ancestry of their owners. Cresswell Castle in Pembrokeshire is a typical example of this architectural fashion and could have been a contender for inclusion in this book were it not for the fact that it was a castle in name only and had negligible defensive capabilities. This overgrown ruin on the banks of the Cleddau consists of a rectangular enclosure with domestic buildings ranged around three sides of a central courtyard. Each corner is capped by a tiny round tower, variously serving as a staircase, dovecot or privy. The river frontage was originally left open to benefit from the view and accessibility to river traffic, but at a later date was filled in by a substantial domestic block. Cresswell was built by the enterprising Roger Barlow of Slebech, one of the self-made men who benefited from the break-up of the vast monastic estates at the Reformation and invested their wealth in stone and mortar. A far more ambitious building was constructed several generations later for Sir Thomas Morgan at Ruperra near Caerphilly. This stunning edifice, now in ruin but hopefully earmarked for restoration, is a four-storey residential cube with large round towers on the corners. The battlements are a later embellishment added to replace the original gabled roofline. Ruperra stands at the zenith of the mock-medieval building style that flowered during the Elizabethan and Jacobean periods and was not repeated on such a scale until the appearance of the fantasy castles of the Victorian age.

A near contemporary of John Leland was Rice Merrick (c.1520-87) of Cotterell in the Vale of Glamorgan. His manuscript collection *Morganiae Archaiographia* was compiled around 1578-84 and provides a wealth of information on the customs, genealogy, history and society of Elizabethan Glamorganshire. A similar survey was undertaken of late-Elizabethan Pembrokeshire by George Owen of Henllys, a member of the local aristocracy. Owen wrote that 'all the buildings of the ancient castles were of lime and stone, very strong and substantially built, such as our masons of this age cannot do the like; for although all or most of the castles are ruinated and remain uncovered, some for diverse hundred years past, yet are all the walls firm and strong and nothing impaired' (*The Description of Pembrokeshire*, 1603). Owen listed 19 castles in his survey, but of these only three were still inhabited at the time.[3] Nevertheless the inherent strength of the medieval masonry enabled many castles to survive substantially intact, as Owen had noted. Mighty Pembroke may have been a roofless shell, but it was still strong enough to play a major role just 40 years later in the wars between king and parliament.

Visual rather than verbal depictions of castles and historic buildings are very rare in this early period, but John Speed's *The Theatre of the Empire of Great Britain* (1611) provides a valuable resource for the appearance of the main towns of Jacobean Britain. Speed's county maps and bird's-eye views can be used by historians to build up a picture of the pre-industrial townscape of Wales. The drawings of the major castles may be stylised and lack detail, but they are still useful in depicting buildings that have since disappeared, such as the round keeps within Cardigan and Monmouth castles, and the Shire Hall at Cardiff.

Revival and destruction

> *I have taken to acquaint your Lordships with what, in my apprehension, I conceive may be both dangerous and unprofitable to this state, which is to keep up forts and garrisons which may rather foment than finish a war.*
> Sir John Meldrum (letter to parliament 1644)

The slow decline of the castles into venerable old age was hastened by the social and political upheavals of the early seventeenth century. King Charles I (1625-49), like his father James before him, had never been on good terms with parliament, believing in the divine right of monarch to rule unopposed. By 1642 the worsening relationship had spiralled out of control. Skirmishes between opposing supporters of the king and parliament were a prelude to a major confrontation at Edgehill in October, and the country was plunged into nine intermittent years of civil war. At first many of the Welsh aristocracy placed a greater value on their lives and estates than on the rights and wrongs of the opposing forces, and tried to stay out of harm's way; but it proved impossible to avoid taking sides as the war progressed and, lacking the Puritan fervour of the English, the people of Wales by and large supported the king's cause.

In order to maintain control over strategic areas various buildings were pressed into use as military strongpoints, often changing hands as the fortunes of war ebbed and flowed. The old castles were the most obvious contenders, and over 40 were sufficiently intact to play a role in the conflict, but many large houses and churches were also utilised – even the shell of Abbey Cwmhir (gutted at the Reformation a century earlier) was put to use. Although lacking the precision that contemporary military engineers strove for, the old castles did have the advantage of robust construction. Thick walls could hamper the onslaught of artillery, and the profusion of arrow slits could be adapted for use with muskets. The defended area might be greatly increased by the addition of an outer line of earthen ramparts and bastions, to serve as gun emplacements and help deaden the impact of incoming missiles.

Few sieges were as long and drawn-out as they had been in medieval times, and the threat of artillery bombardment was often enough to make the garrison lose heart. The siege of Laugharne in 1644 lasted about five days, with the Parliamentarian forces changing their artillery positions twice before the town was entered. Once it was realised that the end was inevitable the defenders arranged a truce and agreed to surrender the castle peaceably. They were allowed to march away and join another garrison nearby. Such chivalrous behaviour happened on many occasions, but there were also times when the rules of war were taken to the bitterest extreme and no quarter was given. When Hopton (Shropshire) fell in 1644 the defeated garrison were brutally slaughtered, the only kindness being shown to an old servant who was given a chair to sit in while having his throat cut.

After several years of indecisive fighting, the Royalist forces suffered a major defeat at Naseby in 1645, which marked the turning point of the war. A few isolated pockets of resistance held out for two more years, but the surrender of Harlech in 1647 brought the fighting in Wales to an end. Charles sought refuge with the Scots but was handed over to the Parliamentarians and placed under house arrest. Even so, he persisted by duplicitous means to try to regain power with Scottish aid. A Royalist resurgence in 1648 (known as the Second Civil War) was sparked by uprisings in south Wales, Essex and Kent, and provided the more radical members of the government with sufficient reason to abolish the monarchy and put the king on trial. Charles was condemned as a 'tyrant, traitor, murderer and public enemy to the good people of this nation' and was executed early the following year. Cromwell's armies did not bring about a cessation of hostilities until 1651, but in the meantime parliament gave orders for certain key fortifications to be *slighted* (disabled) to prevent them being used again as strongholds of resistance against the state. Along with the dissolution of the monasteries, this government-sponsored demolition job ranks as the greatest act of architectural vandalism ever suffered by this country.

The extent of punitive slighting varied considerably from castle to castle. Carpenters, masons and miners would be employed to hack away and undermine the walls, and any stubborn part of the fabric would be helped on its way down with gunpowder. In some cases it was enough to breach the gate or knock off a few battlements; at other sites complete and savage destruction was the order of the day. Parliament was particularly ruthless to those castles that had proved hard to take or where the garrison had put up a stubborn and bloody resistance. Corfe Castle in Dorset was bravely defended by Lady Mary Bankes for almost two months before capitulating. The besieging army took their dented pride out on the castle, one of the oldest and mightiest in England, and blew it to pieces. Aberystwyth Castle was one of Edward I's great fortresses and once stood as proud and imposing as Harlech; that too, was shattered into fragments. But not all the castles ruined in this period were destroyed by post-war state-sanctioned ruin; there is no record of anything being done to Caerphilly, Penrice (p.134) or Llangybi (p.161) for instance, and yet these buildings show clear signs of deliberate demolition. Recent excavations at the latter have revealed a backfill of shattered stonework within the stunted towers. It cannot be said with certainty which faction ordered the destruction, nor whether it was done as a precautionary measure to deny the use of the strongholds to the opposition, or punitive demolition carried out after the castles had been captured.

Less uncertainty remains with other key sites utilised in the conflict. Montgomery Castle was subjected to a well-documented slighting carried out between June and October 1649, a task that required 180 labourers and cost £675 (a substantial sum in those days). Thanks to the thoroughness of the workforce the large mansion of the Herbert family standing within the walls has disappeared completely. Similarly, the marquis of Worcester's palace at Raglan was reduced to a shattered ghost of faded splendour. A later account of the destruction mentions the lead being stripped from the roofs, the great tower tediously picked apart from the top before being undermined by a collapsible tunnel, and the parklands deforested. Even the fishponds were drained so that the local people could make off with the carp. A few lucky castles managed to escape the general wreck; Beaumaris and Caernarfon were slated for demolition, but the order was thankfully never carried out. Picton was allegedly spared because the Parliamentarian commander felt guilty about the dishonourable way it had been captured (a nursemaid lent out of the window to take a message from a passing soldier, and the baby was snatched from her arms and held to ransom).

The demolition of fortifications was to a certain extent an economic measure as well as a practical one, for the government was saved the cost of garrisoning them in future. The process continued even after Cromwell's Puritan reign ended in dismal failure. Chirk was partially slighted in 1659 when the owner, Sir Thomas Myddleton, supported a premature rising in favour of the exiled heir. Denbigh was slighted in March 1660 just two months before the king's return, and the main buildings at Conwy were unroofed in 1665. Once the damage had been done, the shattered castles were subjected to a further round of depredations over succeeding years. The sudden abundance of useable materials was a boon for builders; why pay for stone to be carted from a distant quarry when there might be plenty to hand? Bits of castle found their way into local houses just as the despoiled monasteries had been recycled a hundred years earlier.

Romantic ruins

> *The evening sun was gilding the whole place with wonderful brilliancy, and as I looked at the old towers gleaming in it, and the wooded banks and the shining river ... the scene very much resembled an evening on the Rhine.*
> William Makepeace Thackeray on Chepstow Castle (*Cockney Travels* 1842)

When antiquarians looked again at the architectural heritage of the countryside following the Restoration of the Monarchy, the condition of many historic ruins had changed drastically since Leland's day. A survey as ambitious as his *Itinerary* was undertaken in the closing years of the seventeenth century by the Keeper of the Ashmolean Museum in Oxford, a Welshman by the name of Edward Llwyd (1660-1709). Llwyd's results were as wide-ranging as Leland's, but differed significantly in the approach to fieldwork. While Leland did most of the legwork himself, Llwyd used local correspondents to provide information on the antiquities in their neighbourhood. Questionnaires were sent out to informants in every county in Wales. A few were never returned, others came back with the barest details, while some provided a veritable treasure trove of antiquarian knowledge.

Only a few hardy travellers dared to brave the vagaries of the road during the seventeenth century. In 1684 Thomas Dineley accompanied the duke of Beaufort on a tour of his estates in Wales, describing the places they stopped at and adding a few simple illustrations of the main places of interest. The Dutchman Johannes Kip (1653-1722) specialised in engravings of country mansions, and William Dugdale (1605-1686) produced illustrations of antiquities to accompany his published works. It was not until the middle of the eighteenth century that a more concerted effort was made to depict historic ruins with pictures, rather than words. From about 1711 until 1753, the Yorkshire brothers Samuel and Nathaniel Buck specialised in providing detailed copperplate engravings of the most important and outstanding ruined buildings in England and Wales. Their work not only indicates the condition of the castles and abbeys at that point in time, but also provides us with valuable information on those places that have since deteriorated further, or have disappeared altogether. The etchings can hardly be considered works of art, and

Many of the castles depicted by the Bucks were shown as romantic ruins, as here at Llanbleddian in the Vale of Glamorgan

they have about as much realism as a stage set (criticisms often levelled at their work), yet they are an invaluable source for the local historian. It would be very unwise to study the architecture and history of a particular castle without recourse to their meticulous drawings.

The Bucks relied upon advance subscriptions from wealthy landowners who wanted their ancestral relics to be depicted for posterity. Samuel (who was the main creative force behind the venture) and his younger brother Nathaniel, would tour a selection of ruins in a particular part of the country during the summer months, making drawings with pencil, pen or wash. The sketches were then worked up into detailed copperplate engravings at their London studio during the winter. They brought out a series of Welsh antiquities between 1739 and 1742, and their complete collection of etchings depicting the 'Venerable Remains of above Four Hundred Castles, Monasteries, Palaces etc ... with near one Hundred Views of Cities and Chief Towns' was published in 1774. An accompanying portrait depicts two well-to-do periwigged figures, Samuel looking rather portly and not as energetic as he must have been on his earlier travels. According to the blurb, they were employed for over 32 years on this huge task, snatching 'from the inexorable Jaws of Time, the Mouldering Ruins of each lofty Pile'. Their achievement would not be surpassed until the advent of the camera.

The Buck engravings bring us about half way from Leland's time to our own, through the long years of neglect and military depredations. By the second half of the eighteenth century the improving road network in Wales made it easier for people of means and leisure to explore the countryside. The Romantic movement flourished as artists and writers went in search of the wild and sublime landscape to eulogise on paper and canvas. Literary potboilers inspired a revival of medieval architectural styles and the ruined castle became something of a fashionable asset for any large country seat. Those estates lacking a genuine ruin often made do with a gothic folly tower or 'viewstopper' to grace their lawns, and in a short time the style migrated from the garden to the house itself, resulting in the grand castellated mansions that proliferated throughout the Victorian age.

The growth of the railway network in the first half of the nineteenth century allowed access to almost all areas of the countryside, leading to a wider appreciation of genuine architectural and historical remains. Amateur archaeologists and landowners dug away at local antiquities with ample enthusiasm and varying degrees of scientific thoroughness. Compared to today's exacting methods their work often bordered on vandalism. Articles and reports on various historic buildings appeared in the pages of learned journals such as *Archaeologia Cambrensis,* which was founded by the Cambrian Archaeological Association in 1846 and is still going strong. In 1882 the Ancient Monuments Protection Act was passed, giving statutory protection to our national heritage; but even as late as the First World War, sites were excavated with shockingly cavalier attitudes, simply by stripping away large areas of rubble to uncover as much of the walls as possible, with little consideration given towards the preservation of the exposed remains. Thus Llangynwyd and Morgraig (p.121), both dug in the first decade of the twentieth century, are still surrounded by the rubble and collapsed stonework left behind when the archaeologists moved on to greener pastures.

In 1908 the Royal Commission on Ancient and Historical Monuments in Wales (hereafter referred to as RCAHMW) was established to record and survey the built heritage of the country. At its headquarters in Aberystwyth the RCAHMW maintains the National Monument Record, a vast repository of publicly accessible information relating to archaeological and historical sites. The responsibility for conserving and promoting the heritage of Britain lay with the Department of the Environment (formerly the Ministry of Works) until the government's National Heritage Act of 1983 created three new departments: English Heritage, Historic Scotland and CADW: Welsh Historic Monuments. CADW now has the responsibility for preserving and running historic sites, and making them accessible to the public, as well as providing advice and grant-aid for the restoration of buildings in private care.

Virtually all of the historic castles have been granted the status of Scheduled Ancient Monuments, which puts them under statutory protection, meaning that no works can be carried out on them without consent. Paradoxically, there is no mechanism to safeguard their condition, and the landowner is not legally responsible for their preservation and upkeep. However, CADW does offer grants for their conservation. A Scheduled monument could, in effect, be left to fall down of its own accord should the authorities not step in and carry out essential repairs at their own cost. On the other hand, listed buildings (which are often still inhabited) can be restored or modified within certain parameters by the owners, and grant aid is available to help with the cost. As CADW's former chief inspector Richard Avent pointed out, 'Owners who may be willing to apply for grants to keep a historic roof over their heads are generally far less altruistic when it comes to parting with money to prop up a ruin at the end of the garden or at some remote location on the estate. Often these structures are regarded as nuisances, a protected hazard which they would rather be without.'[4]

Prior to the introduction of the Ancient Monuments Protection Act, any restoration work carried out on historic buildings in private ownership was down to the enthusiasm and financial benevolence of the landowner. For instance, in 1844 the duke of Beaufort employed George Grant Francis, a founder-member of the Cambrian Archaeological Association, to commission detailed drawings of Oystermouth Castle near Swansea as a prelude to a course of restoration work. Francis skilfully reconstructed the delicate traceried windows that now form such a conspicuous feature of the castle. The second earl of Cawdor patched up the ruinous walls of Carreg Cennen in the 1870s, while around the same time Joseph Cobb undertook extensive repairs to Caldicot, Manorbier and Pembroke castles. Officials expressed disparaging views about work that involved replacing large sections of old materials with new and (where details were missing) the substitution of inaccurate and cheap replacements, resulting in 'a most inharmonious and offensive piece of patchwork'. Cobb in particular was so irked by criticism of his work that he wrote a defensive letter to the Cambrian Archaeological Association, and subsequently stated that he would never 'remove an ancient stone, except to put a similar sound one in its place'.[5]

The official approach has long been to 'preserve as found' rather than 'restore'. Britain has only a small number of ruined castles reconstructed to the same degree as many on the Continent have been. The keep at Dolwyddelan was a ragged ruin until the splendidly named Lord Willoughby de Eresby completely rebuilt it in 1848; but even this is a very modest example of what could be done when compared to the wholesale reconstructions carried out for the third marquis of Bute at Cardiff and Castell Coch in the 1870s. The architect William Burges created structures that have more to do with romantic Victoriana than genuine medieval building styles. The fourth marquis, in contrast, undertook a very lengthy and painstaking restoration of Caerphilly, and rebuilt towers, walls and battlements that had been missing for hundreds of years. Even the houses and cottages that had grown up around the ruins were swept away as part of an ambitious restoration scheme that cost £100,000 and lasted from 1928 until the outbreak of the Second World War.[6] Here the intention was to preserve the castle as a medieval relic rather than resurrect it as a fairytale mansion, but even so the work went far beyond what was considered acceptable at the time. Yet few can now deny that, in the case of Caerphilly at least, the end justifies the means.

As this book reveals, there are many substantial ruined castles in Wales not looked after by CADW, the National Trust or some such official organisation. A proprietor of an ancient monument may want CADW to take their ancestral relic into guardianship (thereby making the state responsible for maintenance, whilst retaining ownership of the property), but the offer is not always taken up. Many sites are too fragmentary or considered too historically insignificant to justify the expense of restoration and the burden of ongoing maintenance. Preservation work is a very expensive and time-consuming process; any potential disturbance to sensitive archaeological layers in the ground must be thoroughly investigated; crumbling walls have to be stripped of vegetation and carefully repaired with suitable materials; stairs and walkways may need to be built to allow access to parts of the site; and any necessary modern buildings must be designed to complement the ancient fabric and cause as little disruption to the historic environment as possible. The archaeological excavation and masonry consolidation of Laugharne Castle in Carmarthenshire lasted over twenty years and, although actual figures are not available, the cost must have been in the region of £3 million. The more modestly sized Oystermouth is scheduled for a three-year phase of restoration estimated at £1 million. Even the consolidation of the little tower-house at Candleston in 2007-8 cost approximately £60,000.

The story is not all doom and gloom. Had this book been written just twenty years ago, several more major castles would have had to be included. Ancient Dinefwr, capital of the Welsh rulers of Deheubarth, was only then in the process of being cleared from centuries of undergrowth and transformed from a little understood and mythologized shell in a private park. Llywelyn's castle at Dolforwyn was being uncovered for the first time by archaeologists. The imposing ruin of Llanbleddian near Cowbridge was taken over by CADW only after a protracted legal battle with the owner, before the process of making the remains safe and accessible to the public could begin. The above-mentioned Candleston in the Merthyr Mawr sand dunes was a popular place for children to play until health and safety issues forced its incarceration behind barbed wire. Now the crumbling masonry has been made safe in part and access is again allowed. And Cardigan, one of the key fortresses of the west and long under siege from neglect and decay, has recently won the first stage in a battle to halt the decline.

The increasing threat to historic sites by modern developments was addressed back in the 1970s by the creation of four independent Archaeological Trusts to cover the main regional divisions of Wales at that time (Clwyd-Powys, Dyfed, Glamorgan-Gwent and Gwynedd). The Trusts carry out rescue excavations, watching-briefs and risk assessments in advance of proposed building works. Although it would be impossible now to excavate a castle with the same carefree attitude as in the past, the damage caused by vandalism, off-road vehicles and unauthorised use of metal detectors can be just as detrimental. Archaeological sites in rural locations may escape the worse depredations but in urban areas the threat of redevelopment is far greater. Sully Castle was wiped off the map in the 1970s; Rumney Castle near Cardiff was built over in the 1980s; Maesglas in Newport is now an insignificant lump in the middle of a children's playground; Rhoose Castle went after 1910; and Aberafan way back in 1895. As population levels rise and increasing pressure is put on the utilisation of greenfield sites, more will undoubtedly go. Preservation orders and Listing status may save the actual fabric of a building, but its relationship with the surrounding historic landscape will have been changed forever. One might ask how such a grand and imposing structure as a medieval castle, an image that figures so prominently in the national consciousness, could disappear from the landscape. But for those castles that lack the grandeur and substance of say, Caernarfon, Harlech or Pembroke (and the level of care expended upon them), then the answer is very simple.

Epilogue

And so, what can be done with these forgotten castles?

Many of the sites looked at in the following pages, such as Carndochan, Castell Dinas, Cefnllys, Mellte Castle, Morlais and Plas Baglan, are so buried in debris and soil that the best thing to do would be to leave them alone, unless erosion or unexpected damage necessitates remedial work. Some minor consolidation may be necessary to preserve the few upstanding remains of Castell Tinboeth, Kenfig and Morlais (the south keep was capped in concrete a few years ago to preserve the vaulted basement underneath). Soil erosion is undermining the flaky walls of Aberedw and the task of potential conservation work is hampered by the mature trees along the ramparts. In fact, tree-growth is a major problem facing any restoration scheme; Castell Meredydd, Castell Troggy, Llanfair Discoed, Llangybi and Morgraig are five notable sites where tree roots are buckling the stonework far more remorselessly than any medieval siege machine. It isn't enough to just strip the ivy and cut down the trees, for the damage caused by the root growth has to be repaired and any unsound masonry taken down and replaced. This can result in quite major restoration work, and in the case of Dinas Powys this proved to be the undoing of a well-intentioned local group that had attempted to preserve the ruin in the 1980s.

Excavation would be highly desirable to clarify the structural development of several key sites, and to ascertain how much of the fabric still remains intact below ground. Blaenllynfi, Castell Troggy, Cefnllys, Llanfair Discoed, Newhouse and Painscastle are good candidates for exploratory work, and re-excavation of Llanhilleth with modern techniques would gather more precise information than that unearthed by the 1924 dig. Minor excavations

Excavations by Time Team at Llangybi in 2009

(the archaeological equivalent of keyhole surgery) have already been carried out recently at Llangybi, and exploratory work is planned in the near future for Dinham.

In the following pages, 53 forgotten castles are examined, and the entries have been arranged into five geographical areas (for convenience rather than for any historical or archaeological significance). The comparatively small number of entries in north and west Wales is not due to a lack of castles in those areas, simply that there are fewer sites that qualify for inclusion here. Several castles were omitted for various reasons from the main section but are briefly mentioned in the appendix for the sake of completeness. All place-name spellings have been taken from current Ordnance Survey maps and each entry is provided with location and access information (which to the best of my knowledge was correct at the time of writing). Anyone requiring additional information on a particular site should use the abbreviated references in conjunction with the bibliography on page 177. Further details may also be obtained from the records of the four Welsh Archaeological Trusts and from the online database of the RCAHMW (*Coflein*).

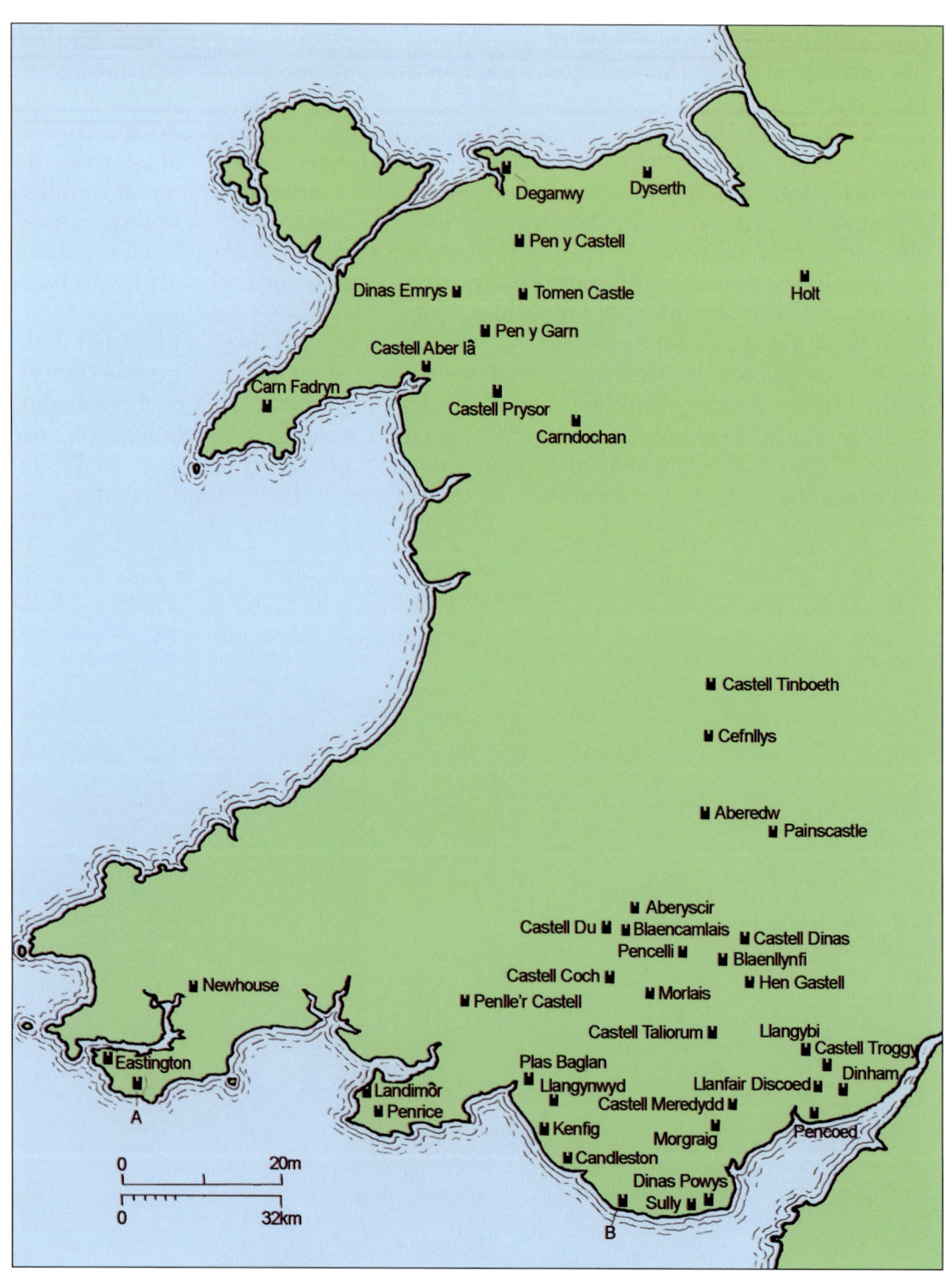

The forgotten castles of Wales included in this book.
A: The fortified houses of Pembrokeshire (pages 59-63);
B: Castles of the Vale (pages 101-108)

North Wales

Castell Carndochan, *Llanuwchllyn*

This enigmatic scatter of rubble on a high crag has no recorded history, but it undoubtedly marks the remains of a native stronghold built to control one of the strategic roads across the bleak uplands of Gwynedd. The tumbled stonework demarcates an oval enclosure at the end of a rocky ridge overlooking a river valley draining into Llyn Tegid near Bala. There was a small square building within the courtyard, a tower of rounded plan on the cliff edge, another on the east side (which may have been a gatehouse), and a much larger tower on the southern flank jutting forward to meet any attacker head-on. This was evidently the keep and must have formed the main accommodation block. The stonework is slightly better preserved than the other walls, and it may be that specialist masons were drafted in to carry

A reconstruction drawing showing how Castell Carndochan would have probably looked in the mid thirteenth century

out that particular work, leaving the rest of the defences to be built by less skilled local labourers.

The Welsh were rather slow to adopt the Norman practice of castle-building (the first attempt is not recorded until the year 1111) and their earliest efforts were just copies of the earth and timber mottes that proliferated throughout the twelfth century. They took to using masonry defences with a similar lack of enthusiasm, and the few stone castles that appear to predate c.1200 are very primitive structures indeed. However, a more complete understanding of the early development of native stone castles is hampered by the lack of surviving remains.[7] It seems that the concept of castles did not fit in well with the Welsh predilection for guerrilla warfare, and the princes simply did not have the revenues or manpower to afford large complex fortifications on a par with those of their Anglo-Norman contemporaries.

It was not until the reigns of Llywelyn the Great and his grandson Llywelyn ap Gruffudd that native strongholds were considered to be essential as more territories were brought under their control. The architectural features still to be seen at Castell y Bere, Criccieth, Dolwyddelan, Dolbadarn, Dolforwyn and Ewloe (all conserved ruins in the care of CADW) reveal how the Welsh borrowed and adapted ideas to create something new. None can be said to be masterpieces of military planning, for they are little more than haphazard arrangements of towers, yet they display an idiosyncratic approach to castle-building, particularly with the use of the apsidal or D-shaped keep. This design was similar to the half-round flanking towers used in English castles, but was usually larger and more elongated, as the rubble remains at Carndochan reveal. The most complete example of an apsidal keep can be seen at Ewloe near Flint, which still stands in part up to battlement level and gives a good impression of what the Carndochan tower would have looked like. There was a ground-level store with a single living chamber above, reached by an external defended stairway. Another stair within the thick lateral wall gave access to the wall-walk and battlements. Ewloe was reportedly built by Llywelyn ap Gruffudd in 1257 to control the borders of his expanding dominions, although there is a possibility that the keep was in fact constructed some years earlier by his grandfather Llywelyn the Great. This Llywelyn was responsible for building *two* apsidal towers at the large mountain fortress of Castell y Bere near Dolgellau, and the construction of Carndochan can probably also be ascribed to this prince.

The surviving ruins of Castell Carndochan have not been consolidated and no proper excavations have taken place here, although the foraging of amateur archaeologists in the eighteenth and nineteenth centuries turned up evidence of burning. Presumably the castle came to a fiery end, either destroyed by the forces of Edward I, or deliberately slighted by the retreating Welsh. There is no evidence that Carndochan served any later use, and by the beginning of the fourteenth century the land was held by one Madog ap Iorwerth, who was associated not with the castle, but with a holding north of Llanuwchllyn that still bears his name (Plas Madog).

Location: 3km west of the village of Llanuwchllyn on the A494 near Bala. Just beyond the village turn off the main road to Dolhendre, cross the bridge before the chapel and follow the track around the base of the steep crag on which the castle lies (Ordnance Survey map reference: SH 847 306).
Access: The site can be reached by a climb from the track up through the forestry, and then across the open moors.
References: Merioneth (1955); Davis (2007).

Castell Prysor, *Trawsfynydd*

Like Carndochan, Castell Prysor is one of a number of sites in north Wales that must be ascribed to native work on account of its peculiar structure; indeed from a distance it hardly looks like a man-made castle at all, but one of the many outcrops that dot the rocky landscape of old Arudwy. And basically, that is what it is; Castell Prysor is a natural tor which has been heightened and clad in drystone walling to create a motte-like fortification. The stonework is now very ruinous, but it is still possible to make out sections of revetment that formerly encased the knoll and rose to support a stone tower on the summit.[8] This seems to have been reached by a path or stairway curving around and up the side of the mound. At the foot of the knoll two rubble banks link up with more natural outcrops to create a tiny oval enclosure. In some publications this has been termed a bailey, but it is absurdly small and could only have functioned as a little barbican to protect the access stair to the motte. The expected ancillary buildings are located on the south side of the knoll in a slightly

The natural tor on which Castell Prysor was built and which retains some stonework from the castle as shown in the reconstruction drawing

43

sheltered hollow, where the foundations of two rectangular buildings and enclosure walls can be seen. There is a third building on the other side of the knoll, but it is better preserved and is likely to be the ruins of a later farmstead.

King Edward I wrote a letter from Prysor in 1284 while travelling through the recently conquered heartland of Gwynedd. This is the one and only mention of the castle in medieval records, but should not be taken as evidence that Castell Prysor was English work of the late thirteenth century, just that it was a convenient staging post across the mountains. Presumably the king and his army were encamped here, for it is hard to believe that this modest little fort offered suitable accommodation for a passing monarch. The primitive nature of the castle suggests a far earlier origin, though how much earlier is difficult to say. It has been suggested that Prysor was built by Llywelyn the Great in 1221 when he took over Arudwy and 'began to build a castle there for himself' according to the *Brut y Tywysogion*; but this cannot be taken very seriously and Llywelyn's castle is generally accepted to be Castell y Bere. More likely Castell Prysor was built a few generations earlier in the turbulent years following the death of Owain Gwynedd in 1170 and the break-up of centralised power in north Wales. Gerald of Wales considered it noteworthy that the Welsh princes had built new stone castles by 1188 (discussed more fully below) and it may be that Prysor was also constructed around the same time by Owain's heirs, desirous to secure the boundaries of their fragmented realm.

Location: The castle lies near Trawsfynydd village off the A40 Dolgellau to Porthmadog road. At the village take the A4212 turning to Bala and continue along Cwm Prysor for about 5km; the castle mound may be seen on the north side of the valley across the river (OS map ref: SH 758 369).
Access: The castle is on private land and there is no official public access.
References: Brut; AW (1998); Davis (2007).

Deganwy, Llandudno

In 2009 the Welsh Assembly Government announced that ten sites of 'iconic significance to Welsh Culture, heritage and nationhood' were to benefit from a two million pound funding programme of restoration work. One of these sites is Deganwy, a double outcrop of volcanic rhyolite located on the coast between Llandudno and Conwy. Up to the end of the thirteenth century this natural geological feature was the high-tide mark of English expansion into Wales, and a mighty castle was built here to symbolise the royal power that threatened the independence of the native princes. Now there is just a scatter of broken walls and buried foundations, meagre remains supplemented by a spectacular view across the estuary of the river Conwy to the mountainous heartland of Gwynedd. It is not hard to see why this rock was ideally suited as a fortification; it rises over 100 metres above the sea to a roughly level summit 60 metres across, protected on most sides by inaccessible cliffs. The less severe slope on the eastern flank served as the main approach and also formed a natural saddle linking up with a second, smaller peak.

The larger of the two summits was utilised as a settlement site long before the Norman Conquest. Excavations carried out here between 1961 and 1966 produced finds dating from the first to third centuries AD and, more significantly, imported Mediterranean pottery of the fifth and sixth centuries, which supports the literary tradition of a royal Welsh citadel of the Dark Ages. The *Brut y Tywysogion* records the destruction of the settlement 'by fire of lightning' in AD 812 and again in 823 by the less divine intervention of Saxon raiders from Mercia. However, the building of the first castle here was down to one of the earliest Norman invaders, Robert of Tilleul, a man 'endless in his ambitions, proud, greedy, combining the most ruthless butchery with the most conventional piety, insatiable in his lust for adventure and battle'.[9] No sooner had his cousin Hugh of Avranches been installed as earl of Chester, than Robert was given *carte blanche* to plunder westwards.

By 1073 he had reached the banks of the Clwyd and built a motte and bailey at Rhuddlan, which served as a secure base for further advance and also provided him with the name with which he is more familiarly known – Robert of Rhuddlan. 'For fifteen years he severely chastised the Welsh and seized their territory … making inroads into their country, through woods and marshes, and over mountain heights,' wrote one contemporary chronicler. 'He inflicted losses upon his enemy in every shape. Some he butchered without mercy like herds of cattle as soon as he came upon them. Others he threw into dungeons, where they suffered a long imprisonment, or cruelly subjected them to shameful slavery.'[10] He aided and then double-crossed the squabbling rulers of Gwynedd and by 1080 had reached the line of the Conwy, where the rock of Deganwy offered a superb defensive position. For Robert to have built an earthen motte here as he had at Rhuddlan would have been a complete waste of time, and bearing in mind the geology of the site there is no reason why his castle should not have been stone-built from the start, perhaps utilising the simple defences of the earlier fort and having a central stone hall or tower.

In 1086 the king carried out a great survey of land values (Domesday Book) and Robert was listed as ruling north Wales for a yearly rent of £40. In reality this must have been a nominal acknowledgement rather than an enforceable claim. His career came to a not unexpectedly bloody end, probably in 1088, during an attack by Welsh or Norse pirates.[11] The raiders were returning to their ships beached beneath the Great Orme at Llandudno when Robert was roused from his mid-day sleep and told of the attack. Before being fully armed and supported by an adequate number of men, he charged recklessly down to the beach, where the raiders promptly filled him with arrows and took his head as an ornament for the ship's mast. This was only a temporary respite, for Earl Hugh took command of the offensive and pushed beyond the Conwy as far as Caernarfon and Anglesey. The Norman takeover of Gwynedd seemed inevitable, but then in 1094 a widespread series of Welsh counterattacks took place, and the invaders were pushed back across the river, leaving the land west of the Conwy as the core territory of the royal House of Gwynedd. The lands to the east, forming the four ancient *cantrefs* of Perfeddwlad, remained in disputed ownership.

The castle was an obvious thorn in Welsh flesh, a visible symbol of English power just out of arrow-shot across the water, and a stumbling block to any expansionist schemes. Llywelyn the Great removed that obstacle from his path. Then in 1210 the earl of Chester hastily rebuilt the castle to reinforce his claim to Perfeddwlad, and the following year received an encouraging visit from King John and his army to counteract Llywelyn's advance. The *Brut y Tywysogion* boasts how this show of military might ended in ignominy when the army was blockaded at Deganwy and suffered such food shortages that 'it was a luxurious feast for them to have the flesh of their horses'. Nevertheless John succeeded in humbling the prince, and it was to take another three years for Llywelyn to regain his position from this setback. In 1213 Perfeddwlad once more passed under Welsh control, and Deganwy was rebuilt as a native stronghold and palace. Unfortunately, subsequent works have effectively removed all certain traces of that structure apart from a section of revetment wall and the base of a small round turret on the north side of the rock. A few other foundations underlying the later masonry could also belong to this period. During the excavations in the 1960s a finely carved stone bracket was discovered here, which depicts a bearded and crowned head, perhaps a likeness of the great prince himself. It would originally have supported one of the roof beams of the hall or some such grand building, and is now on display at the National Museum of Wales.

Whatever the size, scale and splendour of Welsh Deganwy, the castle did not long outlive its builder. When Llywelyn died in 1240 his legitimate heir Dafydd failed to hold on to power with the same ruthless efficiency and, as the English began to reclaim their territories, Deganwy was purposely destroyed in a scorched-earth policy. Dafydd was brought to heel and forced to concede all the lands between the Dee and Conwy to Henry III. To counteract any Welsh resurgence, the king ordered the construction of a new castle at Dyserth in 1241 (see page 50), and then pushed further west and began to transform the shattered walls of Deganwy into a major royal stronghold. It was a task that was to take ten years and cost a huge sum of money, but despite being claimed to be the strongest castle in the kingdom, it was never completed.

Royal accounts provide an overview of the building scheme. The work was undertaken on the king's behalf by John Lestrange, Justiciar of Chester, who was ordered to use the best masons available. But progress was slow in the face of repeated opposition and harassment from the Welsh, so much so that the king himself had to arrive with an army in 1245. It was still unfinished when he left two months later. The principal tower was not started until 1247 and was still under construction in 1249, as well as another tower on the second summit (which was named after the king's clerk and counsellor, John Mansell). The small bailey between the two outcrops was, however, still only protected by timber palisades and rock-cut ditches, and so in 1249 the order was given to upgrade the defences with masonry. Work began the following year on the south side of the bailey, which was provided with a twin-towered gatehouse containing two upper floors of heated chambers. The north side was intended to have the same defences, but although a start was made on the gatehouse (now marked by a solitary upstanding fragment), it appears that the scheme was never finished. In the meantime the King's Hall was completed, Mansell's Tower was heightened by another storey and roofed with lead, and then a start was made on building a ring wall around it. While all these works were

The naturally imposing site of Deganwy Castle and how the castle of Henry III, reputedly the strongest castle in his kingdom, might have looked

going on a small borough was established beside the hill, and a charter of rights was issued in 1252. Each burgess was to have a half-acre plot for building a house and two acres of arable land beyond the limits of the settlement. The earthworks of that urban venture can still be seen today. Ironically, the town managed to outlast the castle and was still occupied at the beginning of the fourteenth century.

A surviving fragment of stonework of the gatehouse

In the meantime the garrison of the incomplete stronghold faced a grave crisis. Llywelyn ap Gruffudd had succeeded where his uncle Dafydd had failed, and by 1256 had united Gwynedd under his rule and reinvigorated resistance to the English. Perfeddwlad was once more in Welsh control, and the hated Royalist strongholds of Deganwy and Dyserth were now isolated outposts in enemy territory. For seven years they were intermittently besieged and relieved, before the situation became so hopeless that the garrisons had little choice but to surrender. Both castles were then taken and thoroughly demolished; 'not one stone was left upon another,' wrote the scribe of the *Annales Cambriae*. Llywelyn could have kept Deganwy and refortified it for his own use, but instead he opted for savage destruction. Was it simply too big for the more modest Welsh armies to garrison effectively, or was the symbolic status of this royal castle too much to bear?

Llywelyn's workmen were particularly enthusiastic in rendering the castle indefensible. At the foot of the hill some sizeable chunks of tumbled masonry can be seen, but most of Deganwy has been reduced to foundations and scrappy fragments (in places just a few mortared blocks precariously clinging to the natural rock face). By piecing together this jigsaw of rubble it is possible to make a tolerably accurate reconstruction of the castle, although many details are forever lost and others must await confirmation by future excavations. The main part of the castle was known as the Donjon, which in this instance does not mean a solitary keep but the whole of the larger summit. A curtain wall was built in straight stretches around the cliff edge, linking up with the irregular outcrops and incorporating some of the older ramparts. There were various buildings set against the wall (indicated by the position of garderobe drains) and a large central quarry where most of the building stone came from. The pit might later have doubled as a cistern to collect rainwater. On the highest part of the hill there stood a long block, almost certainly the King's Hall of 1250. A mass of rubble at its west end has been interpreted as the remains of a tower, perhaps a keep dating back to the earliest days of the castle. There are more certain remains of a half-round tower jutting out from the opposite corner of the hall. This, presumably, was the 'principal tower' built in 1247-49. Despite the extremely ruined state, it is still possible to see a single fragment of dressed stone that would once have formed part of a string-course encircling the base of the tower. Regardless of the rushed construction, it seems King Henry wanted a few architectural flourishes to grace his new fortress, and no doubt the principal chambers were similarly decorated.

From this tower the garrison could overlook anyone climbing the steep path up from the bailey towards the gateway. If an enemy broke through the first barrier they would have entered a narrow killing ground hemmed in between the southern slope and the upper curtain wall, with another gate at the far end. These defences may seem insignificant for a major royal fortress, but the restricted topography of the hill would not have allowed for anything more substantial. The main gatehouse down in the bailey was a more typical structure for the time, but this was not started until 1250, along with a curtain wall that climbed the precipitous side of the eastern summit to link up with Mansell's Tower. Some form of defence on this smaller peak was a prerequisite from the start, and it seems to have taken the form of a relatively large apsidal tower, larger in fact than any of the other towers at the castle. Some historians have compared its shape and size to the Welsh keeps at Ewloe and Castell y Bere, suggesting it was a left-over from Llywelyn's fortress. While this is possible, the name of the tower and the documentary accounts make it more likely to belong to Henry's scheme. The exceptionally large dimensions (internally it measures at least 10m by 18m) might imply that it was initially built as an open redoubt or bastion (as suggested in the drawing on p.47), and was only later converted into a habitable tower.

In the course of King Edward's first war against Llywelyn the royal army encamped within the rubble of Deganwy, but when the king triumphed in 1283 he decided to build a completely new castle on the opposite side of the river, a significant step beyond the natural barrier that had so long marked the boundary between Welsh and English lands. Edward's castle at Conwy was positioned right on the water's edge so that even if the overland routes were in enemy control, ships could dock below the walls and bring in men and supplies. Stones from Deganwy were said to have been used in the building of Conwy, and this may have been more than just a practical method of recycling materials; for elsewhere the king dismantled the residences of his vanquished foes and incorporated them into his mighty new castles – a symbolic conquest expressed in architecture.

Location: *the rock of Deganwy lies 3km south of Llandudno off the A456 road to Conwy (OS map ref: SH 783 795).*
Access: *freely accessible. There are several footpaths to the hill, the easiest from the top of York Road (turn off the main road at Deganwy Castle Hotel).*
References: *Brut; HKW (1963); RCAHMW (1956).*

Dyserth, *Prestatyn*

The story of Dyserth coincides in part with that of Deganwy, for this was another royal castle built to take advantage of a downturn in native fortunes. Unlike Deganwy however, the history of Dyserth extends to a mere 22 years, and now, thanks to an unwarranted act of commercial vandalism in the early twentieth century, there is hardly anything left to see. Quarrying for limestone began on the castle hill in 1903 and photographs taken around 1911 show an extensive ruin on the summit with upstanding fragments of walls and towers, yet the destruction continued, and by the end of the First World War the castle had been practically obliterated. The only fragments that now remain are the overgrown banks and ditches of the outworks, just visible at the back of some private gardens.

The castle was built by Henry III in 1241 to consolidate English authority in north-east Wales and to supplement the much older Norman base at nearby Rhuddlan. Llywelyn the Great was dead, and his son and heir Dafydd had been forced to humble himself before the king and relinquish all his lands between the Conwy and the Dee. Henry's masons were directed by John Lestrange, Justiciar of Chester, to build the castle on the summit of a steep rock overlooking the Vale of Clwyd. The site was variously known as Caerfaelan, Castell y Garreg and Dincolyn, and occupied the remains of an Iron Age hillfort.[12] Henry's army soon pushed further west and began to rebuild the gutted shell of Deganwy as a front line base; but both royal castles were to be short-lived. Dafydd attempted a siege of Dyserth in 1245 but was repulsed by the arrival of an army from Chester, and the next year he inconveniently died, leaving the House of Gwynedd in a very unstable position.

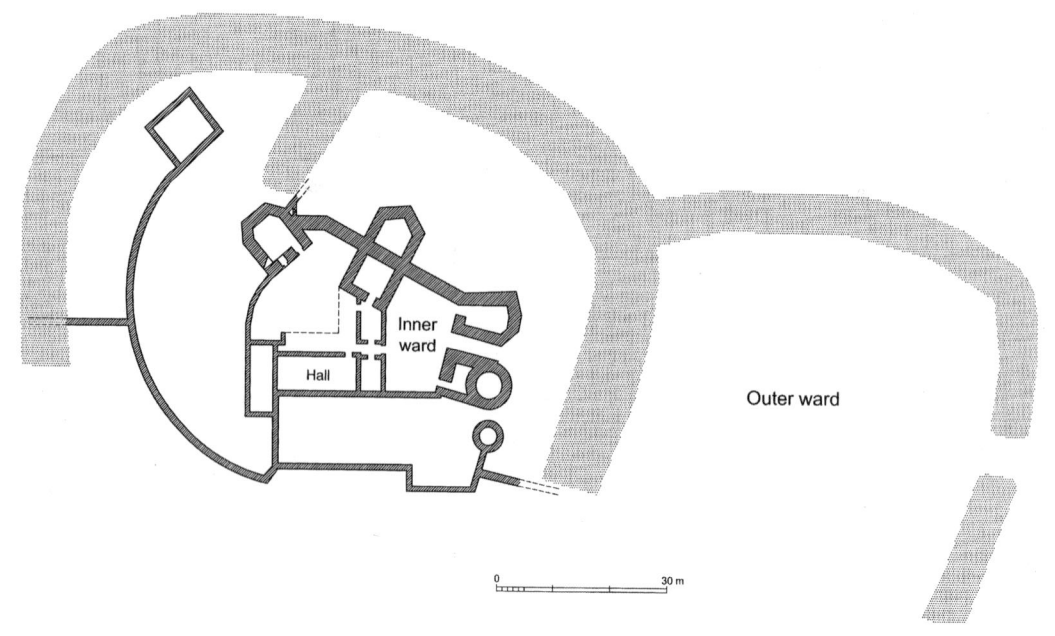

Interpretive plan of Dyserth Castle (after Edwards et al)
and a reconstruction drawing of the inner ward (opposite)

Building work at the castle continued for some years to come; the royal accounts mention the purchase of lead to complete the roofs in 1246, but the bailey had still not been completed, and the King's Hall and chapel within the courtyard were only started after 1250.

By 1256 Perfeddwlad was under the control of Llywelyn ap Gruffudd, and both Deganwy and Dyserth faced seven long years of intermittent siege before they were taken and destroyed in 1263. Dyserth may have been sited on a seemingly impregnable rock, but it had no direct link to the coast for it to be effectively maintained when the overland supply routes were in Welsh control. It was a lesson that Henry's successor Edward learned well. When Llywelyn was first defeated in 1277 Edward chose to build a completely new castle at Rhuddlan with a river route to the sea, rather than repair the broken walls of lofty Dyserth.

The form and appearance of this short-lived castle can now only be recovered from archive material and the results of minor excavations carried out here before destruction. It was clearly a very unusual thirteenth-century castle, but some of the conclusions reached by the archaeologists are suspect, and the veracity of the excavation reports can no longer be confirmed on site. The main feature was a small inner ward with thick curtain walls and two large multangular towers positioned on the side most vulnerable to attack. It appears that the massive walls were never built on the remaining side overlooking the steep rocky slopes; presumably the planners considered these natural defences to be more than adequate protection.

Entry to the ward was through a gatehouse of asymmetrical plan, flanked by a polygonal tower and a rounded one. Most of the courtyard was occupied by an L-shaped range of domestic buildings, which seem to have been connected to one of the towers by a covered walkway. The south-facing side of the castle was further protected by a thin-walled outer enclosure with two towers of round and square shape, perhaps added as an afterthought to improve the negligible defensive strength on this flank. From the gatehouse a drawbridge led across a rock-cut ditch to an outer bailey defended by a rubble rampart, ditch and counterscarp bank, and this is now the only substantial part of the castle still surviving.

In some respects Dyserth is comparable to Montgomery Castle (Powys), which had been built by Henry some twenty years earlier. This too has a compact, heavily defended inner ward with a twin-towered gatehouse and a series of outworks; but the use of multangular towers is quite unusual at a time when round towers were almost universally adopted by the castle-building elite. It is not clear where the influence for the design came from. Multi-sided towers are not at all common – solitary examples appeared in English castles such as Odiham (*c*.1174), Dover (*c*.1180), the Tower of London (*c*.1190) and Corfe (*c*.1204) – but it is easier to find later examples than earlier. More than forty years were to pass before anything similar to Dyserth was built (notably Caernarfon and Denbigh). Regardless of whether the decision to build such unusual towers was a deliberate choice of the king, or just a fad of the architect, there can be no doubt that the end result would have been a striking and unusual symbol of English power in the face of Welsh resistance.

Location: Dyserth village lies at the foot of the Clwydian hills off the A547 between Rhuddlan and Prestatyn. Castle Hill is just north of the village and can be reached by several footpaths, although the easiest way is to drive up the hill to Graig Fawr nature reserve. The overgrown outworks lie in the back garden of a private house opposite the car park (OS map ref: SJ 060 799).
Access: on private land but visible from the road.
References: Brut; AC (1912, 1915); HKW (1963).

Gerald's castles

In 1188 the archbishop of Canterbury travelled around the country recruiting soldiers for the Crusades, accompanied by the archdeacon of Brecon, Gerald de Barry, better known to historians as Giraldus Cambrensis, or Gerald of Wales. The outcome of their trek was subsequently written down by Gerald (with numerous digressions and outlandish interpolations) and serves as a window into late-twelfth-century life and customs in Wales and the Marches. While travelling through Gwynedd, Gerald made a point of commenting on two stone castles that had recently been built by the Welsh; 'one called Deudraeth belongs to the sons of Cynan and is situated in the Eifionydd area facing the northern mountains'. Timber castles were still commonly used by the Welsh at this time and masonry fortifications seem to have been something of a novelty. Deudraeth has been identified as **Castell Aber Iâ** on a headland separating two estuaries (the 'two sands' or deu-draeth of the place-name). It was built by Gruffudd and Maredudd ap Cynan, grandsons of the great prince Owain Gwynedd, to secure this portion of the divided territories.

The castle is little more than an overgrown knoll with a rock-cut ditch isolating the rounded summit, but among the undergrowth can be glimpsed fragments of drystone revetment, the last vestiges of the masonry defences. Antiquarian accounts suggest there was some kind of tower here,[13] but the remains were largely robbed for building stone in the nineteenth century. The estate was subsequently acquired by Sir Clough Williams-Ellis who, from 1925 onwards, transformed the hamlet into the architectural hodgepodge that is now Portmeirion. Sir Clough built the mortared walls around the summit of the rock, and also incorporated some of the remaining stones into his Italianate campanile.

The other castle Gerald mentions is **Carn Fadryn** on the Llŷn peninsula further west, an isolated hill crowned with one of the largest stone-walled Iron Age forts in Wales. The top is covered with the tumbled stone foundations of ramparts and circular hut foundations, as well as several rectangular buildings that could be medieval. On the very summit a long narrow stone enclosure with a simple entrance gap has been constructed beside the peak, which was perhaps utilised as the base for a vanished stone tower. The site is now very ruinous and hard to distinguish from all the pre-Roman stonework scattered around. In fact, it is such an odd structure that if it wasn't for Gerald's writings it would no doubt be passed off as a small Celtic fort of Iron Age or Dark Age date. A later mansion bearing the name of its predecessor was built in a more congenial location at the foot of the hill, but of this 'Madryn Castle' only the Elizabethan gatehouse remains today.

Elsewhere in north Wales there are a number of similar primitive stone forts that could well be broadly contemporary with Gerald's castles. The aforementioned Castell Prysor is one; **Pen y Castell** near Llanrwst is probably another. The remains are shrouded in a dense forestry plantation high above the Conwy valley and not easy to appreciate without some selective pruning. There seems to have been a series of drystone walls and revetments strengthening natural outcrops to form a long and narrow bailey subdivided by a rock-cut ditch. On the highest part of the escarpment is a more substantial stone structure of circular form, measuring 17 metres across, and surrounded by a thick drystone wall that still stands two metres high. Despite its small size, this looks more like an enclosure rather than a tower, and perhaps sheltered some internal timber lean-to buildings originally. The site resembles the Celtic forts of Ireland and Scotland, and a possible Dark Age date cannot be ruled out. Another very similar site was discovered in 1990 by an archaeologist working for the Snowdonia National Park, at **Pen y Garn** overlooking the Glaslyn estuary not far from Porthmadog. The stony foundations define an oval enclosure 30m by 40m built against a rocky escarpment.

Whether these sites are actually twelfth-century castles or much earlier fortified homesteads may only ever be determined by excavation at a future date. There is little doubt about the two final castles looked at here. **Dinas Emrys** is an isolated rocky hill near Beddgelert that formed a defended outpost during the Roman period and Dark Ages (the site also figures prominently in Arthurian myths and legends). In medieval times the hill was reoccupied and a stone keep was erected near the summit. The stones were bonded in clay rather than mortar, and only the lower courses survive today, outlining a rectangular chamber 7m by 9.8m with a more irregularly-shaped outer wall. Despite the odd shape, this was clearly a medieval castle, and the only debatable point is who built it. The most popular contenders are Owain Gwynedd or Llywelyn the Great, but it could well have been one of the minor princes in the hiatus between the two reigns.

The imposing keep of Dolwyddelan looks like all self-respecting castles should, bristling with battlements and glowering down from an unassailable crag, daunting any attacker; but this appearance is due entirely to restoration work in 1848-50 when the fragmentary remains were practically rebuilt from the first floor up. Dolwyddelan is not the 'forgotten' castle looked at here, which is its inconspicuous predecessor, known as **Tomen Castell**, in the valley below. Like most of these small castles, it is a natural outcrop of rock which has been augmented with stonework, and was designed to guard one of the upland routes. The pine-covered knoll stands between the river and the road and carries the last vestiges of an oblong keep of irregular shape, much like the one at Dinas Emrys. The summit could only have been reached by a timber ramp or a zigzag path up the less sheer southern flank of the mound. This modest tower may well have been built by Owain Gwynedd's son Iorwerth, who held this territory and whose own son, Llywelyn the Great, enhanced his birthplace by building the new castle of Dolwyddelan close by.

*Access: **Aber Iâ** lies in the woods just west of Portmeirion village off the A487 near Porthmadog, and can be reached by a footpath from the village (OS map ref SH 588 372). **Pen y Castell** is on National Trust owned Cadair Goch viewpoint, off the A470 at Maenan Abbey Hotel, 4km north of Llanrwst. From the signposted lay-by take the path through the woods and up the side of the ridge; where it levels off, double back through the forestry and walk along the crest of the ridge until the site is reached (OS ref: SH 793 667). **Pen y Garn** is on private land on a mountaintop 2.7km east of Tremadog beside the A498 (OS ref: SH 581 411). There is no access to the hill of **Dinas Emrys**, which can be seen from the A498 2km north-east of Beddgelert (OS ref: SH 606 492). **Tomen Castell** is also on private farmland, but can be seen from the A470 between Blaenau Ffestiniog and Betws-y-Coed, directly opposite Dolwyddelan Castle (OS ref: SH 724 521).*
References*: Gerald; AC (1927, 1960); RCAHMW (1956); CADW (2004).*

Holt, Wrexham

With the defeat of the Welsh princes in the war of 1282-83, Edward I and the Marcher lords wasted no time in securing their borders against any potential future rebellion by building a series of formidable castles using the most up-to-date military designs. Holt on the Dee was one of those new strongholds, on a par with Conwy, Denbigh, Flint and Rhuddlan and, like them, should be an imposing monument attracting hundreds of visitors, but instead it is a scrappy collection of fragments in a fenced-off quarry. Were it not for the signs, any passer-by would be hard pressed to recognise it as a castle, let alone a major fortress of the Edwardian period. Three factors caused this major stronghold to fall into such a pathetic state; each by itself would not result in such a loss, but combined they succeeded in almost eradicating this castle from the landscape.

Edward had granted the forfeited Welsh territories to his loyal magnates on the proviso that new castles were built at their expense, to supplement his own defensive scheme. Henry de Lacy built Denbigh, Roger Mortimer started Chirk and Reginald de Grey completed the unfinished stronghold at Ruthin. The earl of Surrey, John de Warenne, received the territories of Bromfield and Yale, which included the hilltop castle of Dinas Brân at Llangollen. This was a native Welsh site that had been partially demolished to prevent its reuse by the English. 'There is no stronger castle in Wales, nor has England a greater,' wrote Henry de Lacy to the king, and urged its rebuilding; but as with Dyserth, Dinas Brân had a relatively inaccessible location and instead John de Warenne chose to build his new castle right on the border with England, on the navigable reaches of the river Dee guarding what had been a crossing point since Roman times. When he did so is a matter of some controversy. There is evidence to suggest that his first foundation was elsewhere, and that it was destroyed in a Welsh attack. Although John is considered to have been the probable builder of Holt, it was not until 1311 (seven years after his death and during the tenure of his grandson) that a 'new castle' is first mentioned. Furthermore, the compact plan and unusually fine details (described below) are more typical of the lavish 'show castles' and fortified houses that began to appear in the fourteenth century than the purely military strongholds of the Edwardian period. Possibly the castle was begun by the earl *after* 1300, by which time the Welsh had settled down and the architects could give more attention to the domestic aspects of the building.

It is only due to the fortuitous survival of antiquarian drawings that we have any idea of the startling design of the castle, a compact pentagonal enclosure set on a

The village sign for Holt displaying a reconstruction drawing of the castle based on John Norden's perhaps unreliable survey of 1620

low-lying outcrop of red sandstone beside the river. The masonry was carried down the sides of the outcrop as supporting revetment for the upper structure, which had basement rooms cut into the natural rock face. The castle was in effect built *around* the outcrop as well as on it. The inner walls were lined with domestic and ancillary buildings overlooking a cramped central courtyard, and each of the five corners had a round tower jutting out into the water-filled moat. The pentagonal layout seems unusual, but it is just a progression of the type of thirteenth-century castle design that relied on simple geometry to achieve a coherent and effective plan. Bolingbroke (Lincolnshire), built some 60 years earlier, has a very similar layout, and so too has Morgraig (p.121), while Caerlaverock in Scotland has a triangular plan.

The lordship passed to the Fitzalans of Arundel in 1347 and during the Glyndŵr rebellion the castle was provisioned against attack but does not seem to have been taken. During the latter part of the fifteenth century the lordship was in royal ownership, and was periodically granted to favoured magnates well provided with estates elsewhere in the country. Nevertheless, Holt was not neglected; further works may have been carried out and the castle was still inhabited well into Elizabethan times. John Leland came here around 1539 and saw 'a pretty Welsh town, governed by a mayor, having once a year a fair ... and a goodly castle'. Due to this longevity and regal ownership, Holt was surveyed on three known occasions between 1547 and 1620, and the written descriptions, coupled with plans and drawings, mean that we know considerably more about this lost castle than many other better surviving ruins. The surveys are not completely reliable as there are some puzzling contradictions, but by sifting the evidence it is possible to achieve a convincing picture of Holt Castle in its latter days as a Tudor mansion.

The castle was approached through an outer enclosure containing a number of timber-framed buildings, including a gateway, barn, stable, courthouse and dovecot. A timber bridge spanned the moat to the square Exchequer Tower (which had an upper chamber where the lordship records were stored) and then a drawbridge crossed to the main entrance, a simple archway with a gate and portcullis. Above this rather weakly defended entrance there was a carved stone panel depicting a heraldic lion, and from this feature Holt was known throughout the Middle Ages as *castrum leonis* or Chastellion.

Around the sides of the pentagonal courtyard stood three-storey buildings containing basic stores and ancillary rooms at the lower levels with the main residential apartments on the upper floors. The great hall stood on the left upon entering the court and was approached by a large stairway. Each of the towers contained four floors of residential chambers above the basements, and there were numerous winding stairs connecting all the different levels of the castle. There was a clear bias toward the provision of ample accommodation, and Holt was evidently not just a military base. Even the exterior was rather unusual if a sketch drawn in 1562 is to be trusted; it shows a highly ornate structure with dressed stone walls, horizontal string courses and battlemented watchtowers crowned with chimneys.

These details are untypical of the Edwardian castles (only the gatehouse at Harlech has similar architectural flourishes), but quite commonplace in the grander fortified houses of the fourteenth century and later. In fact, the nearest comparable structure to Holt seems to have been Donnington in Berkshire, built around 1386.

Donnington Castle, Berkshire, which has some resemblance of design to the castle at Holt (see drawing below)

A sketch of the castle made in 1562

The only really inexplicable part of the vanished castle is the Chapel Tower, which is depicted in the 1562 survey as a round tower with a flanking square turret jutting out towards the river. When the cartographer John Norden surveyed Holt in 1620 he showed the entire tower as square, not round; however, Norden's survey differs in details from the earlier plans and may not be very reliable. Lawrence Butler wrote a fascinating article on this 'problem' castle[14] and proposed that there was a detached tower standing on the riverbank, which the earlier surveyors mistook for part of the main building. There was certainly something here, for the surveys mention a vaulted passage leading down from the courtyard to the river, where a strong iron door barred access. The purpose of this was no doubt to provide an escape route if the castle was being overrun by an enemy and to allow goods to be loaded directly from boats.

At the time of John Norden's visit the castle was evidently in decay, for he noted 'part of the roof ... fallen down and much of the timber rotted'. A floor in one of the towers had even collapsed the day he arrived! Rather ominously, he added that 'the lead of the said castle and other materials, if the same should be demolished, are worth to be sold'. Yet despite the accelerating decay, twenty years later the castle was garrisoned for the king during the Civil War. In November 1643 the Parliamentarian army stormed the fortified

The arched doorway probably led into the lost courtyard buildings of the castle

bridge over the Dee and swiftly mopped up the main Royalist strongholds in Flintshire, but inexplicably left Holt and its small garrison alone. It was a temporary victory, for by the end of the year north Wales was back in Royalist control with the arrival of reinforcements from Ireland. Holt saw more action during the Civil War than throughout its previous existence. It also held out far longer than most of the Royalist bases in Wales, eventually capitulating in January 1647, just two months before the surrender of Harlech, the last remaining stronghold in Wales.

After the war the first stage of Holt's demise took place, as the defences were slighted on the order of Parliament. Since so little now remains we cannot be sure how much damage was inflicted; the gateway was probably disabled and perhaps one or two towers brought down. The second stage occurred soon afterwards, as pillaging for building materials commenced. Holt town had suffered badly during the war and most of the houses had been demolished to obtain a clear field of fire, therefore reparations had to be made, and the castle ruin was a handy source of stone. Worse still, between 1675 and 1683 Sir Thomas Grosvenor quarried the site for materials to build a new mansion on his estate at Eaton further downriver. There was not a great deal left when the Buck brothers sketched the ruins in 1742. But perhaps the most destructive factor of all was the quality of the masonry itself – a soft red sandstone that weathers easily and is not ideally suited for tough, durable buildings. The fact that so much of the castle was built around the outcrop, rather than securely footed on the bedrock may also have contributed to its rapid decay and the ease with which it was pillaged. Now only the inner core of rock remains, and the few visible walls and openings formed the courtyard face of the interior buildings. Everything else has gone.

Location: *the site lies in a disused quarry on the banks of the Dee behind Holt village, 7.5km north-east of Wrexham on the A534 to Nantwich (OS map ref: SJ 411 537).*
Access: *exterior view only. A signposted footpath from the village green leads down to the site.*
References: *AC (1907, 1908); HKW (1963); Hubbard (1986).*

West Wales

The fortified houses of Pembrokeshire

Tower-houses, pele-towers and strong-houses are terms used to describe the smaller fortifications that proliferated in the unsettled regions of northern England, Scotland and Ireland between the fourteenth and seventeenth centuries. In a relatively lawless society plagued with endemic infighting, cattle raiding and piracy, anyone who could afford to sought to protect their lives and belongings behind securely locked doors. The classic form of tower-house resembles a scaled-down castle keep, containing a basement store and several floors of cramped living quarters above. For those nearer the lower end of the social scale, the only affordable protection would be a stone-walled farmhouse where the living chamber was on the first floor above a vaulted undercroft and accessed by a removable ladder.

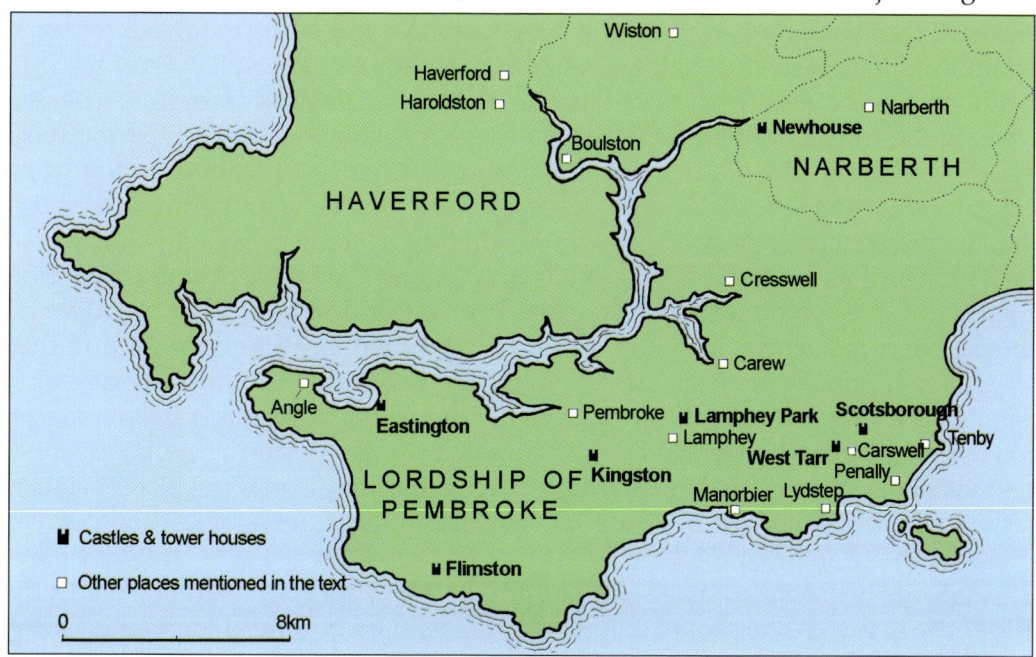

Although these buildings form a major part of the architectural landscape of northern Britain, there is a far from insignificant number in Wales, and the largest concentration is found in south Pembrokeshire. Why they should be needed at all is something of a mystery, for there is no evidence to suggest that the same level of unrest existed here as in Scotland, or that Pembrokeshire was subject to greater discord than other areas of Wales in the later medieval period. In fact, this part of the country was controlled by the Anglo-Norman settlers from an early date. After several raids on the old Welsh territories of Deheubarth and Penfro, the Normans undertook a more permanent settlement in 1093. Penfro was split into the Marcher lordships of Pembroke and Haverford and controlled from a series of major castles. Henry I even introduced Flemish settlers to the region in order to boost the take-over by ethnic colonisation, and the ultimate success of this move can be gauged by the many English-sounding place-names still remaining here.

Pembrokeshire retains some of the most architecturally and chronologically diverse castles in the country, ranging from the primary timber forts to early Norman keeps, massive fortresses of the Edwardian period and the diminutive tower-houses of the Tudor age. Most of the major castles are in the care of CADW or the Pembrokeshire Coast National Park and Local Authorities, and there is public access to them. A few have been restored as residences and are still occupied; but being far less notable than their larger kin, the tower-houses have not fared as well. To date, only two sites, Carswell and Angle, have been taken into official care and sufficient preservation work carried out to enable public access;[15] the others remain as overgrown ruins or patched-up buildings still in agricultural use.

The question still remains unanswered as to why there was a need for these towers at all, although a likely possibility is that they were built as precautionary measures against the threat of piracy. The exposed coastline of Pembrokeshire and the navigable waterway of Milford Haven offered many opportunities for a sea-borne enemy to get far inland. (Owain Glyndŵr's French mercenaries landed in the Haven in 1405, and 80 years later Henry Tudor's invading army used the same route.) The towers may also have had some relevance as status symbols among the local landowners, in much the same way that water-filled moats (of limited defensive use) were dug around farmsteads and manor houses in lowland areas of Britain. Another reason for their existence may simply be the result of local building traditions. Pembrokeshire did not have an abundance of good trees for carpenters to create the timber-framed halls that most people lived in during the medieval period. The 'black-and-white' houses that form such a conspicuous feature of the Marches (and were at one time more widespread across the country) are now absent from the western regions of Wales, where building in stone became the norm.

The historian George Owen noted in 1603 how 'most castles and houses of any account were built with vaults very strongly and substantially wrought'. If a house has a residential chamber set above a vaulted and fireproof ground-floor store, there is already some element of defence present that is otherwise lacking in a single-storey timber hall. If that upper chamber is only accessible by an external wooden stair or ladder (which could be hauled up inside during an emergency), the defensive aspect is further increased. Such a building could never withstand a major assault for long, but it would be very useful in deterring a raiding party or an opportunistic gang of robbers.

Carswell near Tenby is just such a building. Barely six metres square inside, this little house of tower-like proportions contains a vaulted ground-floor kitchen with a

One of the two diminutive towers at West Tarr Farm

separately accessed living room on the floor above, both chambers heated by fireplaces set into a typically massive Pembrokeshire chimney. Only a few metres away there is another vaulted building of similar proportions, possibly another house, although it has undergone considerable alterations. The main house has been preserved by CADW and so is freely accessible, but just a kilometre away at **West Tarr Farm** is another pair of buildings in a far poorer state of repair. Curiously, both are built on steeply sloping ground, which makes them comparatively less defensible. The main house contains vaulted chambers on both floors and originally had an external doorway providing access to the first-floor room. After the building was abandoned as a dwelling, the entrance was blocked off and a more convenient doorway was knocked through the fireplace on the uphill side. The West Tarr tower is rather unusual for it seems to have formed part of a larger building that now survives only as a fragmentary ruin alongside. The ground floor undercroft extended well beyond the tower and was accessed by a mural stair from the upper chamber. The relationship between the two buildings might be made clearer by removing the undergrowth and carrying out small-scale excavations. The owners of the site have restored some of the nearby outbuildings, and hope to carry out some remedial work on the towers in due course.

In the courtyard of **Kingston Farm** near Pembroke stands another tiny tower, which has a main chamber measuring just under 3m by 4m. The external appearance of the house has been modified by the removal of the large chimney stack and a doorway has been cut through the ground floor fireplace, so that like West Tarr it has been downgraded from domestic use to an agricultural outbuilding.

These dwellings seem so pathetically small on their own that it must be suspected they once formed part of a

The Tower House at Kingston Farm

larger complex or were served by other buildings close by which have not survived. They have been likened to the 'ten-pound towers' of Ireland, modest little fortified dwellings that landowners were encouraged to build for their own protection in 1429 with the aid of a £10 royal grant.[16] The towers were to measure 6m by 4.8m and stand at least 12 metres high, dimensions which tally with the Pembrokeshire houses. Whether these examples also belong to the fifteenth century is less certain, for they have almost no dateable features, and excavations at Carswell produced finds no earlier than the sixteenth century (even though the place-name goes back to the 1320s). Kingston has a window detail that would not be incompatible with a Tudor date.

On the Castlemartin peninsula beyond Pembroke there are a number of early farmsteads abandoned since the army requisitioned the area in 1938. The most obvious is the wreck of **Flimston** beside the old parish church, which can be seen from the graveyard when the road to Stack Rocks is open on non-firing days. Flimston may look like a ruinous nineteenth-century farm, but it is in fact a substantial late medieval hall with a vaulted cross-wing at the far end, indicated by a prominent round chimney. A blocked external doorway seems to have been the original access way to the first-floor chamber. Here the tower-like structure is integral with the house, and not free-standing as at Carswell and Kingston. **Scotsborough** near Tenby incorporates a defensible wing in its layout, although this is clearly an addition to the older, undefended house. The remains of this large mansion of the Perrot family are now in a very fragmentary state and heavily overgrown, but the most substantial surviving part is a rectangular vaulted building with a projecting turret (probably for a garderobe). The first-floor chamber has a fireplace with the usual round chimney, but the tiny loop-holes are quite unexpected for a domestic chamber and point to some defensive function. Evidently this wing was a bolt hole into which the occupants might retreat in case of emergency. There are many more ruined houses all across this region which incorporate vaulted structures in their make-up (Boulston, Haroldston, Lydstep, Minwear and Penally are notable examples), and while the huge episcopal palaces at St Davids and Lamphey have passed into state care, the less substantial dwellings of the Tudor and Elizabethan gentry crumble in weed-choked decay.

One question already touched on is whether these houses were intentionally planned with defensive needs in mind, or were simply the by-product of the layout and materials favoured by the builders. It may not

The Old Rectory at Angle

be possible to give an answer to that when considering the likes of Carswell or Scotsborough, but there are other buildings in Pembrokeshire that use architectural features derived from castles to create more obviously fortified dwellings. The best example is the Old Rectory at Angle, a tiny keep-like tower containing four cramped rooms and sporting a drawbridge, winding stair and machicolated battlements. The tower stood at one corner of a square moated enclosure fed by the tidal reaches of the Haven. This castle-in-miniature is in the care of the Pembrokeshire Coast National Park and can be visited at reasonable times. Nearby **Eastington** has similar features and will be looked at in greater detail below.

The well-maintained fabric of the Old Rectory only serves to highlight the shocking state into which many other historic buildings have fallen. A particularly sad example is the tower at **Upper Lamphey Park** near Pembroke. It is still in private ownership and no work has been carried out to preserve the crumbling walls since it was identified in 1994, despite the fact that it lies adjacent to a public footpath within the boundary of the CADW-owned Bishop's Palace. It is doubtful whether any passer-by would even recognise this dilapidated barn as a historic building, so great have been the changes inflicted upon it. Rather surprisingly considering the late date of discovery, the tower appears as a tiny detail in the Buck brothers' 1740 engraving of the palace. There in the background is shown a hilltop building resembling a small church, with a crenellated tower and flanking wings. Only the tower still stands today, shorn of its battlements and accompanying buildings. A few details, such as the projecting stair turret and corbelled chimney stack, indicate that the ruin has a more complex architectural history than first appearances might suggest. It seems to have formed part of a group of two-storey buildings and originally stood at least one floor higher than it does today. From its elevated setting within the park it could well have served as a semi-fortified hunting lodge for the wealthy prelates of Lamphey.

*Location & access: **Scotsborough** lies 1km west of Tenby off the B4318 to St Florence; a signposted public footpath starts where the road crosses the Ritec marshes (SN 117 011); To reach **West Tarr** return towards Tenby, take the A4139 to Penally, then turn off to St Florence along the Ritec valley. After 3.5km there is a sharp right turn (to Carswell), continue on, and where the road dips into a little valley the Tarr towers can be glimpsed through the trees on the right (no public access) SN 089 009. **Upper Lamphey** lies 1km north-east of Lamphey village on the A4139 to Pembroke. Pass the turning to the Bishop's Palace and after crossing a little bridge there is a narrow road (public footpath) leading uphill. The tower is at the end of the derelict barn near the top of the hill (SN 026 014). **Kingston Farm** lies 1.8km south-east of Pembroke town via Grove Hill Road. At a prominent T-junction take the left turn and after about 0.6km there is a right turning down to the farm (no public right of way) SR 994 994. **Flimston** lies on the way to Stack Rocks off the B4319 Pembroke to Castlemartin road. Vehicular access is limited to non-firing days and the ruin is strictly off-limits to the public (SR 924 957).*
References: *Smith (1988); AW (1990); Austin (1994); Davis (2001).*

Eastington, *Rhoscrowther*

Eastington manor lies on the Milford Haven waterway beyond the near-deserted village of Rhoscrowther, an idyllic setting marred by an enormous oil refinery on the hillside behind. The most obvious part of the site is a long, low eighteenth-century mansion, but tucked on to the far end is the rugged stone shell of a medieval tower-house. Eastington has a near-identical plan to Scotsborough mentioned above (and was built by the same family) but with one very important difference – the entire roof is surrounded with a battlemented parapet offering a more aggressive mode of defence. The ground floor is a poorly-lit vaulted chamber used for storage with the principal residential chamber on the upper level. This is now reached by a large stone staircase (evidently an addition, but perhaps an early one) and the original access was probably via a simpler and more easily defendable ladder-stair. This first-floor hall was a large and well-appointed chamber by medieval standards. It measures 10.5 by 4.9 metres and was provided with a fireplace, wall cupboards and dressed stone windows (a two-light opening with cusped heads has managed to survive intact). There is also a small vaulted chamber in a projecting turret, which probably contained a garderobe formerly. Unfortunately the original roof has not survived and the timbers are modern replacements. There are also marks of an attic floor and a blocked doorway beside the fireplace, although these features are probably alterations carried out when Eastington was refurbished in the eighteenth century. Beside the entrance a mural stairway leads up to the wall-walk, where an additional turret provided any observer with good views across the bay.

From the outside the tower bears the very obvious scars of a demolished single-storeyed building. Experts still debate as to whether this was an addition or part of the original layout. Was Eastington a standalone tower-house, or just the fortified solar (the private chamber) of an adjoining undefended hall? The mark of the roofline and the stubby fragments of lateral walls are deeply embedded in the stonework, and two of the first-floor windows are shifted to the side, as if to purposely avoid the high roof. These details suggest to me that Eastington was planned and built as a hall and tower combination, such as can be seen at a number of other late-medieval sites. Candleston in Glamorgan (see page 108) has the same basic layout, and the long-destroyed Bonville's Court near Saundersfoot was a very similar building, as the drawings of Edward Lowry Barnwell indicate. Barnwell (1813-1887) was a retired schoolteacher and antiquarian, and carried out a detailed survey of the old houses of Pembrokeshire in the 1860s. Of Eastington he wrote that the 'modern' house (i.e. the missing hall) had been removed a short time before his visit. Apart from the tower itself there are several ruinous outbuildings and walled courtyards, so the whole site must have been far more extensive and impressive than it now appears.

The manor is associated with the Perrot family, a widespread and important local dynasty who were here from at least the fourteenth century until the sixteenth century. The hall and tower would certainly have been built during their tenure, although the lack of any firm documentary evidence makes it impossible to pinpoint the date or the builder. Barnwell thought the tower could date from the early fourteenth century on account of the surviving window detail, while the recent Pevsner guide suggests the late fourteenth century. A date in the succeeding century could be equally tenable. After the Perrots departed, Eastington was briefly held by the

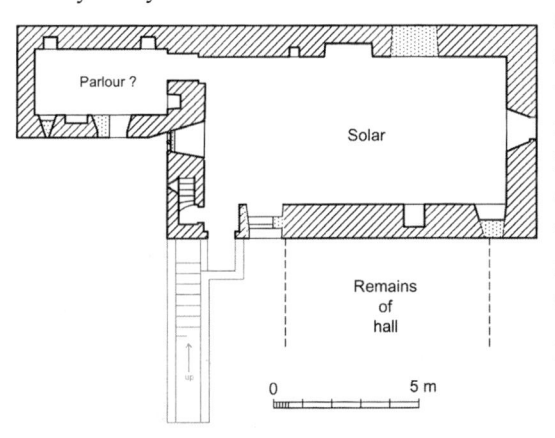

First floor plan of Eastington

Barnwell's drawings of Eastington (left) and Bonville's Court (right)

Philipps family of Picton Castle and in 1670 it was assessed as a house of five hearths.[17] Shortly afterwards the Meares family were in residence, and around the middle of the eighteenth century they improved the accommodation by adding the long range to the upper end of the tower. Yet as early as 1769 a prospective purchaser wrote that the buildings were in a parlous state, with leaking roofs, rotten timberwork, decaying wainscoting and a crumbling boundary wall. The repairs were carried out, but by 1800 the manor was again in decay and by 1842 (when the estate was bought by John Mirehouse, who also owned neighbouring Angle) the house was deemed fit only to be let out to tenants. In the intervening years the Meares' wing has been restored and is still occupied, but the tower is an echoing shell and some of the outbuildings and the adjoining walled gardens are now in a poor state of repair.

Location: Rhoscrowther lies 6km west of Pembroke off the B4320 road to Angle. A signposted turning leads past the refinery to the little village. Beside the single row of houses there is a private track which heads down towards the sea where the manor house lies (OS grid ref SM 001 024).

Access: no public access; the tower can just be seen from the road, but anyone wanting a closer look should ask permission at the adjoining house.

References: AC (1867-68); Smith (1988); .Jones (1996); Pevsner (2004).

Newhouse

This neglected and poorly understood site lies deep in Canaston Woods on the tidal reaches of the Cleddau river. The surrounding area was a medieval forest and hunting preserve belonging to the lordship of Narberth from at least the twelfth century. It has been suggested that the manor of Newhouse was established here by the Canaston family in the late thirteenth century, but perhaps more likely it originated as a hunting lodge belonging to the Mortimer lords of Narberth. A document of 1623 refers back to a dispute between Roger Mortimer and Bishop Thomas of St Davids over the manor of *Newehous*; this would have taken place around 1280. There are more contemporary references in 1326 (*Newhous*) and 1357 (*Novadomus*), and the place-name implies that it was a recent foundation and not an older Anglo-Norman settlement. Lordship records from the 1360s also name the

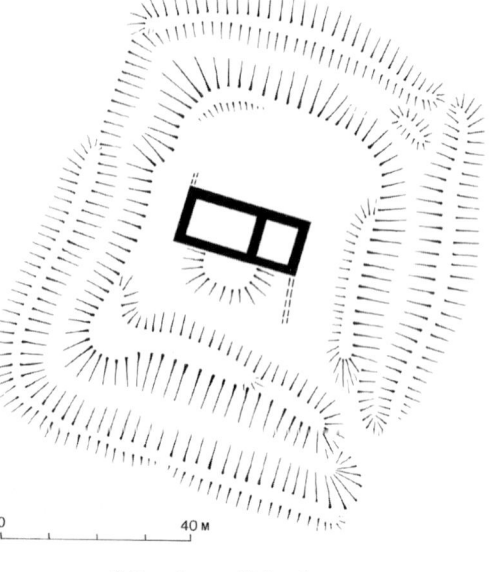

Site plan of Newhouse

various *reeves* responsible for the day-to-day running of the manor.[18] By 1609 it had acquired a second title, 'Newhouse, alias Red Castle' and on John Speed's 1611 map of Pembrokeshire it is shown as Redcastle. Today it is usually known as 'Castell Coch', but this is probably a late derivation of the English name.

The site lies on the edge of a stream valley a short distance away from the old parish church (also ruined) and comprises a rectangular platform surrounded with a ditch and counterscarp bank. In the middle of the platform is a two-storey hall block, the only visible masonry still standing above the dense undergrowth. Newhouse has been classed as a moated site or strong-house, but these names are confusing and inaccurate, and only serve to belittle its defensive capabilities. This was a substantial little fortification. The rock-cut ditches are over four metres deep and were never the shallow water-filled features normally associated with moated sites of manorial status. Around the edge of the platform is a rubble bank, apparently the remains of a demolished curtain wall, and a mound at the south-west corner could be the site of a round tower. A gatehouse probably occupied the opposite corner but this side has been obscured by a later causeway built to provide easy access across the ditch.

The hall block remains substantially intact apart from the missing battlements and east gable wall, but all the internal timberwork and partitions have decayed away. The ground floor was occupied by a long chamber entered from the courtyard through an arched door secured by two drawbars (the slots for holding the sliding timbers can still be seen). This level was lit only by small loop-holes and was probably used for storage. Along the side walls are rows of square holes that once held the joists supporting the first-floor hall. These lateral timbers

Internal and external views of Newhouse today

rested on a massive beam running the full length of the building, which must have had upright posts to support its great length. In one corner of the room there is a destroyed newel stair that rose to the hall and then on up to the wall-walk.

The main entrance to the first-floor hall was on the courtyard front and would have been reached by a timber stair (as suggested in the reconstruction drawing above). However, this door lacks a drawbar or any other security features and so may be a later insertion, or perhaps even a modified window opening. There are other architectural oddities here too; there is no sign of an original fireplace and so the only way the room could have been heated was by a central hearth set on a stone pillar rising from the basement. This method of supporting a potentially hazardous fireplace on a wooden floor has been noted at a number of castles, and points towards an early date for the building.[19] There is no sign of any dressed stonework, and the windows may have been just basic unglazed openings. Even the smallest windows – which no-one could ever have squeezed through – were provided with drawbars for security.

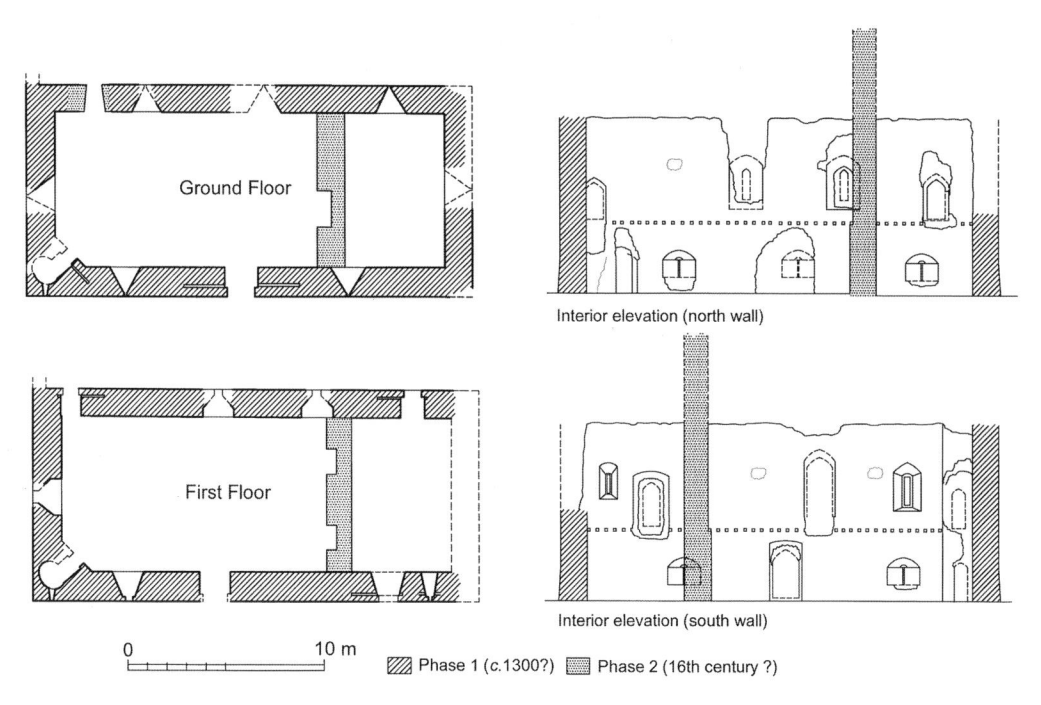

A cutaway reconstruction of the hall block (opposite), and (above) plans for Newhouse which show the position of the later wall inserted probably in the mid 1500s when the castle was transformed into a more convenient residence

The doorways in the north wall are also puzzling because they now lead nowhere. They also had drawbars and so were intended to be closed against anyone trying to break in, but it is not clear why the occupants should need *two* back doors. Both are too far from the courtyard wall to have led directly on to the wall-walk (unless there was a timber bridge). Did they provide access to vanished apartments behind the hall? But if there were any adjoining buildings then they could not have been part of the original scheme because they would have obscured some of the hall windows. Possibly they led into garderobe turrets at the back of the hall. There is certainly evidence for some sort of structure jutting out from the north-west corner. In fact the hall block may have undergone far more modifications than first appearances suggest, and clearance of the ivy followed by a detailed study of the stonework might clarify the building's development.

This is a much larger and more substantial structure than the Pembrokeshire tower-houses and defensible dwellings previously noted and significantly it lacks a vaulted undercroft. Another very similar building exists in the village of Angle[20] and, like Newhouse, was a freestanding hall block with a beamed floor and defensive features. Unfortunately some of the walls are missing and the full plan is incomplete. Yet another comparable building survives at the Bishop's Palace at Lamphey, which has a rather forbidding appearance for an ecclesiastical residence and was probably built in the period 1260-80. It shares the beamed floor, battlemented parapet and projecting latrine turrets of Newhouse, but benefits from a wall fireplace and

This first-floor hall in Angle was similar to Newhouse

finely carved stone doors and windows. There are no dateable features remaining at Newhouse today, but the simple layout coupled with the lack of fireplaces and dressed stonework suggests it is probably late thirteenth century.

The basic arrangement of the medieval hall proved quite inadequate for the needs of subsequent owners, and a cross-wall with multiple fireplaces was inserted into the hall (reducing the length of the building by a third). The wall-walk and battlements were removed to accommodate a high-pitched roof and the interior was divided up into smaller heated apartments on three floors. It seems that the eastern end of the hall was abandoned from this time on. Again, there is no direct evidence to date these changes, but they were probably carried out by the Barlows of Slebech, who acquired the manor around 1546 and transformed the building into a more convenient residence. This powerful and acquisitive family hailed from East Anglia and made their mark on the locality during the reign of Henry VIII. William (d.1568) pursued an ecclesiastical life during the Protestant Reformation, becoming in turn Bishop of St Asaph, St Davids and Chichester. His brother Roger (d.1553) led an equally adventurous existence as a seafarer, exploring the westerly trade routes and accompanying Sebastian Cabot on a voyage to the New World in 1526 (he is claimed to have been the first Englishman to set foot in Argentina). Along with his brother John, Roger Barlow purchased many of the former monastic lands in Pembrokeshire and established a branch of the family at Slebech just across the river.

What other changes were carried out here during the long occupancy of Newhouse will only be revealed by excavation. It was leased out to another member of the Barlow family in 1657 and is thought to have been abandoned as a dwelling about twenty years later. Clearly the fortified hall formed only part of the site, and there is a fishpond, garden enclosures and a little moat, all now practically inaccessible in the tangled undergrowth nearby.[21]

Location: *4km west of Narberth beside the A4075 from Canaston Bridge to Oakwood Leisure park. The ruin lies in private woodland bordering the Bluestone Holiday Village (OS map ref: SN 072 136).*
Access: *on private land within the Bluestone development and not presently accessible to the public.*
References: *AC (1868, 1922); DAT; Charles; Pevsner (2004).*

Mid Wales & the Marches

Aberedw Castles, *Builth Wells*

The patchwork of territories between the Wye and Severn rivers (*Rhwng Gwy a Hafren*) was bitterly contested by the native princes and Norman interlopers in the twelfth and thirteenth centuries. Documentary evidence for the foundation of the numerous small castles in this region is scarce, but it is known that a Normandy family, the Tosnys, were active here in the late eleventh century. Later members of the dynasty launched a protracted legal case to gain possession of Aberedw and the surrounding lordship of Elfael, and so perhaps the original castle was their foundation. It was built close to St Cewydd's church on a natural rocky knoll, with an unassailable river gorge providing an effective defence against attack. A rock-cut ditch surrounded the motte on the landward approach, but there does not seem to have been a bailey. This modest grassy mound may look like a typical earthwork castle, but recent erosion has revealed a core of layered shale, suggesting it was stone-built from the start, perhaps with a masonry tower on the summit. If so, it would have resembled Castell Prysor in Gwynedd (see p.43) and may instead have been a Welsh foundation when the territory was back in native control.

The site of the first castle at Aberedw

Aberedw only achieved historical prominence in the mysterious events that clouded the last days of Llywelyn ap Gruffudd. As the war against King Edward struggled on through the winter of 1282, Llywelyn left Gwynedd and headed south to rally support among his followers. The prince did not enjoy the trust of all his allies and there was a scheme afoot to depose or assassinate him (one chronicle has a tantalising reference to a group meeting in the belfry of Bangor Cathedral to plot his betrayal). This statement has given rise to a rich crop of conspiracy theories, the most popular being that Llywelyn was separated from his main force and lured to

Aberedw, ostensibly to discuss terms with some Marcher lords who were planning to change sides. The prince and his attendants were captured and murdered upon arrival at Aberedw, while another version of the tale has Llywelyn fleeing to the rocks opposite the castle and sheltering in a small cave (still to be seen), before rejoining the main army the following day. A local blacksmith is supposed to have reversed his horseshoes to confuse any pursuers. The few reliable accounts of the events of 11 December 1282 suggest that a battle took place near a river crossing and ended in a rout; Llywelyn and a small group of men were hunted down and the prince was speared as he tried to escape. The knight responsible for this act was unaware of the identity of the man he had cut down, and only as the dying man called for a priest was the prince recognised. Llywelyn's mangled body was taken to the Cistercian abbey of Cwm-hir for burial, while the severed head was sent in triumph to King Edward. The fateful skirmish may well have taken place at Aberedw, although the spot favoured by tradition is Cilmery west of Builth, where a modern memorial to the fallen prince now stands.

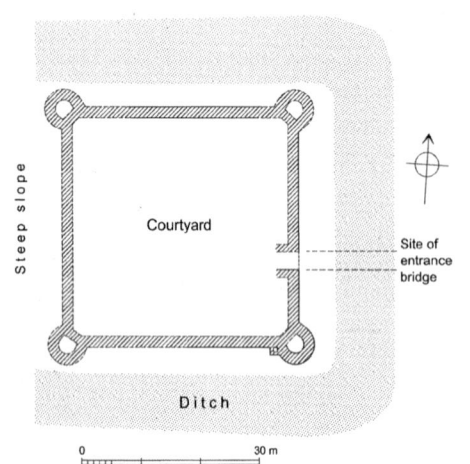

The dust of battle had hardly settled before the Marcher lords moved in to consolidate their gains. Edmund Mortimer evicted the Welsh tenant of Aberedw and gave the land to one of his knights, Walter Hackelutel, who straightaway began work on

Interpretive plan and reconstruction drawing of Walter Hackelutel's castle at Aberedw – the second castle

a new castle a short distance away from the old motte. In November of 1284 King Edward confirmed the grant, in effect giving retrospective planning permission: 'Mortimer has granted by his charter to Walter ... all the lands in Elfael Uwchmynydd that belonged to Gruffudd ap Owain ... and Walter has commenced to build a castle there, to which the king has given his willing consent; the king grants that Walter may complete the castle thus begun and may hold it when so built without trouble from the king or his heirs.' The trouble, when it came, was from a different source. By 1293 Ralph de Tosny was clamouring for the return of his alleged ancestral land, and instigated court proceedings against Walter. He eventually lost the case and Hackelutel retained Aberedw until his death in 1315, but afterwards the lordship passed along with the Tosny estates to the Beauchamp earls of Warwick.

Whether these powerful aristocrats ever cared for this small fortress is highly debatable, and by the end of the fourteenth century it was claimed to be worthless. It does not appear to have played any further role in local affairs and disappears from the records. In truth, the castle built by Walter was a very inadequate structure for the time – a small square enclosure with rounded towers on the corners, a textbook example of a thirteenth-century stronghold but on the scale of a toy fort. The walls are too thin, the towers too small, and there was no big gatehouse. Only a deep rock-cut ditch around the landward approach adequately served to hold off any attacker. Walter had financial problems raising this modest structure, for in October 1285 the king relieved him of a debt of £57 owed to a Jewish moneylender for building expenses. Interestingly, the entry in the accounts states that the money was needed for 'erecting a house in the Welsh Marches and afterwards crenellating it by the king's license for the security of those parts'. The wording suggests that Walter's castle was actually a fortified dwelling rather than a strategic military stronghold.

The tree-covered enclosure is unobtrusively sited behind the modern houses of the village and backs onto a steep slope to the river Wye. Few traces of any internal buildings can be seen, and so much of the castle is buried in its own rubble that only future excavations will reveal the complete layout. Vestiges of the entrance passage can be seen within the east curtain wall although the apparent causeway across the ditch is almost certainly the result of later infilling (the ditch would originally have been spanned by a timber ramp with a drawbridge). The south-east corner tower is the only one of the four to remain fairly intact and it is still possible to make out the curving face of the inner room, which measured about 3 metres in diameter. This cramped chamber was evidently intended for residential accommodation

The outline of the half-buried south-east tower

since there is an adjoining garderobe shaft serving the vanished upper level. Presumably the other towers were similarly equipped.

The visible stonework of Walter's castle is now in a wretched state and continues to crumble due to the flaky nature of the local stone and growing tree roots. In the nineteenth century the Cambrian Railway was driven through the slope below the castle, and the steep

The crumbling walls of the second castle

cutting undermined some of the walls (though it has not completely destroyed the west side as some accounts in print suggest). This site needs to be excavated and properly conserved before erosion and neglect combine to wipe away the few visible remains for good.

Location: *Aberedw village lies on the B4567 in the Wye valley approximately 5km south-east of Builth Wells (OS map ref: SO 074 473).*
Access: *both castles are on private land but are accessible by public footpaths. The motte can be reached from the back of the churchyard; the site of Walter's castle is crossed by a path that runs from the main road just above the old railway embankment at the start of the village.*
References: *Radnor (1951); AW (1994); Remfry (1996).*

Aberyscir, *Brecon*

This unremarkable castle mound is one of the many relics of the Norman invasion of the Welsh kingdom of Brycheiniog in the late eleventh century and, like the lesser strongholds that lie scattered throughout this region, has made hardly a mark on recorded history. Nevertheless it is essential to understand what happened here over 900 years ago to put many of the more substantial castles described in the following pages in their proper historical perspective.

Soon after the Battle of Hastings, William the Conqueror rewarded one of his chief supporters, William fitz Osbern, lord of Breteuil in Normandy, with the earldom of Hereford. As the powerful ruler of a huge territory, fitz Osbern had the right to undertake further conquests, and he secured most of lowland Gwent before he returned to the Continent and death in battle in 1071. His son Roger inherited his drive and ambitions (but not his political acumen) and in 1075 became embroiled in a rebellion which ended with the loss of his lands and liberty. The king then chose to partition Roger's forfeited earldom among lesser lords rather than repeat the risk of having so much territory under the control of one man. The more notable beneficiaries were Ralph de Mortimer, Walter de Clare and Philip de Braose, and the dynasties they founded shaped the politics of the Welsh Marches for the next two centuries.

Another of King William's followers was Bernard de Neufmarché, a relatively obscure knight from Normandy who may not have participated in the initial invasion of 1066, but subsequently received estates on the Hereford-Breconshire border. With a band of loyal knights he began to move into the native territory of Brycheiniog in the late-1080s, completing the conquest initiated by the earl of Hereford. Rhys ap Tewdwr of Deheubarth who, only a few years earlier, had been acknowledged as ruler of south-west Wales by King William, put up a strong resistance as he naturally feared that if Brycheiniog fell, his own kingdom would be next in the firing line. At Easter 1093 the Welsh and Norman forces clashed near Brecon, and Rhys was defeated and killed. This was a crushing blow to native independence, for it not only allowed the transformation of Brycheiniog into a Norman lordship but also opened the way for a widespread advance in other parts of the country. Bernard's followers erected lesser fortifications at strategic locations to secure their own allotted lands and act as buffer zones to his main base at Brecon. They followed the course of the Usk and neighbouring river valleys winding deep into the countryside and left the bleaker, less accessible uplands under nominal Welsh control. It was a method of colonisation that was to be repeated throughout the coming years, as indeed it had been by earlier invaders.

The Romans had established one of their military bases on the hill beside the confluence of the Usk and Yscir rivers, and the ruined walls must have been plainly visible to the Normans in their westward progress. The founder of the castle (variously claimed to be Bernard fitz Unspac or Hugh Surdwal) did not utilise the existing Roman fort, but instead opted for a smaller and more easily defendable promontory on the opposite bank of the Yscir. Another deciding factor may have been the pre-existence of a native church dedicated to St Cynidr, which was later given a dual dedication to St Mary. The end of the ridge beyond the church was scarped into an oval motte measuring about 40m by 50m with an outer ditch. There was probably a bailey, but all traces have been obliterated by the later buildings of Aberyscir Court. Along the river frontage of the motte there is a 20-metre length of curtain wall now standing

A thin fragment of a circular tower overlying the curtain wall, which might, therefore, be a later feature

barely two metres high, which is all that remains of a walled courtyard or shell-keep crowning the summit of the mound. The adjacent Roman fort would have provided abundant building materials for replacing the initial timber buildings with stone, which presumably took place sometime in the twelfth or thirteenth century. There is also a solitary fragment of a round tower here, but it is very thin and overlies the curtain wall so it must be a later feature, probably a summer house associated with the adjacent Court. All other stonework has been robbed away and if it were not for the few meagre remains, Aberyscir would probably be classed as just another modest motte. It is interesting to think that other similar earthwork sites in Wales may retain unsuspected masonry structures.

Location: 4.5km west of Brecon along the A40 towards Sennybridge on the north bank of the Usk. Turn off at Aberbran and take the next right back towards Brecon to where a T-junction sign marks the way to Aberyscir church (OS map ref: SO 001 296).
Access: on private land and no public access. The tree-covered mound can just be seen from the A40 across the Usk valley.
References: Brycheiniog (1961); Remfry (1999).

Blaencamlais Castle, *Sennybridge*

An obscure entry in a medieval chronicle refers to a 'new castle beyond Brecon' destroyed by English forces under the command of Prince Edward in 1265. The castle was apparently the work of Llywelyn ap Gruffudd when his authority had spread beyond Gwynedd and most of Breconshire was subject to his rule. The location of this lost castle has puzzled historians, but a good contender was the large mound at the head of the Camlais valley, about 9km west of Brecon. It looks convincing as a Welsh castle – small, compact and set in a fairly remote location on the edge of the uplands. Even from a distance away the mound is quite a prominent object on the skyline. The castle superficially looks like a large motte encircled with a ditch and massive counterscarp bank; but the cratered summit is ringed with jagged masonry forming the base of a round keep with an internal diameter of 6.8 metres and walls about three metres thick. The foundations appear to extend down to the natural bedrock and so the mound is just rubble heaped around the base of the keep, and not the remains of a reused Norman motte as has been suggested. There is no sign of a bailey or any ancillary buildings, and so it seems that the castle was nothing more than a lone tower on the edge of the moors (as shown in the reconstruction drawing).

The visual evidence does suggest a typically modest Welsh fortress, and the castleologist David Cathcart King at first believed this was Llywelyn's lost castle of 1265, but the subsequent identification of a deed in the National Library of Wales put paid to that. This 1358 document recorded a settlement of land in the area and mentions a *Castrum de Gamleys* founded by Humphrey de Bohun, earl of Hereford. There were at least eight family members with this name, but since Brecon was only acquired around 1241 when Humphrey V (d.1265) married a heiress of the de Braose family, the search can be narrowed down. Round keeps like this are generally ascribed to the early thirteenth century, so Humphrey V would be the most plausible candidate. However, Cathcart King thought it more likely that the builder was Humphrey VI (d.1298), who came of age in 1270 but would only have had the chance to start work on the castle after Llywelyn had withdrawn from Breconshire following his defeat in 1277.

Would such an archaic-looking castle have been built at the end of the thirteenth century when more advanced types of fortifications were commonly used? An earlier date may seem more probable on stylistic grounds, but large round towers and detached keeps were still being built at this time; Gilbert de Clare had them at Castell Coch and Morlais, and even the king's normally adventurous architects constructed them at Builth, Flint and Hawarden. Blaencamlais could feasibly have been intended as a precaution after de Bohun's rebellious Welsh tenants had quietened down. It seems unlikely that this minor outpost remained in effective military use for very long before being abandoned; however, its location on the edge of the vast expanse of the Fforest Fawr preserve may have made it occasionally useful as a hunting lodge.

Location: *from Sennybridge village on the A40, take the A4067 south and then fork left at Defynnog to Merthyr Tydfil (A4215). Continue for about 3km, ignore the first signposted turn to Blaencamlais, then take the next left at the crossroads. Where the road levels out beside an open pond, the castle mound will be seen in the fields to the north (OS map ref: SN 956 261).*
Access: *there is no public access to the castle, although the mound is visible from the road.*
References: *Brycheiniog (1965, 1984-5).*

Blaenllynfi, *Bwlch*

The parlous state of Blaenllynfi Castle today is probably not due to savage Welsh raids or devastating bombardment from Parliamentarian cannons, but simply the result of shoddy workmanship. The large stumps of masonry rising above the overgrown earthworks are buttresses built to shore up the crumbling defences, and these have lasted far better than the walls they were meant to support. There is only one short length of upstanding curtain wall remaining here today, and as it survives up to wall-walk height it gives the only clue to the former scale of this remote and (until recently) little understood site.

The castle guarded a hill pass from the Usk valley to Llangorse and Talgarth. The location may have been ideal for that purpose although the defensive position was very poor, for it lay within a marshy hollow overlooked by higher ground. The stream was therefore dammed to form a wide moat to adequately protect the main structure. This took the form of a roughly rectangular masonry enclosure with two small round towers and three larger square towers covering most of the angles. The entrance seems to have been a simple gateway at the north corner, and within the courtyard there were a number of domestic buildings ranged against the inner walls. Because the stones were laid in clay instead of mortar, the walls began to crumble at an alarmingly early date, requiring constant repair and the addition of several buttresses. One corner tower even collapsed (or was knocked down) and the breach in the wall was simply blocked off. Evidently the owners had only enough cash and enthusiasm to make do and mend.

The origin of Blaenllynfi must be traced back to Bernard de Neufmarché's invasion of Brycheiniog in 1093, although whether a castle was built here at such an early date is uncertain and the surviving earthworks do not look typically Norman. Bernard died around 1125 and Brecon passed to his daughter Sybil, wife of Earl Miles of Gloucester. Miles was succeeded in turn by four sons, who had all died heirless by 1165. Then the inheritance was split between Miles's surviving daughters and their husbands, and the rich prize of Brecon and Abergavenny passed to William de Braose II. It may have been around this time that Blaenllynfi was split off from Brecon to form an independent lordship, and a new castle was established here to defend the territory.

The de Braose family were among the most important and influential Marcher dynasties in Wales. Hailing from Briouze in Normandy, William de Braose I was given

One of the medieval buttresses built to support the crumbling walls

How the decaying castle might have looked in the early fourteenth century

lands in Sussex by the Conqueror, and during the reign of William Rufus, his son Philip seized on the Welsh territories of Builth and Radnor. Philip's son William de Braose II (d.1192) was the one who laid claim through his wife to a share of the Hereford estates including Brecon. His heir, yet another William (d.1211), earned a justified reputation for treachery that was shocking even by the standards of the day. His most notorious act was to slaughter unarmed Welsh guests at a Christmas feast at Abergavenny Castle in 1175. William's downfall came in 1208. After picking a quarrel with King John, a man as ruthless and double-dealing as himself, his lands were seized and he fled to die in exile, leaving the king to vent his rage on his wife and son, who were locked up in a dungeon and starved to death. John's treatment of de Braose sent shock waves through Marcher society. The lords realised that the king could turn on anyone, and John's already precarious reputation tumbled headlong. Although the de Braose family later regained most of their lands under John's heir, Henry III, they were never as powerful as before.

On William's fall, the lordship of Blaenllynfi was granted to the king's current favourite, Peter fitz Herbert, who may have been responsible for building the first masonry structures here. The earliest documented appearance of the castle occurs in 1215 when it was captured by a Welsh army led by Giles de Braose, bishop of Hereford and younger son of the unfortunate William. Giles died in the same year, and his brother Reginald (d.1228) continued the struggle to regain the family inheritance. He allied himself with the Welsh and stubbornly refused to compromise with the other Marcher lords by adding his name to the Magna Carta. With the help of Llywelyn the Great (an alliance strengthened by marriage to the prince's daughter Gwladys Du), Reginald was in a position of some power in the Welsh Marches. But with the accession of Henry III he came to terms with the king and was received back into royal favour, returning Blaenllynfi to Peter fitz Herbert. This *volte face* caused a rift between Reginald and his father-in-law, and subsequently in 1233 Llywelyn devastated a number of castles in Breconshire, including Blaenllynfi.

The subsequent lords of Blaenllynfi, Reginald fitz Peter and his son John, were a bad lot (John was even accused of torturing and hanging a clerk without trial). Continuous financial troubles forced them to sell off their assets to the Crown, and various owners came and went, more concerned with gathering revenues from the lordship than ensuring the upkeep of the castle. Surveys carried out in 1330 and 1337 paint a very bleak picture of a castle well past its prime and desperately in need of costly repairs. Certain buildings and towers were said to be in decay, others on the point of collapse or already fallen. One survey lists all the items of value within the castle, including such medieval bric-a-brac as two brass pots, four trestle tables, a portable altar and a pair of worn-out cart wheels!

The lordship passed to another powerful Marcher family, the Mortimers of Wigmore in 1354 and through them, via the duke of York, to the Crown. There may have been an attempt to establish a borough here, for when the Tudor antiquary John Leland passed through Blaenllynfi he observed 'a very fair castle now decaying, and by was a borough town, now also in decay'. What are probably the earthworks of that abortive venture have been traced in the adjacent fields. The old watermill and silted up millpond still survive below the castle mound. By the time the topographers Samuel and Nathaniel Buck sketched Blaenllynfi in 1741 the site looked much as it does today, although they did notice the tall fragment of a tower now lost. From the 1960s onwards the landowner was allowed by the Ministry of Works to carry out minor excavations under strict guidelines, and some of the internal walls and buildings were uncovered. Further conservation work in the 1990s has helped to preserve the meagre remains, but much of the layout is still unclear, and the design of the castle will only be properly understood with further large-scale excavations. In the meantime, public access has been provided and some picnic tables have been optimistically set up within the courtyard; however, the whole site has become densely overgrown again and only in winter is there any chance of spotting some of the half-buried walls amidst the undergrowth.

Location: *Blaenllynfi lies just north of Bwlch village on the A40 Abergavenny to Brecon road. At the village take the B4560 to Llangorse and then the next left turning to Pennorth; the castle is in the woods to the left (OS map ref: SO 145 228).*
Access: *in private ownership, but public access is allowed (gate opposite Castle Cottage).*
References: *AC (2004) contains a detailed account of the castle, on which this account is based.*

Castell Coch (Mellte Castle), *Ystradfellte*

One of many similarly named sites in Wales, Castell Coch ('Red Castle') lies hidden away in a valley deep within the Brecon Beacons National Park. A short distance north of the tiny village of Ystradfellte the mountain streams of the Llia and Dringarth merge to form the fast flowing Mellte and here, on a headland naturally protected by the confluence, lie the overgrown remains of the castle. The walls were built with locally obtained red sandstone (hence the name), but the use of poor-quality earthy mortar has not helped their preservation, and much of the stonework has collapsed into moss-covered heaps. Nevertheless, the basic plan can still be traced and consists of a walled courtyard of pentagonal plan with a rounded tower at the southernmost point and a gateway at the north-east corner. The courtyard is occupied by a mound of rubble marking the remains of a rectangular building, almost certainly a two-storey keep, measuring about 19 by 11m. The approach along the ridge from the north is protected by a large bailey with a massive earthen rampart and outer ditch. Surprisingly, there is no sign of a ditch separating the inner ward from the bailey, although one might be expected, especially since the builders took the trouble of cutting through the tip of the ridge beyond the round tower. Presumably it has been filled in. It is tempting to see this as a two-phase site, the large earthwork enclosure coming first, followed by the more compact inner masonry fort.

There are hardly any historical references to this site other than the appearance of *Stratmelthin* in a list of properties belonging to the late William de Braose IV, lord

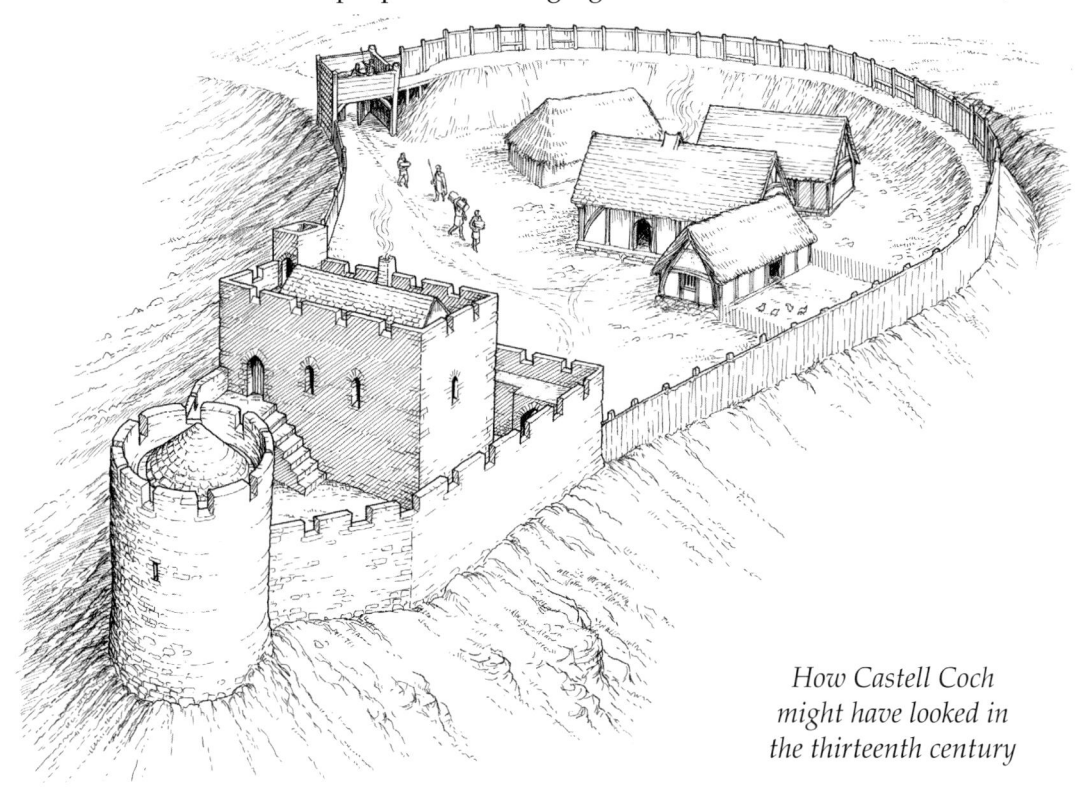

How Castell Coch might have looked in the thirteenth century

of Brecon (d.1230). Clearly this is an English clerk's attempt to master the tongue-twisting Welsh place-name Ystradfellte, and presumably the castle was built by that powerful Anglo-Norman family to secure the frontiers of their lordship. The rectangular keep would indicate a twelfth-century date for construction, although the round tower places it in the thirteenth. However, the relatively small size of the castle and its location make it unconvincing as a strategic military outpost, and it was probably a hunting lodge occupied periodically by the lords whilst their retinue encamped in the bailey. The vast expanse of mountains, moors and wooded valleys that now forms part of the National Park was once a jealously guarded hunting preserve.

Another possibility is that the stone castle was built by Llywelyn ap Gruffudd around 1260, when most of Breconshire came under his sway. It certainly looks like the sort of small and relatively simple castles that the Welsh were building at this time, but Castell Coch lacks the deep ditches that form such characteristic features of other Welsh castles, making an Anglo-Norman origin more probable. During the great dispute between the warring earls of Gloucester and Hereford (p.126) one of the hearings was convened at Ystradfellte in 1291. Presumably the castle was the site of that meeting, but historical references to the later history of the building are lost. If Castell Coch was a hunting lodge then it may have served some use to the lords of Brecon until the estate became Crown property in 1521.

Location: *2.5km north of Ystradfellte village in the Brecon Beacons National Park, off the A4059 road. From the village head north along the mountain road to Sennybridge and take the next right turning. The road dips down into the valley and the tree-covered castle site can be seen from the bridge (OS map ref: SN 935 145).*
Access: *on private land. Permission to visit the site must be sought at Heolyrhedyn farm.*
References: *Brycheiniog (1968-69).*

Castell Dinas, *Talgarth*

The term 'hermit crab castle' perfectly describes sites which rely on pre-existing fortifications to bolster their own defences, much as the aforementioned crustacean uses a discarded shell. Classic examples of hermit crab castles in Wales include Cardiff, Caerwent and Loughor, all built within Roman forts, and here at Castell Dinas the massive earthworks of an Iron Age hillfort were just too good to ignore by the Normans as they made their way through south Wales. The site was admirably chosen by Celts and Normans alike: a steep-sided hill standing within a gap in the Black Mountains, where traffic passing between the Wye and Usk valleys could be controlled. Appropriately enough, the site was known in medieval times as Bwlchyddinas ('the pass of the citadel'), a name which is still occasionally used today. At 450 metres above sea level, this is the highest situated castle in England and Wales and that fact reveals the reason for its ultimate decline. Despite the admirable natural advantages of the site, this breezy peak is not the most pleasant place to live, and once the military need had passed, Castell Dinas was abandoned to the wind and the rain.

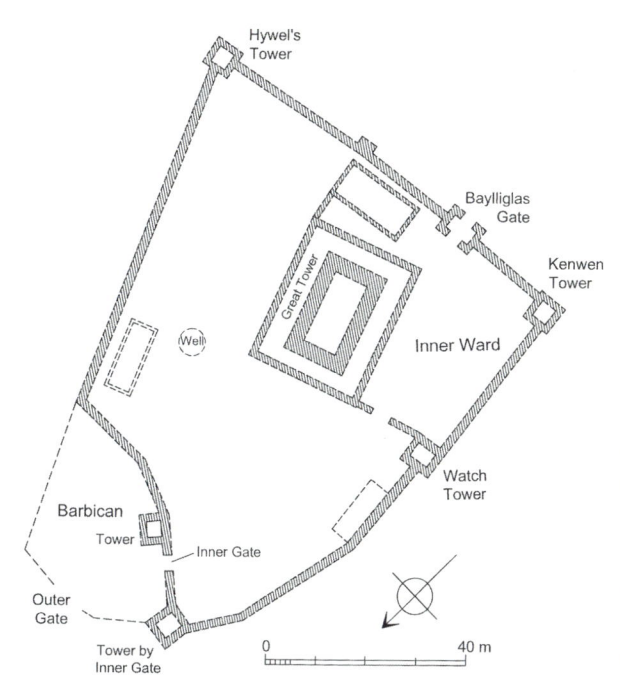

From the elevated viewpoints on either side of the hill the full defensive advantages of the site can be appreciated. Worn-down banks and ditches, dug over two thousand years ago by the native Celts, wind their sinuous way around the slopes. The Normans strengthened the hillfort by recutting the ditches and fortifying the highest part of the innermost enclosure with rough masonry walls and towers. Although the stonework has since crumbled into heaps of rubble, the overall plan is still discernible. At the northern point of the hill the multiple ramparts twist and turn,

An aerial view of Castell Dinas looking south-east and (top) an interpretive plan (orientated in the same direction) of the masonry remains and buildings mentioned in the survey of 1337

Existing masonry remains above contrast with what might once have been (opposite) the inner ward in the twelfth century viewed from the south and showing the great tower at the rear and Bailey gate in the middle

forming a convoluted pathway up to the summit. Here stood an outer barbican leading to the main gateway, which retains the only piece of the masonry castle to stand above the turf. Part of a square tower with an arched opening can be seen, almost certainly a secondary structure built from more durable mortar than that used for the rest of the castle.

Very little is known about the early history of Castell Dinas. It is claimed to have been the work of William fitz Osbern, earl of Hereford, or his son Roger as part of an advance into Welsh territory in the 1070s, and to have declined in importance when Bernard de Neufmarché established the main lordship base at Brecon in 1093. However, it seems rather unlikely that a large and costly masonry castle would have been built so far into enemy territory at such an early date.[22] More probably it was built after Bernard had established his headquarters at Brecon, and served as a major outpost to secure the potentially hostile uplands. After 1165 the inheritance of the earl of Gloucester was partitioned, and the castle was linked with nearby Blaenllynfi to form a new lordship held by William de Braose II. Perhaps this is the period that saw the building of the castle. In 1233 Llywelyn the Great invaded Breconshire and destroyed an impressive number of castles, including Blaenllynfi, Castell Dinas and Pencelli. Blaenllynfi displays clear evidence of rebuilding, presumably following on from that attack, but the extremely ruined state of Castell Dinas makes it difficult to say what works were carried out to make good the Welsh depredations. The absence of any obvious thirteenth-century military features (such as round towers and substantial gatehouses) suggests that very little was done here beyond essential repairs.

The lordship passed to the Crown in the fourteenth century, and surveys were carried out to ascertain what was needed to bring the castles up to scratch. The inspectors arrived here in January 1337 and saw the 'outer gate with a mantlet [a defensive wall or barbican] on either side ... so weak and ruinous that they must be newly built'. They noted a sequence of towers along the outer walls, including Hywel's Tower, Kenwen Tower, Baileyglas Gate and the Great Tower. Of the latter only an enormous heap of stones survives, but it probably contained two upper residential chambers over a basement store, and would have formed the main accommodation here for the constable and his retinue. The building had a lead roof and two chimneys, and was surrounded by a walled courtyard for added protection. The inspectors considered that all the repairs would amount to £65, a very low sum compared to their estimate of £451 to patch up Blaenllynfi.

The area enclosed by the masonry defences amounts to about a third of the actual hilltop, and the remaining part lay to the south beyond a shallow outer ditch. This open field was accessed through the Baileyglas Gate (a hybrid name meaning simply the 'green enclosure') and was probably used to pen livestock, for the inspectors noted an abundance of cattle here. Interestingly, during the war of

1277 the unscrupulous constable had taken advantage of the unsettled conditions to steal cattle belonging to Llanthony Priory just over the mountains. Presumably these too would have been kept in the Baileyglas field. Although of lesser importance this outer enclosure could not have been left undefended; there must have been a surrounding wall, if not a fence or impenetrable thorn hedge.

The end of Castell Dinas is as mysterious as its beginning. It probably remained in some use throughout the fourteenth century and is thought to have been provisioned against attack during the Glyndŵr rebellion. In fact, the best clue to the ultimate fate of this grim and lofty fortress is provided by John Leland, in an unusually loquacious entry for that most succinct of antiquarians: 'Dinas Castle stands a good mile from Blaen Llynfi upon a top of a notable hill. It is now ruinous almost to the hard ground. There be manifest tokens of three wards walled about ... The people of Dinas did burn Dinas Castle that Owain Glyndŵr should not keep it for his fortress'. Whether Leland actually climbed to the top or relied on local knowledge for his information is unclear, but the tradition that the castle was demolished as a precautionary measure during, or after, the great rebellion is a plausible fate.

Location: *Dinas Hill lies in the Black Mountains about 4km south-west of Talgarth, and is prominently sited close to the A479 road to Abergavenny and Crickhowell (OS map ref: SO 178 301).*

Access: *the castle is freely accessible as the hill forms part of Tir Gofal managed historic landscape scheme. There is a signposted footpath from the car park of The Castle public house, and another via the farm track at Pengenffordd crossroads.*

References: *Brut; Brycheiniog (volume X and XXXI).*

Castell Du, *Sennybridge*

The forlorn wreck of this little-known castle stands on a hilltop overlooking the confluence of the rivers Senni and Usk, and is also known as Castell Rhyd-y-briw. Only a fragment of a D-shaped tower survives, heavily obscured with ivy and almost hidden from view at the back of a bungalow. The tower measures about 8 metres in diameter and jutted out from the southern flank of the castle. There are fallen blocks of masonry scattered about, and many loose stones have been used to build garden features. On the west side of the hill is a Second World War pillbox, but this too is now just another ruined and overgrown monument to past conflicts. Between the two structures erosion of the slope has exposed a rubble core of masonry, perhaps another tower or part of the vanished curtain wall that once enclosed the summit. Nothing else remains, and any discussion on the form and extent of this castle would inevitably be conjectural. Even excavation is unlikely to help, since any buried archaeological features have probably been obliterated by the modern houses.

When John Leland passed this way sometime in 1536-39 he saw a 'ruined little pile on Usk strongly built as a lodge', which suggests there was still a substantial castle here at the time, and its possible former use as a hunting lodge was still

A fragment of a D-shaped tower is all that remains of Castell Du

remembered locally. The only earlier reference to the castle is a letter written from Rhyd-y-briw by a local Welshman, Einion Sais. He was here in 1271 swearing allegiance to Llywelyn ap Gruffudd and giving hostages as surety for his loyalty. Einion was evidently a very unwilling and unreliable vassal, and when King Edward moved against the Welsh in 1277 he served on the royalist side. His very name (*Sais* means Englishman) should have given Llywelyn some cause for doubt!

Was Castell Du Einion's own castle? David Cathcart King alluded to this enigmatic little castle in two papers and concluded that it was built by Llywelyn ap Gruffudd in the 1260s when Breconshire was under his control. There is a tantalising reference in the Battle Abbey Chronicle to a 'new castle beyond Brecon by Llywelyn destroyed from its foundations' in 1265. King believed that the original Latin scribe had omitted a key word and that the passage should read 'built by Llywelyn'; so that this was an unidentified native castle destroyed by the English, rather than vice versa. King believed that Castell Du was that lost castle,[23] although if Einion was occupying it in 1271 as a base for Welsh resistance in the area, it must have been rebuilt in the meanwhile. This is a conveniently neat conclusion and one that will probably never be satisfactorily resolved. Was Llywelyn's destroyed castle actually Einion's rebuilt stronghold at Sennybridge, or are they two quite separate sites? To add to the confusion the Breconshire antiquarian Theophilus Jones stated that Einion also had a castle beside Penpont church, 3km to the east, but that the remains had long been destroyed.[24] If this statement can be believed, there may have been *three* Welsh castles in this area.

Location: *Sennybridge village is 7km west of Brecon on the A40 to Llandovery. Pass through the village and turn left before reaching the second petrol station up into a small housing estate; the castle is in the field behind the furthest bungalow (OS map ref: SN 920 284).*
Access: *no public access but the remains can be glimpsed from the road.*
References: *Jones (1805-9); Brycheiniog (1965, 1984-5).*

Castell Tinboeth, *Llanbadarn Fynydd*

Few documentary facts have survived to outline the history of this forgotten castle, and over the years antiquarians and historians have offered many theories to fill the gaps. What can be said with some certainty is that Castell Tinboeth was a thirteenth-century stronghold belonging to one of the most powerful and ambitious dynasties in the Welsh Marches, the Mortimers of Wigmore. Some members of this family were so closely connected to the royal bloodline that their lives were dogged with suspicion and misfortune, bringing the dynasty to a premature end in the first quarter of the fifteenth century.

Their rise to power began in 1075 when Ralph Mortimer I was granted a portion of the forfeited territories of the earl of Hereford, who had been ousted for rebelling against the king. The earl's castle at Wigmore near Leominster became the new Mortimer seat and a springboard for further conquests. To the west lay a tempting group of Welsh *cantrefs*, principally Elfael and Maelienydd, which formed a territory known as *Rhwng Gwy a Hafren* ('between the Wye and the Severn'). In the great offensive against the Welsh in 1093, Ralph moved into Maelienydd and built an earth and timber castle at Cwm Aran near Llanbister that was to serve as the main Norman power base in the region for the next two centuries. The chronicles record the frequent capture, destruction and rebuilding of this castle, but by 1200 the territory was more or less firmly under Mortimer control. The rise to power of Llywelyn the Great posed a serious threat to English rule in the middle Marches, even though Ralph Mortimer II (d.1246) had made a political marriage with the prince's daughter Gwladys Du (widow of another powerful Marcher lord, Reginald de Braose of Brecon). To reinforce his hold on the area Ralph ordered the construction of new stone castles at Knucklas and Cefnllys in the 1240s, but as he was serving in Gascony at the time the work was very probably overseen by his 11-year old son and heir Roger III (d.1282) – an early start for what was to be a long military career.

Tinboeth was the third major castle built to secure Maelienydd for the Mortimers and was built on a high, steep-sided hill coupling natural defences with a strategic viewpoint, to the detriment of any domestic comfort. The entire summit was scarped to form a raised oval platform surrounded by an enormous rock-cut ditch which is still a formidable obstacle today, despite centuries of erosion

An aerial view of Castell Tinboeth with (opposite) the fragments of stonework that survive (located at the right-hand of the polygonal wall seen in outline on the scarped platform above) (© Crown copyright: RCAHMW)

and in-filling. There is an additional counterscarp bank around the rim of the ditch which swells out to form a narrow bailey or defensive outwork on the more vulnerable east side. An earthen rampart around the summit of the platform probably conceals the footings of a stone wall, laid out in straight stretches to enclose a courtyard of polygonal plan.[25] One solitary fragment of a D-shaped tower has managed to remain upright, and this probably formed part of a typical twin-towered gatehouse. The rest of the masonry has fallen in pieces into the ditch. No other structures can be seen above ground today, but detailed excavations would no doubt reveal more of the plan.

There is no record of the castle's construction, and lingering theories that it was de Braose's work of the twelfth century can be dismissed; the site is too substantial to be anything other than a thirteenth-century fortification. Furthermore, the assumption that the first buildings were of wood, and only later replenished with masonry, is debatable; the scale of the ditches and the vast amounts of shale that must have been produced make it more probable that the castle was stone-built from the start. Perhaps the curtain wall was constructed first, followed at a later date by the gatehouse with its better quality masonry; this might explain the disparity between the surviving remains. The idea that the castle sits within an Iron Age hillfort is questionable too, and may only be proven by excavation. The hill is scarred with a number of banks and ditches, but none form a coherent defensive scheme and some are clearly the result of post-medieval quarrying or mining.

Further confusion has been caused by the place-name. During the medieval period the site was known as Dinbod, Dynbawd, Tynbot and other variations, names which have been realistically interpreted as *Din-baud* or 'Maud's fort', giving rise to the tradition that it was built by Roger's widow, Matilda de Braose.[26] This is not an unlikely suggestion, for Matilda was no shrinking violet but a resourceful woman fully capable of aiding and abetting her ambitious husband. During the rebellion of Simon de Montfort, she organised Prince Edward's escape from his captors and then celebrated the Royalist victory with a great feast at Wigmore presided over by de Monfort's head on a lance, which Roger sent to her as a present. She outlived her husband by some 18 years, but the idea of a sorrowful widow building a castle to defend her family lands must be doubted, however appealing it sounds. Roger died in October 1282, and *Dynbaud* is included in a list of his castles garrisoned on the king's behalf in 1282-83, so it must have been in existence when war broke out. Five horsemen and thirty foot soldiers were stationed here during the emergency.

This is the first mention of the castle in contemporary records[27] and taken at face value suggests that it was a late foundation established by Roger Mortimer himself. Bearing in mind the trouble he had with Llywelyn over his nearby castle at Cefnllys (see below), the most likely period for Roger to have built Tinboeth would have been in the years immediately following the prince's first defeat in 1277. Had it been built earlier, it could hardly have escaped either the chroniclers' or Llywelyn's attention. In the early fourteenth century the castle seems to have passed into the ownership of one of Roger's younger sons, who styled himself William of Tinboeth, but the Mortimer estates were seized by the crown in 1322 when Roger IV was imprisoned for taking part in a rebellion against Edward II. They were restored, but soon confiscated again when Roger was executed for the major role he played in the downfall of that monarch. While these events of national significance were being played out, Castell Tinboeth quietly slipped into obscurity, and the lack of any further records suggests it had a very short life. A remote and inconveniently sited castle such as this could only function as a military base, and when that need had passed, it was quickly abandoned.

Location: the castle lies on a hill 2.5km north of Llanbister village on the A453 from Llandrindod Wells to Newtown. After passing the signposted turning to Bwlch-y-sarnau there is a lay-by beyond a house; park here and follow the track opposite (a public footpath) up through the woods to the hilltop (OS map ref: SO 090 754).
Access: on enclosed farmland, but accessed via a stile from the footpath.
References: Brut; AC (1858, 1967); Remfry (1996).

Cefnllys Castle, *Llandrindod Wells*

This was another Mortimer stronghold built to consolidate their claim to Maelienydd and was similarly built on a steep-sided hill typical of the Radnorshire landscape. So determined were the English to secure possession of this land that *two* castles were built here in the course of a long and bitter struggle against Prince Llywelyn ap Gruffudd.

The history of Cefnllys begins in 1241 when the Welsh of Maelienydd attempted to dislodge Ralph Mortimer II, but the uprising failed and the following year he built a new stone castle on a high ridge within a loop of the river Ithon to forestall any further trouble.[28] These natural defences coupled with high stone walls must have made Cefnllys a seemingly impregnable fortress, and it is significant that when the Welsh rose again in revolt in 1262, the castle was only taken 'by treachery'. According to the *Brut y Tywysogion,* once the invaders had slipped inside, they killed the gate keepers and captured the constable and his family before setting the buildings on fire. The chronicles imply that this was a random act by the local populace, but some historians have considered that the attack was instigated by

Llywelyn ap Gruffudd as part of his scheme to weaken Mortimer support in the middle Marches.

A large force under the command of Roger Mortimer II and Humphrey de Bohun, lord of Brecon, soon arrived at Cefnllys, but Llywelyn was determined that this strategic base should not remain in English hands. He sent his forces to blockade Mortimer and his allies within the ruined walls. Besieged, undermanned and short of supplies, the outcome to the conflict could have been very grim indeed, but Llywelyn allowed the English forces to make an ignominious retreat. Was this chivalrous gesture on account of their kinship (Mortimer and Llywelyn shared the same grandfather) or a deliberate ploy to avoid staining his growing political status with unnecessary bloodshed? Once the English had left, Llywelyn presumably completed the destruction of the castle.

Within a few years the prince had reached the pinnacle of his power with the signing of the Treaty of Montgomery in 1267, in which Henry III acknowledged his pre-eminent position. One of the clauses of the treaty concerned the vexed question of the ownership of Maelienydd. The territory was effectively under Llywelyn's control by right of conquest, but Mortimer was allowed to repair Cefnllys in advance of any lawful settlement of his ancestral claim to the land. It did not take long for this legal loophole to be exploited. Mortimer started work on a second castle here, evidently stronger than the first, and the angry prince wrote to the new king complaining that the terms of the treaty had been exceeded. Llywelyn's specific complaint was that Mortimer had 'constructed a new work, not merely a fence, as

An aerial view of Cefnllys showing the site of the earlier castle to the left and the later castle to the right, the latter separated from the rest of the hilltop by a deeply cut ditch in the rock (© Crown copyright: RCAHMW)

has been suggested to the king, but a wide and deep ditch, and stones and timber have been brought to construct a fortress'. Not surprisingly, King Edward showed little enthusiasm for reining in Mortimer and by 1277 Llywelyn was no longer in a position to make demands. Work on the second castle continued, presumably utilising materials from the first site. A small borough was also established here to encourage some economic growth in the area. This urban venture was to last long after the medieval period, and only declined with the rise of the nearby spa town of Llandrindod in the eighteenth century. The town may have lain within the defended hilltop or, more likely, at the foot of the slope beside the surviving church of St Michael.

In October 1282 Roger Mortimer III died barely two months before his enemy Llywelyn, and Cefnllys passed to his son Edmund. There was another uprising in 1294, and Edmund was subsequently obliged to offer some concessions to his belligerent Welsh tenants, granting them the right to be heard in court under English law so long as they did not rebel against his ownership of Cefnllys. In 1304 Edmund died and the inheritance passed to his son, Roger Mortimer IV, first earl of March, who gained notoriety as the lover of Queen Isabella and the driving force behind the deposition of Edward II. Roger enjoyed his exalted position for only a few years before the young Prince Edward launched his own coup and executed Mortimer in return for his father's overthrow. The confiscated estates were soon returned and remained with the family until the death of Edmund Mortimer IV, fifth earl of March in 1425, when the inheritance passed to his nephew Richard, duke of York. In 1461 during the Wars of the Roses, Duke Richard's son and heir Edward, earl of March, was crowned King Edward IV, bringing Cefnllys and the other former Mortimer castles into royal ownership.

The castle in the meantime was probably in decay, although it was not abandoned as Tinboeth seems to have been, probably because the existence of the town made it a necessary fixture. During the Glyndŵr rebellion Cefnllys was garrisoned with twelve spearmen and thirty archers. An account claims that the surrounding land was laid waste by the rebels, but historians are uncertain whether the castle itself was taken. The site nevertheless remained inhabited, and sometime around the middle of the fifteenth century the itinerant poet Lewys Glyn Cothi wrote four poems in praise of the hospitality of the constable of Cefnllys, Ieuan ap Phylip and his

The site of Cefnllys Castle on a prominent hill within a bend of the river Ithon

wife Angharad. The poems allude to Ieuan's new timber-framed hall which presumably stood on the level ground between the two castles. The manorial functions were soon transferred to another building nearby and Cefnllys was finally abandoned. John Leland was here around 1539 and wrote 'In Melennith appear great ruins of two castles. The one is called Tynbot set on a steep crag three miles from the abbey of Comehire [Abbey Cwm-hir] ... the other is called Kevenlles ... now down, it belongs to the Duke of York.'

All the buildings of Cefnllys have long collapsed into heaps of rubble so large and shapeless that it cannot be said with any certainty what stood here. The hummocky mound of the first castle stands at the north end of the ridge and could represent the buried remains of a central tower surrounded by one or more walled courtyards. The second castle lies to the south and is separated from the rest of the ridge by a wide and deep rock-cut ditch (evidently the one referred to in Llywelyn's letter to the king). Beyond the ditch is a roughly rectangular walled platform, possibly with corner turrets, and a central mound marking the collapsed remains of another keep. A few tantalising clues to the appearance of this lost castle may be gleaned from the poems of Lewys Glyn Cothi:

> A white castle above a full white lake
> An eight-sided fort above the bank of Ithon,
> A Greek fort in twelve encircling bands.[29]

The reference to white walls suggests lime plaster or whitewash, and the main keep could have been an octagonal tower. The 'Greek fort' may be an allusion to the imagined strongholds of classical antiquity, while the 'twelve encircling bands' could be a reference to a multi-sided enclosure. But in truth, any sort of castle could be conjured up from the poems, and so Cefnllys must keep its secrets buried in rubble until such time as proper excavations are carried out.

Location: *Cefnllys hill lies 3km east of Llandrindod Wells on the A483. At Fiveways crossing in the town centre turn up past the county hall and continue along the minor road until it crosses over the hill and descends into the Ithon valley. There is a car park beside the river (OS map ref: SO 089 615).*

Access: *a public footpath from the car park crosses the bridge to St Michael's church, from where several paths lead up the steep hillside.*

References: *Brut; Radnor (1932, 1972); Remfry (1996); Cefnllys (RCAHMW)*

Hen Gastell, Llangattock

The meagre remains of this castle can easily be missed even though it lies just a few feet from a country lane, for the mound is only fully revealed once the winter months have stripped away the leaves from the covering screen of trees. Although superficially resembling a square motte with a marshy ditch fed by natural springs,

Despite the covering of trees, the ditched mound of Hen Gastell can still be seen in this view

the abundance of tumbled stonework reveals that the mound is in fact the collapsed remains of a small and compact masonry fortification. The outlines of a rectangular hall or keep, measuring approximately 23 by 15 metres, can be traced on the south side of the mound, while the northern flank overlooking the valley is enclosed with a narrow walled courtyard. Presumably the access was on this side too, through a simple gate and across the ditch on a wooden bridge. The site is very similar to the Welsh castle at Plas Baglan (p.140), but this should not necessarily be taken as evidence of a native origin. In fact, this is one of those sites that have slipped through the records without leaving a trace. No documents chronicle the history or owners of Hen Gastell, and there are no dressed stones on site to helpfully indicate a construction date. The rectangular layout might suggest a twelfth-century origin and the proximity to Abergavenny and Crickhowell would indicate it was also an Anglo-Norman foundation. However, the site is not a naturally strong one for an early castle, and this may instead be a fortified house, or moated dwelling, built by someone of less prominent social standing at any time between the thirteenth and fifteenth centuries. The simple truth is that we do not know the history of this obscure ruin, and unless some documentation comes to light or the excavator's trowel unearths some clinching evidence, the history of Hen Gastell is lost in the realms of conjecture.

Location: The castle lies in a field on the hillside 2km south of Crickhowell. Follow the signs into the village of Llangattock, take the left fork uphill and over the canal, keeping to the lower road heading towards the hamlet of Llanelly. At a series of sharp bends the prominent tree-covered mound will be seen on the downhill side of the road (Ordnance Survey map ref: SO 213 166).
Access: On private land, but easily visible from the roadside.
References: Brycheiniog (1968-69).

Painscastle

This site could hardly be termed a 'forgotten' castle, for not only are the massive earthworks relatively well preserved, but they occupy a fairly prominent position beside the little village; but Painscastle finds a place here as a representative of those sites where, through neglect, demolition and stone robbing, a substantial masonry building has completely disappeared. Anyone looking at Painscastle, or the neighbouring strongholds of Builth and New Radnor, without prior knowledge of their long and brutal histories, would never realise that these grassy mounds were major stone fortifications in their day.

Painscastle's setting in a rural upland area seems off the beaten track, but in fact it stands on one of the main routes through Radnorshire into England. Earlier invaders than the Normans may have established a foothold here, for Roman remains have been found in the locality, and the castle is claimed to lie within a reused fort. The castle was built in the early twelfth century by Payne fitz John (hence the place-name), as the administrative and military *caput* of the surrounding lordship of Elfael and, like many border strongholds, suffered in the oscillating politics of the Marches. When Payne was killed in 1137 the territory was recovered by the Welsh and remained in native control until 1195, when Matilda, wife of William de Braose III, led an army to regain the castle and inflict a bloody defeat upon the Welsh. Painscastle was then rebuilt and renamed *Castrum Matildis* in honour of this ferocious woman, but the new name didn't stick. The works carried out must have been quite substantial, for the castle withstood two further Welsh attacks before the century was out. William's exalted position among the Marcher lords came to a sudden and dramatic end in 1208 when the capricious King John turned against him and forced him to flee the country. Matilda and her young son were not so lucky, being captured and starved to death in a royal dungeon.

For some years the lordship was held by a Welsh ally of the Crown, but when Llywelyn the Great attacked in 1231 Henry III personally intervened and undertook to rebuild the strategic base. The royal army encamped here for three months in the summer as building work commenced on this one castle (while Llywelyn destroyed ten others, as a contemporary chronicler noted with sarcasm). The driving force behind the refortification of Painscastle was surely Hubert de Burgh, Henry's able and ambitious minister, who had built up a power base in the Welsh Marches and was anxious to keep Llywelyn out of the neighbourhood. Hubert's works at the

Painscastle seen from the air (© Crown copyright: RCAHMW)

royal fortress of Montgomery, and at his own castles of Grosmont and Skenfrith in Monmouthshire, remain as testament to his skill at fortification design, and it is regrettable that so little survives here today. Also, because some of the royal accounts are missing, there is no complete record of what was done and the cost incurred. We do know that the castle was 'splendidly rebuilt in stone and lime' and renamed *Maugre Lewelini*, which roughly translates as 'Despite Llywelyn'. This boastful name-change didn't last very long either. A borough was also founded alongside the castle to bring economic growth to the area, and the townsfolk had the right to hold weekly markets and an annual fair. When Hubert was toppled from his pre-eminent position in 1232 due to a series of military setbacks and the influence of powerful rivals, Painscastle was granted to the Tosnys. It fell to Llywelyn ap Gruffudd in 1265 and only after the first defeat of the prince in 1277 could Ralph de Tosny set about rebuilding the defences. The lordship subsequently passed to the Beauchamp earls of Warwick, and the last recorded use of the castle occurred in 1401 when a garrison of 36 was installed during the Glyndŵr rebellion. The fate of the castle is not known (probably it was little more than a precarious English enclave in hostile Welsh territory) and after the war was over it was left to fall into decay. William Camden's *Britannia* of 1586 makes reference to this and other Radnorshire strongholds as 'almost buried in their own ruins'.

Despite this catalogue of destruction and costly rebuilding, all that remains of Painscastle today is a series of earthworks on a ridge south of the village. As 'earthworks' they must be described, even though just beneath the topsoil the collapsed footings of masonry buildings await rediscovery. There is a hummocky motte at the end of the ridge with a roughly rectangular bailey in front, surrounded by a still formidable ditch and counterscarp bank. Semicircular barbicans gave access into the courtyard from the east and west sides. Aerial photographs of the site clearly show the outlines of buried buildings and the scars of robber trenches along the rampart, and the uneven summit of the motte must conceal the base of a substantial round keep. On the east side of the castle is a derelict house that has also played a role in the history of Painscastle. Within the whitewashed stone walls of Upper House are the remains of an early fifteenth-century timber-framed aisled hall, one of the finest examples surviving in Wales. Just like Cefnllys, here at Painscastle we have a clear sign of the shift in power from the castle to the undefended nobleman's residence. The fact that the hall juts into the outer ditch means that the castle had by that time lost its military purpose, and was just a war-worn pile of rubble to be ransacked for building materials.

Location: *The castle lies beside the village of Painscastle on the B4594 approximately 5km east of the Erwood off the A470 to Builth Wells (OS map ref: SO 17 462).*
Access: *on enclosed farmland and no public access. The earthworks are visible from the road.*
References: *AC (1923); HKW (1963).*

Pencelli Castle, *Pencelli*

Pencelli Castle in the Usk valley near Brecon is better known as a popular caravan park and camping site than a historic monument, for only a few fragments of the ancient masonry survives in the back garden of a house. There are other forgotten castles displaying far more extensive and impressive remains; yet what is so remarkable about Pencelli is that just 260-odd years ago a major ruined fortress

Pencelli Castle as depicted by the Buck brothers in 1741
(by permission of Llyfrgell Genedlaethol Cymru /The National Library of Wales)

existed here. It has almost wholly disappeared in the intervening years and were it not for the testimony of the Buck brothers, Pencelli might be considered a fairly insignificant site. The engraving they produced in 1741 shows a long stretch of curtain wall with a typical thirteenth-century twin-towered gatehouse. The position of loop-holes suggest the gatehouse stood at least two storeys high, probably three, and the arched window openings in the adjacent curtain mark the position of a two-storeyed building set against the inner wall. Within the courtyard stands a twin-gabled Elizabethan mansion, while towering over all is a corner fragment of a substantial internal building. Of these features only the house remains today.

Pencelli was an important castle and valued at the service of four knights to the lord of Brecon, but there is not a great deal of documentary evidence to outline its history. It was founded by Ralph de Baskerville, who had fought at Hastings and received lands along the Herefordshire border.[30] Ralph supported Bernard de Neufmarché's conquest of Brycheiniog in 1093 and so gained further territorial rewards for his services. Probably the castle was founded at this time, although an earlier date is not unlikely since the Normans had been attempting colonisation of this part of Wales in the 1080s. The chosen site was a triangular ridge jutting into the Usk valley, adequately defended by natural slopes on two sides, with the man-made defences massed on the more vulnerable southern flank. This side of the castle was also overlooked by higher ground, a factor that may have restricted the effectiveness of Pencelli as a major stronghold in later years. In the early days of the Norman invasion it was nevertheless a secure location, and the few remaining earthworks that have survived later landscaping suggest it was quite a sizeable one too, perhaps encompassing as much as three acres.

The more secure tip of the ridge seems to have been worked up into a low motte (or perhaps a ringwork, the earthworks are now too mutilated to be sure), and this served as the base for a stone keep probably erected sometime in the twelfth century. Only some toppled masses of masonry now remain above ground, but it is probable that these fragments formed part of the tall structure depicted by the Bucks.[31] Some years ago unofficial excavations uncovered the foundations of this keep, which is estimated to be 14m square with walls 3m thick. The base of a square turret (probably for garderobes) projects out from the north corner, while alongside it is a long narrow secondary chamber that might be the lower level of a forebuilding. Close to the west side of the keep is a fallen fragment of a semicircular structure, perhaps a gatehouse or flanking tower. There are vestiges of a stone wall encircling the motte platform, and more rubble has been exposed by erosion along the flanks of the bailey enclosure, but the extent and form of the twelfth-century castle will only be revealed by proper excavations.

When the last of the Pencelli Baskervilles died around 1210 the estate briefly passed to the Le Wafre family, before it was seized by Reginald de Braose in 1215 in the course of his rebellion against King John (as described in the entry on Blaenllynfi). Around this time Reginald married Gwladys Du, the young daughter of his current ally Llywelyn the Great, and settled the property on her in exchange for some lands in Mid Wales. A short time after Reginald died in 1228 Gwladys married the heir of another great Marcher dynasty, Ralph Mortimer II, thereby alienating Pencelli from the de Braose line. Before long Ralph had to contend not only with other members of the de Braose family trying to reclaim Pencelli, but with the far more serious threat from Prince Llywelyn, the father-in-law from hell. In 1231 the *Brut y Tywysogion* reports that Llywelyn destroyed Radnor, Hay and Brecon, before moving on to Caerleon. For some reason he seems to have ignored Pencelli on this occasion, but two years later he destroyed the castle along with the neighbouring strongholds of Brecon (again), Blaenllynfi and Castell Dinas. The castle was recovered and must have been repaired, although the extent of work carried out is uncertain; it may still have consisted of a masonry keep with a stone-walled inner ward at this time, along with timber outer defences.

The ownership dispute was finally laid to rest with the marriage of Ralph's son Roger Mortimer III to Matilda de Braose in 1247, and the castle is claimed to have been significantly refurbished in the ensuing years with the addition of the curtain wall and gatehouse. While this is possible (we have already seen that Roger was an enthusiastic castle builder) the details shown in the Buck engraving would not be incompatible with a later date. Between 1262 and 1276 most of Breconshire was in the control of Llywelyn ap Gruffudd and his allies, and the fate of Pencelli is unknown. If it was still in English occupation and had not fallen to the Welsh, it would not have been a suitable time for Roger Mortimer to undertake extensive rebuilding. More likely the works were carried out as a precautionary measure once Llywelyn had been defeated and driven out.

Pencelli is mentioned again in 1322 as a Mortimer holding seized by King Edward II when Roger IV was imprisoned for rebellion, but it was returned to the family once the hubris of that unfortunate monarch's reign was over. The lordship passed to the Crown in the fifteenth century and was granted to various noblemen before being split up into smaller holdings in the sixteenth century.[32] Most of the estate passed to a branch of the Herbert family and remained with this important local dynasty until after the Civil War when it was conveyed to Thomas Powel of Llanishen, who had married a Herbert heiress. The condition of the castle during this period is

The house built in the castle courtyard prior to 1583 that reputedly contains the remains of the castle chapel

not known. Perhaps some of the buildings were still occupied, but by 1583 a new house had been built in the courtyard, reputedly incorporating the remains of the castle chapel dedicated to St Leonard.[33] The Herbert house still survives more or less intact, although there have inevitably been improvements and alterations, particularly around 1800 when it was given a castellated façade. Nevertheless it is a fascinating building in its own right, one of the earliest examples of a 'double-pile' house in Wales, and very similar to Newton in Brecon, which is linked to the family and possibly the work of the same architect. The builders of the Herbert house utilised some of the abundant masonry lying around, and fragments of reset Norman stonework can be seen in the walls.

There was still a substantial amount of the old castle left when the Bucks visited almost 160 years later, and it cannot be just coincidence that the gatehouse was still standing then, for it would have served as an imposing entrance to the courtyard. But by the time of the 1840 tithe map all the ruins had gone. The map shows the house, an extensive range of outbuildings, and a large open space skirted by the turnpike road that undoubtedly marked the position of the large outer bailey. The Breconshire historian Theophilus Jones makes no mention of masonry here *c.*1800 nor does he record the tradition of any, so it is likely that the last vestiges of the castle had been pulled down long before his time, probably soon after the Bucks' visit. The Georgian owners evidently had no further regard for the noble façade and swept it away, filling in the great ditches and using the leftover stonework to construct the stables and barns that still remain a prominent feature of the site today.

Some of the remnants of the castle today

Location: Pencelli lies about 5km south-east of Brecon on the B4558 to Talybont and Llangynidr. The castle site lies on the hill at the eastern end of the village (OS map ref: SO 095 249).
Access: On private land and not accessible to the public. The house and castle site can be seen from the caravan park and from a public footpath alongside the canal at the foot of the hill.
References: Brut; Jones (1805-09); Brycheiniog (1965, 1978-9); Remfry (1999).

Glamorgan

Castles of the Vale
Glamorgan has the largest number of castles of all the historic Welsh counties (latest estimates stand at about 81 confirmed medieval sites) and is furthermore blessed with an abundance of surviving medieval documents collated by the Victorian engineer and historian G.T. Clark (1809-85). In addition, the antiquarian gleanings of Rice Merrick (*c*.1520-87) provide a detailed picture of Glamorgan in Elizabethan times. Merrick chronicled the Norman invasion of the county and his account, wonderfully romantic and hopelessly inaccurate, still colours our view of the period. The story goes that the last Welsh king of Morgannwg, Iestyn ap Gwrgant, ill-advisedly asked the Normans for help in defeating a rival in battle, but once the conflict was over and Iestyn was victorious, the mercenaries decided to stay on, ousted Iestyn and parcelled the land amongst themselves. The twelve knights who had followed Robert Fitzhamon on this fanciful escapade founded dynasties that still existed in Merrick's time.[34]

In reality, the Norman conquest of Glamorgan was a slower, more piecemeal affair. The county is geographically split into two main regions; a low-lying coastal plain (the *Bro*) extending from Cardiff to Port Talbot, and a larger, sparsely inhabited region of mountains and deep winding valleys (the *Blaenau*). The Normans were only interested in holding onto *Bro Morgannwg* for, as Merrick notes, the Vale 'was always renowned as well for the fertility of the soil, and abundance of all things serving to the necessity or pleasure of man, as also for the temperature and wholesomeness of the air'. The dispossessed Welsh had to make do with the bleaker uplands. The first castle here is believed to have been established at Cardiff in 1081 by William the Conqueror, while on royal progress through south Wales to meet with Rhys ap Tewdwr of Deheubarth. Rhys came to terms with the king to retain possession of his land, but when he was killed in battle in 1093, the earl of Gloucester, Robert Fitzhamon, moved swiftly to secure lowland territory in Gwent and Glamorgan and create a new Norman lordship centred on Cardiff. Fitzhamon's successor and namesake was Robert of Gloucester, illegitimate son of Henry I, who acquired the lordship in 1113 through his marriage to Fitzhamon's daughter. Until his death in 1147, Earl Robert oversaw the consolidation of the territory as far west as Neath. The uplands were left under nominal Welsh control until the thirteenth century, although an early encroachment by Robert's son William provoked an amazingly bold Welsh response; one night in 1158 Ifor Bach

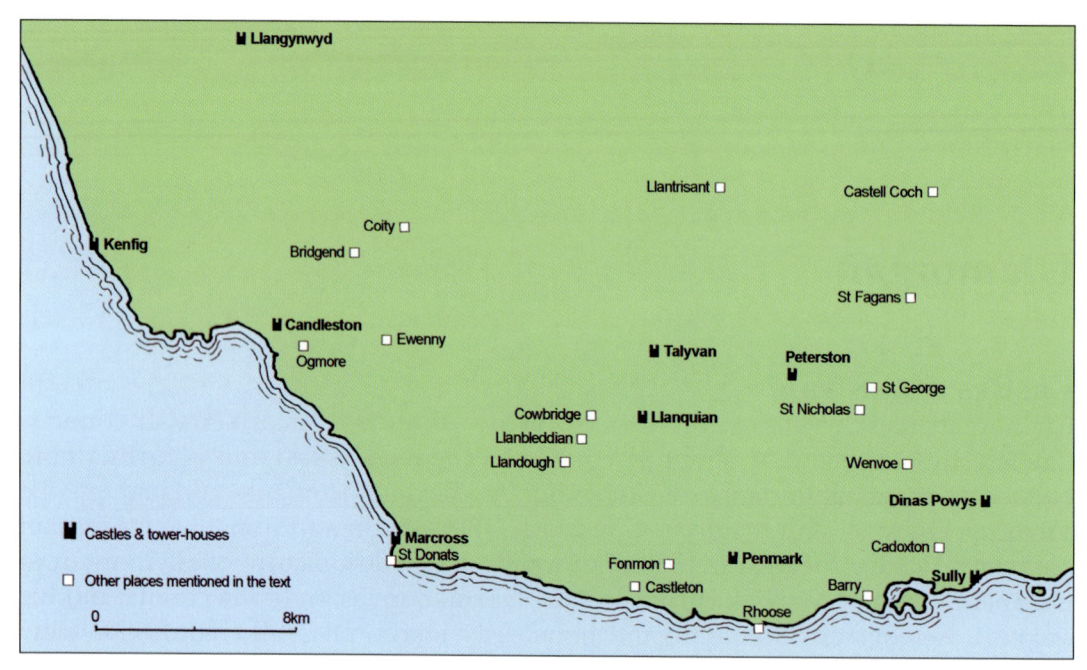

Castles of the Vale of Glamorgan

and his men broke into Cardiff Castle and kidnapped the earl and his family, and held them captive until their lands had been restored.

Once the defensive network of castles had been established in the Vale, the growth of settlements was encouraged and villages with distinctly un-Welsh names sprang into existence: Bonvilston, Cosmeston, Cowbridge, Flemingston, Gileston and Monknash for instance. Monastic houses such as Ewenny, Margam and Neath were founded at the instigation of the Norman overlords for the peace of their souls. The castles that were built to keep this rich area firmly under English control display a whole range of architectural styles from the earliest earthwork mounds through to state-of-the-art concentric fortresses along with diminutive tower houses and defended farmsteads. Even after the feudal age had long passed, some castles remained in use and were adapted to the more sophisticated needs of society, including Fonmon, Llandough, St Donats, St Fagans and Castell Coch. While CADW look after most of the major sites there exist many lesser known castles that qualify for a place in this book. Five of the most substantial sites are looked at here, and the history of the Vale in medieval times is further outlined in the entries on Dinas Powys, Kenfig, and Llangynwyd.

Pride of place among the forgotten castles of the Vale must be given to **Penmark**, the head of one of the largest and richest lordships in Glamorgan. The castle, too, is surprisingly large, the outer rampart and ditch encloses perhaps as much as three acres of land as well as the church. Penmark was granted by Fitzhamon to Gilbert de Umfraville, who built a castle to control his acquisition, and it seems to have been a ringwork set on the edge of a steep fall to the Waycock valley. A large outer enclosure swept around the southern quadrant to protect the more vulnerable approach. Natural erosion and deliberate infilling has reduced these once formidable earthworks to a few insignificant hummocks. At some point the timber defences of the ringwork were replaced with a thick masonry wall of angular plan apparently lacking in flanking towers, and therefore probably of early date. In the thirteenth century a rounded corner tower and garderobe block were added to the west wall, which is now the only upstanding part of the castle. The overgrown walls are in a poor state and show signs of recent collapse. A stony mound at the east end of the ward covers the remains of several rectangular buildings, but their plan and purpose will only be revealed by excavation. When the male line of the Umfravilles died out in the fourteenth century Penmark was acquired by the St John family of nearby Fonmon, who appear to have neglected the castle in favour of their own ancestral stronghold. A small sketch of Penmark produced in 1622 suggests that the entrance was a simple gateway, and that there was a tower-like building within the courtyard, possibly a free-standing keep.

The fields surrounding the coastal villages of Monknash and **Marcross** bear ample witness to the time when the monks of Neath Abbey farmed the land here. Earthworks, field enclosures, ruined barns and dovecots testify to the agricultural

The rounded corner tower (left) and garderobe block added to the west wall at Penmark Castle

wealth gleaned from these fertile acres. The hamlet of Marcross lies in a small valley winding down through the cornfields to the sea. The most obvious remains are the scattered ruins of the monastic grange (incorrectly marked on some maps as a 'medieval village'), but incorporated into the outbuildings of nearby Village House are fragments of a small castle of the Marcross family. The remains do not appear to have been of much extent and the site lacks any natural defensive advantages, so it is best described as a strong house rather than a true castle. There was a rectangular enclosure with several internal buildings and at least one corner tower, all surrounded by an outer ditch. One wing flanking the road has been rebuilt as a cowshed and retains dressed stone details of *c*.1300. The building was still occupied when the Hearth Tax returns were compiled in 1670 for it was assessed as a residence of seven hearths; thereafter it was abandoned and by 1788 only the outer walls were said to remain. There is even less here now, for in 1980 the landowner erased some of the walls and ditches to extend the outbuildings.

The very English sounding **Peterston-super-Ely** was home to the le Sore family from the twelfth to the late fourteenth century. The name of Robert le Sore is mentioned in a document of *c*.1102 and he was probably granted this land, along with neighbouring St Fagans, by Robert Fitzhamon. Later legends claim that the castle was founded by Peter le Sore (hence the place-name) but there is no authenticated reference to this person. The story that Owain Glyndŵr captured the castle and beheaded Mathew le Sore is also unlikely (even though his reputed skull was once kept on display at the parish church), for the lordship had passed to the Butler family well before the rebellion started. By Leland's day the castle was 'all in ruin' and the most obvious relic is a chunk of solid masonry incorporated into a modern house beside the road. This seems to have formed part of a square tower on the north-west corner of the castle. A less obvious fragment of ivy-covered wall lies in the front lawn of the next house along, while in the rear garden there are traces of a thick walled building (probably a free-standing rectangular keep). These few fragments are unfortunately too slight to provide a convincing picture of the original appearance of Peterston Castle. Jeston Homfray's charming 1828 lithograph shows that the remains have been fairly insignificant for a long time, although the village then comprised just a few thatched cottages beside the church. The large upstanding fragment of masonry shown in the foreground seems to have been part of the keep.

Homfray depicted **Talyvan** too, and this castle still retains the pastoral setting that Peterston has lost through

Jeston Homfray's 1828 lithograph of Peterston Castle

urban growth. Unfortunately the romantic image of a hilltop fortress with a tall tower pierced with gaping windows no longer holds true. In the intervening 180-odd years the walls have crumbled and the site is shrouded in dense undergrowth. The little house within the courtyard (Homfray shows the chimney poking out above the curtain wall) has fallen into ruin, and some modern farm buildings stand close by. The castle was built by the St Quintin family who held this and the neighbouring Llanbleddian lordships from the beginning of the twelfth century. In 1233 John St Quintin was ousted from Talyvan by the adventurous knight Richard Siward, who had joined forces with the rebel barons opposed to the policies of Henry III. When peace was restored and the insurgents had crept back into royal favour, Richard should have returned the lordship, but instead held onto it, making the castle a favoured residence and seat for further exploits. The St Quintins had to make do with replacement lands in England. Siward was perhaps responsible for adding a large round keep in the centre of the courtyard and replacing the ringwork palisade with a curtain wall, all of which is now very fragmentary.

Jeston Homfray's lithograph of Talyvan

Richard Siward did not enjoy his new-found privileges for long. In 1245 he was hauled before a court accused of truce-breaking, murder and double-dealing with the Welsh. He was found guilty and outlawed. Siward was a far from innocent party in this affair, but there is also a strong hint of conspiracy among his powerful neighbours. He appealed to the king, but died before the case could be settled. Talyvan was seized by the ambitious earl of Gloucester, Richard de Clare, who shortly afterwards established a new town at Cowbridge controlled from the older St Quintin stronghold of Llanbleddian.

Remains of walling at Talyvan Castle

Thus Talyvan was no longer the centre of an independent lordship and declined in importance. By 1314 it was claimed to be worthless, but this must be an exaggeration since the castle was deemed a worthy target to attack in 1321 by rebels opposed to the hated lord of Glamorgan, Hugh Despenser. Possibly it was repaired and continued to play a subsidiary role as a hunting lodge for an adjacent deer park, but by Leland's time it was 'clearly in ruin'. Around 1700 a small house was built up against the crumbling walls and the courtyard utilised as a garden and orchard. Many stones were said to have been taken away for building purposes in the nineteenth century, and the outer earthworks filled in or flattened by agricultural activities. All the buildings now lie in tangled ruins, and large-scale excavations would be needed to work out what actually stood on this hilltop.

Llanquian lies a few kilometres away from Talyvan and though small, is a particularly interesting site for here can also be found traces of an abandoned church and settlement. The castle itself was a small ringwork set at the end of a ridge, not far from where the old Roman road crossed Stalling Down towards the town of Cowbridge. The earthworks are now very overgrown, but it is still possible to make out the foundations of a square masonry building on one side of the enclosure. The awkward way it aligns with the curving rampart strongly suggests it is an addition, probably of the thirteenth century or later, although there are no distinguishing details left. The ground floor had a vaulted storeroom and the principal chamber was on the floor above. The plan and position suggests a keep-like structure, but the walls are far too thin to have had much defensive potential and so this is probably a very modest hall block. The surrounding rampart looks like an earthwork, but it probably conceals the remains of a stone wall. When the historian G.T. Clark was here in the 1870s more of the stonework seems to have been standing, for he described the castle as 'a shell of masonry, circular or nearly so, about 64 feet in diameter'. He observed a small projecting turret (perhaps for a garderobe?) and considered that the hall-block was part of a gatehouse. A few early records link Llanquian to the Nerber family of Castleton, and the site is sometimes called Nerber Castle.

A few metres in front of the castle are the stony foundations of two medieval buildings and a boundary bank. These earthworks may be contemporary with the castle, or a later farmstead associated with a small settlement that existed here for many years. The ruinous outbuildings of the adjacent farm also incorporate what is thought to be a chapel dedicated to St James mentioned in medieval documents. This can be identified by a tall chimney stack, which presumably served a priest's house attached to one end of the building. Fragments of the original arch-braced roof

Plan (opposite) and suggested reconstruction drawing of Llanquian

trusses survive inside. However, some doubts have been cast on whether this really is a chapel and not just a late-medieval house, perhaps the successor to the castle once it had been abandoned.

This overview of the lesser known castles of the Vale cannot conclude without a brief mention of several important sites that have now disappeared completely. John Leland saw the remains of towers at Wenvoe and Wrinstone. The Tudor farmhouses of St George and Castleton are built on the site of their medieval predecessors, possibly incorporating some vestiges in their thick walls. The vanished sites at Cadoxton, Cosmeston and Rhoose may have been fortified manor houses rather than true castles. Perhaps the most regrettable loss was Marsh House at Aberthaw, again not a castle but a fortified warehouse dating from the early seventeenth century; the last remnant of this unique building was obliterated in 1983.

Location and access: Penmark lies behind the church in the village just north of Cardiff Airport and signposted off the A4226 road to Llantwit Major (OS map ref: ST 058 689). There is no public access but the remains can clearly be seen from the churchyard. **Marcross** lies 5km west of Llantwit on the road to St Donat's and St Brides Major. Some of the earthworks can be glimpsed beyond the farm buildings from the roadside (SS 924 694). The remains at **Peterston** too can be seen from the roadside and the village lies signposted *on a minor road accessed from either M4 Junction 34 or the A48 Cardiff to Cowbridge road (ST 084 764).* **Talyvan** *lies on private land 3.5km north-east of Cowbridge, just off a minor road from Ystradowen to Welsh St Donats. A turning opposite Bwlch Gwyn Farm leads to the hilltop site (OS map ref: ST 021 772).* **Llanquian** *lies 2km east of Cowbridge off the A48 by-pass. A public footpath starts from the service station and passes alongside Hollybush Farm and into the woods where the castle lies (ST 018 745).*

References: Homfray (1828); AC (1872); all the castles of Glamorgan have been studied in great detail by the RCAHMW (1991, 2000).

Candleston Castle, Bridgend

Candleston lies in dense woodland on the edge of the Merthyr Mawr warren, a forlorn ruin almost overwhelmed by high dunes thrown up by climatic conditions in the late Middle Ages. Many coastal settlements in Glamorgan were obliterated by shifting sands (most famously the castle and town of Kenfig); here at least the sand stopped short at the walls although the adjoining hamlet was buried. Candleston is a fortified manor house rather than a true castle, and was intended to offer some security to the owners without the expense of major fortifications.

When Candleston was built in the early fourteenth century the creeping sands had yet to impact upon the area, and it stood upon a low rocky headland overlooking fields and meadows rolling down to the Ogwr estuary. The de Cantilupe family had been here from at least the thirteenth century, although the existing structure is much later and was raised either by Robert de Cantilupe (died *c.*1320) or his grandson Nicholas, the last of his line. A facetted curtain wall was built around the tip of the headland to form a D-shaped enclosure, with a long range of domestic buildings set against the straight flank. Shortly after this first stage was completed, the small and compact tower-house was built out from the hall to provide extra accommodation and give added protection to the adjacent gate.[35] The tower contains a vaulted storeroom on the ground floor, a residential chamber at first floor level, and a dark, basic attic room above. Each level is connected by straight stairs in the wall, which also provide access to the wall-walks. The first floor was clearly designed to be a solar leading off from the adjacent hall (which may have been single-storeyed in its original form), and so Candleston resembles the hall-tower arrangement of many lesser fortifications, such as Eastington and Flimston in west Wales.

The domestic range was considerably altered around 1500 when the castle was in the ownership of Sir Mathew Cradock, an important figure in local events during the turbulent years of the late fifteenth century. The hall was reconstructed as a two-storey building containing a large kitchen on the ground floor and a grand entrance lobby leading to the first floor chamber. Enough dressed stonework survives to reveal that the work carried out was of exceptional quality. Another wing was added in the seventeenth century. At the beginning of the nineteenth century the building was thoroughly overhauled and made suitable for the refined tastes of Sir John Nicholl, who resided here from 1806 to 1808 while his new mansion at nearby Merthyr Mawr was being built. Fireplaces were added, windows were enlarged, a stable block was built alongside the tower and the long domestic wing was truncated. It was subsequently occupied

c.1320

c.1400

c.1500

c.1700

Stages in the development of Candleston from its inception in the early 1300s down to 1700, with the tower-house pictured opposite

by tenant farmers, but by 1900 it was derelict, though still roofed over. Thereafter it was left to fall into ruin and remained a vandalised shell behind barbed wire until CADW undertook partial consolidation in 2008. The main structure has been cleaned up and made secure, but the curtain walls and outer buildings are still very overgrown. Further restoration work may take place in the near future. There is a very similar tower-house to Candleston just 3km away beside the A4196 Porthcawl road; however, Tythegston Court has remained inhabited to this day and consequently has been modernised to such an extent that from the outside it no longer looks like a medieval building at all.

Location: The castle is situated 4km south-west of Bridgend off the A48 or the B4524 road to Ewenny. Follow the signs to Merthyr Mawr, pass through the village and continue on until the narrow road ends in a car park beside the castle (OS map ref: SS 872 773).
Access: at present there is unrestricted access to the site.
References: RCAHMW (2000).

Dinas Powys, *Penarth*

Any description of Dinas Powys should start with untangling the myths that have grown up around this strange forgotten site, much like the weeds and brambles that now choke the towering walls. The castle was supposedly built by Iestyn ap Gwrgant, the last Welsh king of Morgannwg and was named in honour of his wife, a daughter of the ruler of Powys (hence the curious place-name, which means 'citadel of Powys'). Iestyn's ill-advised alliance with the Normans led to his deposition and exile from the rich lands of the Vale, as previously recounted. The veracity of this Elizabethan history has long been discredited, but accounts of Dinas Powys are still subject to confusion over the fact that there are two quite separate castles here – an earth and timber ringwork, and a large stone castle. What can be said with some certainty is that soon after Fitzhamon's invasion of Glamorgan in 1093 a lordship was established here and granted to Roger de Somery. A ringwork was built in Cwrt-yr-ala woods (on the site of a Dark Age court, presumably the 'dinas' of the place-name), but this was soon abandoned and demolished, either as a result of a Welsh attack or, more likely, to render it unusable by a potential enemy.

A new castle was then built on a naturally defensible ridge 600m to the south and it is this ruin that lies hidden in woodland beside a modern housing estate in the village. On the highest part of the ridge a rectangular keep was built at some point in the twelfth century, but of this only a shapeless mound of rubble remains. The antiquarian Iolo Morganwg came here in about 1780 and erroneously considered the keep to be part 'of a much ancienter castle, probably Roman, [with] the mouth of a vault going under it'. Presumably he was referring to a vaulted basement that was still visible at the time. Adjoining the keep is a long rectangular enclosure with roughly built walls constructed from limestone blocks hacked from

Birds-eye view of Dinas Powys. The twelfth-century keep stands at the furthest and most secure point of the ridge. The appearance of the internal buildings is conjectural

the adjacent slopes. The enclosure appears to be contemporary with the keep, since the scars of the bonding walls are clearly visible; however the RCAHMW considers it to be a later addition and that the keep was partly rebuilt at the time. Since the remains are too ruinous to be sure at present, the argument will only be resolved by excavation. The curtain wall has endured remarkably well and remains substantially intact, standing up to 6m high in places. There were two simple gateways on the south and east sides of the courtyard, protected by nothing other than wooden doors and drawbars. There must have been an outer ditch fronting the main south gate, but nothing can be seen today. Similarly a barbican or outwork noted by antiquarians has disappeared. The stone or timber-framed buildings that once clustered the interior have vanished too, leaving only a few window openings and the scars of rooflines marked on the walls. The simple layout of the enclosure and feeble gateways suggest it was built before 1200, when more sophisticated castle designs began to appear.

The castle had an uneventful history apart from a brief siege (or an attempted one) in 1222, when the lord of Glamorgan took umbrage at the audacity of another Marcher lord occupying the castle during the minority of its rightful owner. There does not seem to have been any attempt to improve or upgrade the defences in subsequent years, but probably nothing was required; Dinas Powys was a relatively large castle for the time and offered ample accommodation for the owners, who in any case had estates elsewhere in England. When the last male de Somery died in 1321 the inheritance was split up amongst the surviving heiresses. The castle was considered to be worthless in 1330 and was 'all in ruin' by Leland's time. Neglect and undergrowth have made their mark and stone robbers have taken all the dressed blocks of limestone that once graced the walls. Nevertheless Dinas Powys is still a substantial structure and one of the most complete late twelfth-century masonry castles in Wales. The current state of neglect and indifference is quite shameful bearing in mind the extent of the remains and the close proximity to an urban centre. In 1981 a local charity acquired the site and undertook clearance work to transform it into a community amenity area (the accompanying photograph was taken at that time). Unfortunately, work was halted when it became clear that the damage caused by the undergrowth would require costly and time-consuming specialist repairs. Public access was later blocked and the site was subsequently sold. The vandalised fences no longer prevent unauthorised visits, but the impenetrable barrier of undergrowth is a sufficient deterrent at the present time.

Some of the substantial remains of the walls of Dinas Powys – when more clear of vegetation than they tend to be

Location: *the castle is situated on a wooded hill just east of Dinas Powys village centre, 8km south-west of Cardiff on the A4055 road to Barry (OS map ref: ST 154 716).*
Access: *no public access at present, although the overgrown ruins can be glimpsed through the trees in Lettons Way off Mill Road.*
References: *RCAHMW (1991).*

Kenfig Castle, *Pyle*

When John Leland travelled along the well-worn Roman road between Bridgend and Neath in the late 1530s he saw 'a village on the east side of Kenfig, and a castle, both in ruins and almost choked and devoured with sands that the Severn Sea there cast up'. These besanded relics are still there today, more fragmentary perhaps and further obscured by the shifting dunes in the intervening 470-odd years since his day. Kenfig was not the only victim of climatic changes in the late Middle Ages, but it was the most notable – a fortified town and castle that had struggled for centuries against devastating Welsh raids, only to fall victim to a creeping enemy that no-one could defeat.

A castle was established here in the early years of the twelfth century by Earl Robert of Gloucester (d.1147) as part of a westward advance from the more securely held Norman territories in the Vale of Glamorgan. Kenfig was in an ideal position to control the main road and to guard the narrow coastal strip against Welsh raiders from the uplands. The first castle is thought to have been a ringwork positioned on the banks of the river Cynffig and would have been surrounded by deep ditches that could be flooded for added defence. The castle was located just upstream of an estuary so that boats could bring supplies even if the overland routes were in hostile control. The buildings and defences of the castle were built from wood, but in the centre of the courtyard stood a fine stone keep. This was a typically gloomy and forbidding donjon of the period with massively thick walls, decorative pilaster buttresses on the outer façade, and containing a dark basement store with at least one upper living chamber. There would have been an external stairway to the first floor, and then another stair within the thick walls to give access to the upper levels and battlements. At a later date a garderobe turret was added to the rear of the tower. The keep was quite possibly part of the primary castle, rather than an addition as was so often the case. The earl built a far larger keep at Bristol, and a near-contemporary tower survives in a better state at Goodrich near Ross-on-Wye.

Earl Robert clearly intended Kenfig to be more than just a military foothold in a conquered territory, since he founded a settlement here as well. A document of *c.*1140 mentions the West Street and a property 'outside the gate of the vill of Kenfig', indicating that a suburb had already sprung into existence by that time. The settlement lay to the south of the castle and was contained within an eight-acre enclosure protected by an earth rampart, wooden stockade and outer moat. However, these defences failed to hold back the Welsh, and because the town was always in the forefront of an attack, it was razed to the ground on at least seven occasions between 1167 and 1316. The castle seems to have fared better (probably because the keep was so solidly built and could hold out against a siege) although the wooden defences needed constant repair. There is a record of 24 ships bringing timber from Chepstow to make good the damage caused by an attack in 1185, and in 1232 the wooden defences are mentioned again. In fact, it is thought that the defences were not upgraded with masonry until after another attack as late as 1295. The ringwork bank was replaced with a stone wall and a simple projecting gatehouse, while an entire side of the keep was rebuilt and the basement vaulted in stone. The leftover earth from the demolished rampart was used to level up the courtyard and bury the base of the keep, thereby misleading many antiquarians into thinking that it had been built on a motte.

The last recorded attack against Kenfig took place in 1321, but it was not angry Welshmen this time, rather a coalition of disaffected noblemen striking out at the greedy Hugh Despenser, lord of Glamorgan and hated favourite of the pliable King Edward II. The rebels ransacked the Despenser castles across south Wales, specifically targeting the gates and doors to render them indefensible. The uprising was ultimately a failure; but although Despenser regained and repaired his castles (an extension to the outer gate may belong to this period) his downfall, along with that of his royal master, was not long delayed. Thereafter Kenfig was left in relative peace and continued to flourish. The town had long since grown beyond the cramped confines of the early defences and there was a suburb in the vicinity of St James's Church some 300 metres south of the castle. The dogged persistence of the townsfolk in the face of adversity was rewarded with the granting of borough status sometime in the fourteenth century, although the oldest surviving charter is dated 1397. Other documents list the privileges enjoyed by the residents, including the right to hold a fair twice a year and to give any woman found guilty of spreading malicious gossip a turn in the ducking stool. The town had its own by-laws to ensure that each resident paved the road before their door, kept the High Street free of dirt, and did not verbally abuse council members nor keep vagabonds and harlots in their homes. Like most medieval towns, Kenfig was divided up into a number of burgage plots, consisting of long narrow strips of land running back from the street with a house or shop at the front. The average number of burgages seems to have been around 144, and the population has been estimated at about 700 inhabitants.

Kenfig was on track to becoming a major urban centre like the other nearby castle-towns of Bridgend, Neath and Swansea; but by the end of the fourteenth century the number of occupied plots had dropped to 106. The Black Death probably contributed to this decline since towns nearest to ports were the worst affected by the plague, but the townsfolk would already have felt the first effects of the encroaching sands. Excavations carried out by the Kenfig Society in the 1990s revealed that the ploughed fields on the edge of the town had been periodically covered by blown sand as early as *c.*1275. By 1316 the *Conyger field* (rabbit warren) had dropped in rental value due to inundation by the sea. Probably there had always been a thin strip of stable dunes along the shore, but a combination of strong winds blowing off the Atlantic and tidal changes caused more sand to be blown further inland. The townsfolk may even have made matters worse by cutting trees and allowing cattle to overgraze the meadows, thereby destroying the vegetation that had kept the dunes in check for so long. A succession of bad storms during the fifteenth century caused widespread damage around the exposed coastline of Swansea Bay. At Kenfig the green meadows were replaced with an undulating waste of sand dunes, the estuary silted up and the river changed course. People drifted away to rebuild their lives on higher ground to the south and east, and in 1471 a new church at Pyle was completed using stones taken from the old. The Elizabethan antiquarian Rice Merrick described Kenfig as 'a borough town sometime of good account but long since decayed by overflowing of the sand, and

A bird's-eye view of the town and castle of Kenfig as it might have looked around 1200

The keep of Kenfig Castle today, semi-buried in sand dunes near the M4 motorway

by some the ancient town sinked and became a great mere'. Merrick was repeating an enduring myth that the town was magically flooded overnight beneath the waters of nearby Kenfig pool. In reality the pool is the silted-up estuary of the old river. This was not quite the end of Kenfig though. In 1572 three plots were still occupied and one tenacious resident was living in a small cottage as late as 1665. Thereafter the sands moved in and whatever remained of the once-thriving town was lost.

For such an important and richly-documented site, the surviving remains of Kenfig are pitiably few; some earthworks and inconspicuous foundations are all that remain of the town, while the castle was little more than a ragged arch on top of a mound until archaeologists from a local history society started digging here in 1924. They cleared away tons of sand to uncover the basement of the keep, part of the curtain wall and entrance passage, and discovered fragments of fine carved stonework that once adorned the tower. Unfortunately nothing has been done to preserve the fabric since that time, and the exposed walls are slowly crumbling away in a wilderness of scrubby dunes. The fate of Kenfig is a salutary lesson in the changes nature can inflict on a seemingly unalterable landscape.

Location: *The castle is located on the Kenfig Burrows Nature Reserve between Port Talbot and Porthcawl (M4 junction 37) approximately 1km north-west of Mawdlam Church (OS map ref: SS 801 827).*

Access: *freely accessible. From Mawdlam Church head across the dunes in a north-westerly direction, keeping the M4 on your right, until you reach some disused railway sidings. The castle is not immediately conspicuous, but lies beside the railway embankment. A shorter walk via the M4 underpass can be followed from the B4283 Pyle to Margam road.*

References: *Brut; RCAHMW (1991). There is a website on this and similar deserted villages at www.abandonedcommunities.co.uk. See also www.kenfigsociety.org.*

Landimôr Castle, *Gower*

The Normans seized the peninsula of Gower from the Welsh around 1106 and, except for a few interruptions in the early thirteenth century, succeeded in creating a thoroughly anglicised lordship (as the many English-sounding place-names testify). For its size Gower is a land rolling in castles; major strongholds like Swansea and Oystermouth protected the eastern approaches, while its hinterland was guarded by the likes of Penmaen, Pennard, Oxwich and Penrice (p.134). The manor of Landimôr on the north coast was valued at a knight's fee and would have had a castle too (one is specifically mentioned in 1353); but it would not have been the ruined building standing on the escarpment above the village and known variously as Landimore or Bovehill Castle. This ruin is clearly a late medieval structure and shows no sign of occupying the site of an older fortification; in fact it does not appear to have been a castle at all. There is a strong tradition that the original Anglo-Norman settlement was located elsewhere and was abandoned due to coastal flooding.

The existing 'castle' is an elongated walled courtyard set on the edge of an escarpment overlooking the Llanrhidian marshes. Various buildings line the inner walls while at the southern end of the rectangular enclosure there was a large cross-wing (undoubtedly the great hall). There was a further courtyard beyond the hall containing another domestic range, which has a set of garderobes discharging down the slope. All the walls are now ragged ruins, but the layout can still be traced except for the north end where a nineteenth-century cottage has obscured the plan. This is where the gateway must have been positioned. As none of the buildings show any obvious signs of fortification then Landimôr might be considered an undefended late medieval manor; but in the field on the western approach, where the land rises gently and an enemy might be expected to strike, there was an additional outer

The ruins of Landimôr 'castle'

The remains of the great hall

courtyard defined by a thick stone wall with small corner towers. This wall is far more ruinous than all the other buildings, and perhaps it was deliberately robbed away, but it indicates that Landimôr was once more strongly protected than it now appears. It should be classed as a fortified manor or stronghouse, rather than a true castle.

There is no documentary evidence to pinpoint the construction date or the builder, but the most likely candidate was Sir Hugh Johnys, a distinguished soldier knighted in the Holy Land in 1441 and a staunch supporter of the duke of Norfolk (the then lord of Swansea and Gower). In 1451 the duke granted the manor to Sir Hugh, and it may be supposed that the castle was built by him as a suitable residence within his newly acquired land. After his death in 1485 the property was acquired by Sir Rhys ap Thomas, a prominent Welshman who had been instrumental in helping Henry Tudor seize the throne from Richard III. Rhys was an enthusiastic collector and restorer of castles, and he certainly undertook building work at nearby Weobley, but it is not certain anything was done to Landimôr. The generally poor state of the remains and antiquarian evidence suggest it had been abandoned as a residence at a fairly early date and left to fall into ruin.

Location: the village and castle lie on the north-west edge of the Gower Peninsula, best reached off M4 junction 47 and then follow the signs to Gower and Penclawdd (B4295). At Llanrhidian head towards Llanmadoc for about 3.5km then turn off to Landimôr; the village is beside the sea, but the castle is up on the hill (OS map ref: SS 465 933).
Access: *on private land and not accessible, but exterior visible from a public footpath.*
References: *RCAHMW (2000).*

Llangynwyd Castle, Maesteg

The village of Llangynwyd lies in the heart of the south Wales coalfield, an area that has endured heavy industrialisation for over 150 years and left a familiar image of narrow winding valleys strewn with terraced housing and grey-black mounds of colliery waste. Yet a visit to Llangynwyd will come as a surprise to anyone expecting to see such an archetypal townscape; there is only a church, a pub and a few scattered farms and houses here, in fact a typical rural settlement such as one might find almost anywhere in the Welsh or English countryside. Even the surrounding basin of farmland is uncharacteristic of the geography that has defined the Glamorgan uplands. Probably it was this factor that led Earl Robert of Gloucester to establish an enclave here after founding nearby Kenfig. The surrounding area was known as *Tir Iarll* (the Earl's Land), and a castle would certainly have been built here to defend against the hostile Welsh neighbours, although the first mention of one occurs as late as 1246. This early castle was a large ringwork set at the end of a steep sided ridge some distance away from the old church of St Cynwyd. The wooden stockade surrounding the courtyard was later replaced with a rough stone wall.

Contemporary documents provide further details of the next appearance of the castle; on 13 July 1257 Llywelyn ap Gruffudd 'advanced upon Llangunith and burnt the castle of the lord earl, killing 24 of the earl's men'. The Welsh also destroyed 80 houses in the lordship. Some repairs must have been carried out, for in 1262 the castle was taken over by Humphrey de Bohun, earl of Hereford, and garrisoned with 28 men and 8 horses during the minority of the rightful owner, Gilbert de Clare. As soon as Gilbert came of age his first priority was to ensure that his castles were up to scratch and capable of withstanding another raid by Llywelyn. Llangynwyd was rebuilt and given a twin-towered gatehouse of the type still standing proud at Gilbert's main stronghold of Caerphilly. The entrance passage lay between two D-shaped flanking towers, and was protected by arrow loops, two wooden gates and two portcullises. The rest of the defences consist of the patched up wall and a small half-round tower jutting out from the north flank. The foundations of several internal buildings can be seen, but even so, accommodation within the courtyard must have been very cramped. Rock cut ditches protected the castle on all sides except the east, where the steep slopes proved adequate, and the approach to the main gate was strengthened by a semi-circular barbican. In the field in front of the gate are the worn-down ramparts of an outer bailey, which some have

The approach to Llangynwyd Castle with the site of the semi-circular barbican visible in the foreground

claimed to be the remains of an earlier Iron Age fort.

Llangynwyd fell to the Welsh during a widespread uprising in 1294-95 when the de Clare properties in south Wales were particularly targeted. It appears no more in the records thereafter and was perhaps so severely damaged that it was given up as a lost cause and not restored. The uplands were left in peace; the parish church was rebuilt on a grander scale, the simple timber homes of the upland farmers were replaced with more durable stone houses, and the forgotten castle crumbled

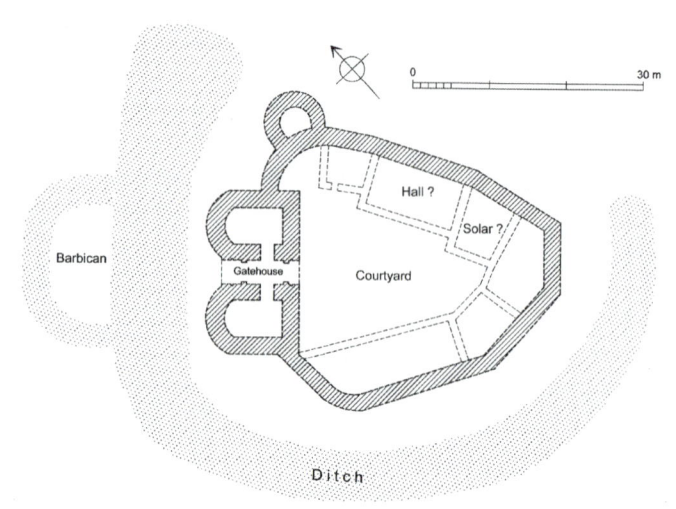

Interpretive plan of the masonry remains of Llangynwyd Castle and how the castle may have looked after rebuilding in the late thirteenth century (below)

into decay, little more than a handy quarry for building materials. The finely dressed blocks of Sutton limestone imported here by Gilbert's workmen from Ogmore-by-Sea now adorn the adjacent farm buildings. Other pieces have been placed in the church for safe keeping. The castle mound had become so neglected and overgrown that its true purpose was not revealed until excavations started in 1906. Since then the site has become overgrown once more and the exposed stonework crumbles at an alarming rate. The rest of the buildings are buried in several metres of debris. Llangynwyd needs to be re-excavated and properly conserved before the few visible features have gone for good.

Llangynwyd would have looked very much like another de Clare castle, that at Neath shown above

Location: *Llangynwyd lies about 8km north-west of Bridgend just off the A4063 to Maesteg (M4 Junction 36). Head towards Maesteg until you reach the modern village of Llangynwyd, then take the signposted turning uphill to 'Llan'. Follow the road around the churchyard on your left, then take the next right turning down a county lane. This dips down into a valley and Castle Farm is on the rise to the left. The castle lies at the end of the ridge beyond the farm buildings (OS map ref: SS 853 887).*
Access: *The castle is on private land and not accessible to the public. Permission to visit the site may be obtained from Castle Farm.*
References: *Brut; RCAHMW (1991).*

Morgraig Castle, *Caerphilly*

For years after this peculiar little fortress was rediscovered at the dawn of the twentieth century, learned opinion considered it to have been a native site; but in recent years academics have challenged that assumption and have suggested an English origin, thus sparking off a fierce controversy that far outweighs the actual remains of the castle and its historical insignificance. There are no records or documents that might shed some light and excavations in 1903-5 only indicated that it was an unfinished thirteenth-century castle. Was Morgraig therefore an oddly planned English outpost guarding against incursions from the bleak hill country, or an ambitious Welsh border stronghold marking the limits of native territory?

Before summarising all the relevant issues it is necessary to put the castle in its geographic and historical context.

Morgraig is situated at the southernmost point of the upland *cantref* of Senghenydd, a long narrow strip of bleak moors and winding valleys extending

A bird's-eye view of Morgraig as it might have looked in the late thirteenth century, had the building scheme been carried through to completion

from the Cefn Onn ridge near Cardiff to the borders of Breconshire beyond Merthyr Tydfil. Anyone stationed on this part of the ridge could keep the whole of the Cardiff plain and Severn estuary under observation, although significantly the view north to the uplands is more restricted. Ever since the earl of Gloucester invaded the old kingdom of Morgannwg at the end of the eleventh century, these uplands had been left in Welsh hands, the native rulers acknowledging the nominal overlordship of their Norman masters at Cardiff. With the arrival of the de Clare family in the thirteenth century things began to change. Richard de Clare would not tolerate this backdoor threat and set about bringing the semi-independent territories under direct English control. By the time the earl died in 1262 only Senghenydd was left in Welsh hands and was held by Gruffudd ap Rhys, an acknowledged vassal of Prince Llywelyn ap Gruffudd.

In 1267 the new earl of Gloucester and Glamorgan, Gilbert 'The Red' (so named from the colour of his hair, or perhaps on account of his fiery temperament) completed his father's work. Senghenydd was invaded and the unfortunate Gruffudd was captured, disappearing into an Irish prison never to be heard of again. The following year Gilbert began to build a monumental state-of-the-art fortress at Caerphilly, a blatant threat to Welsh authority that Llywelyn could not ignore. Hastening south, the prince found himself embroiled in protracted negotiations with the Red Earl before opting for the simple approach and torching the unfinished structure. Although he was defending the rights of his incarcerated vassal, Llywelyn was undoubtedly more concerned about the loss of Welsh territory. His dominions now extended beyond Brecon and Senghenydd offered a strategic foothold within English-dominated Glamorgan. In the meantime the stalemate between Gilbert and Llywelyn continued. After several months of tedious wrangling Gilbert broke the truce, sneaked back into his gutted stronghold and resumed construction. By 1271 Caerphilly was substantially complete and Llywelyn was forced to withdraw from the area.

Overgrown ruins of one of the flanking towers

With these facts in mind, it is clear that Morgraig would not have been started after 1268 (since the building of Caerphilly rendered it obsolete), and from the style and details it is unlikely to have been constructed earlier than the middle of the thirteenth century. Its subsequent history is as obscure as its origin. The derelict shell was probably used in 1316 when Gruffudd's son Llywelyn Bren rose in revolt. The rebels gained control of the ridge and fortified it against frontal attack, but they were defeated when the English army outflanked them. Thereafter the site was abandoned and must have been buried in rubble from an early date, for the abundance of dressed stone does not suggest it was heavily robbed. Only a series of stony earthworks could be seen before the Cardiff Naturalists Society began excavations in 1903, and so no-one really knew what was here. After the dig was completed the intact ground plan of a well-preserved thirteenth-century fortress was laid bare, comprising a compact five-sided enclosure with towers jutting out from each angle. One of the towers is a rectangular keep measuring about 19 metres by 14 metres, while the other four are elongated D-shaped structures.

The castle is considered never to have been finished since no roofing materials have been found and there are virtually no traces of internal buildings. The walls stop at roughly the same height across the site and it seems that only the ground-floor chambers were completed. However, work on the upper levels must have been started, since the excavators discovered fragments of newel steps; and since there are no staircases on the lower levels (access to the first floors was by external wooden stairs), the stone steps could only have been intended for the upper chambers. From what we know of medieval construction practices this would imply that the builders had only been working on the castle for one, or at most two, seasons; then they simply downed tools and stopped work.

And so too did the archaeologists once the site was exposed; no effort was made to preserve the ruins, and the pristine walls standing up to four metres high with intact door and window openings are now badly eroded and overgrown. Most of the dressed stone discovered on site has disappeared, and the walls are still surrounded by the spoil heaps from the century-old excavations. At the time, the archaeologists had little doubts that it was Welsh, for the English simply didn't build castles like Morgraig. The rectangular keep was considered old-fashioned by the mid thirteenth century, though it still enjoyed a certain vogue among the Welsh; examples survive at Criccieth, Dinas Bran, Dolforwyn and Dolwyddelan. The remaining towers are also similar to the Welsh apsidal keeps at Castell y Bere, Carndochan and Ewloe; but their integration with the defensive perimeter is far more characteristic of English castles. For instance, the same basic arrangement is present at Beeston (Cheshire), Bolingbroke (Lincs), Clifford (Hereford), Grosmont, Holt, and Whittington (Shropshire). Yet, significantly, Morgraig is quite unlike any of the other de Clare castles in Glamorgan. Even their nearby hilltop fortresses of Llantrisant and Castell Coch feature run-of-the-mill round towers. Many of the finer details are badly thought out for an English castle – all the walls are roughly built from locally quarried millstone grit, a more intractable material than pennant sandstone obtainable only a short distance further north and, as already noted, access to the upper floors was clumsily arranged. There was no provision for any garderobes in the towers (in fact there seems to be only one latrine in the whole castle!), and there was no gatehouse, just a feeble archway. The absence of rock-cut ditches is another surprising omission for a military base.

All of these oddities could easily be explained as typically idiosyncratic Welsh work, which might have seemed less peculiar had the scheme been carried through to completion. If Morgraig was located in Gwynedd or Powys then no doubts would ever have arisen over its origin. However, when compared to the few known Welsh masonry castles in upland Glamorgan and Gwent (such as Castell Meredydd p.146 and Plas Baglan p.140), Morgraig is a remarkably ambitious structure and one that the petty ruler of an impoverished upland tract would have lacked the resources to build. It is also highly unlikely that de Clare would have allowed such works to proceed unchallenged so close to Cardiff. After reviewing all the evidence the RCAHMW returned a verdict of 'Not Welsh' in their detailed study of the Glamorganshire castles. The smoking gun was the presence of dressed stone from the Sutton quarries at Ogmore, presumably off-limits to the Welsh.

This balanced interpretation should have been the last word on the origin of Morgraig, but instead the official view only served to heat up the arguments. There seems to be a very strong hint of nationalistic pride in wanting this castle to be seen as a native bastion of resistance against the invading English. My own opinion is rather equivocal; I do not believe that Gruffudd ap Rhys had the manpower or money to build such a fortification – but with the backing of Prince Llywelyn then Morgraig *would* have been a feasible undertaking. Llywelyn seems to have been involved in localised castle building among his vassals elsewhere at this time (see Castell Du p.86) and was desperate to keep Senghenydd in native control. The brief lull following the death of Earl Richard in 1262 would be a likely time for Gruffudd to begin building this castle under Llywelyn's *aegis* in order to secure the southern border of his lands; indeed, it may have been this provocative act which sealed his fate and brought the works to an abrupt end once Gilbert came to power. Further archaeological work is unlikely to resolve the mystery and at this point in time an unequivocal answer is far less desirable than a programme of essential conservation work to halt the wretched decline of this major medieval site.

Location: The castle lies north of Cardiff beside the A469 Thornhill road to Caerphilly, in the woods behind and uphill of the Traveller's Rest public house (OS map ref: ST 160 843).
Access: On private land, but a gate provides access from the pub car park and the castle is a short walk up the ridge.
References: TCNS (1905); RCAHMW (2000). For further information on the Morgraig controversy see www.stcenydd.org.uk.

Morlais Castle, *Merthyr Tydfil*

Morlais was one of the largest and strongest castles in Wales and an ambitious symbol of English might set in a remote mountainous area on the edge of the Brecon Beacons. It was built towards the end of the thirteenth century by the most powerful warlord in south Wales, Gilbert de Clare (1243-95), earl of Gloucester and lord of Glamorgan. Gilbert's greatest achievement in the field of military

The Bucks' depiction of Morlais Castle in 1741

architecture was his vast fortress of Caerphilly, one of the most complete examples of a concentric castle in Britain. At Caerphilly we can appreciate the scope of the Red Earl's ambitions and the scale of what was attempted at Morlais; but while Caerphilly has been restored, the moats reflooded, and the ruined towers rebuilt, very little has been done to preserve Morlais. It was in ruins before the end of the medieval period, and when Samuel and Nathaniel Buck sketched Morlais in 1741, they depicted a heap of shattered walls with a few doors and windows visible – a shapeless pile nevertheless impressive in its ruin. During the first half of the nineteenth century antiquarians and amateur archaeologists poked about the remains and pronounced on the history and architecture of the castle (some theories more fanciful than others), but many of the features then in existence have since crumbled away, so that now only a few upstanding fragments rise above the rubble heaps. Yet ruined Morlais still manages to hide one remarkable secret from all but the most assiduous of passers-by.

What caused this powerful castle to fall into such neglect? To answer that question and to explore the origins of the castle, we must continue with the history of the de Clare family outlined in the previous entry. During the power struggle with Llywelyn ap Gruffudd in 1268, Gilbert was forced to assert his authority in Senghenydd by building Caerphilly Castle; but even with Llywelyn's downfall the flames of rebellion flickered for some years to come. In 1287 a short-lived uprising was started by Rhys ap Maredudd of Deheubarth, and Gilbert led a huge army of foot soldiers and woodcutters northwards from Caerphilly to clear the mountain road to Brecon to ensure an effective line of communication. On the way he diverted manpower in order to build a new stronghold at the furthermost point of his dominions, where the river Taff passes through a deep rocky gorge. But this rapid advance provoked the anger of Humphrey de Bohun, earl of Hereford and lord of Brecon, who claimed (incorrectly) that the land was his, and considered a huge castle on his doorstep to be an affront too blatant to ignore.

Royal officials attempted to ease the situation by forbidding Gilbert to continue with the construction work; but as with Caerphilly twenty years previously, the earl deliberately ignored the warnings and carried on building. In 1290 the two earls were summoned to a hearing, but Gilbert refused to turn up. The quarrel suddenly escalated into open violence and de Clare's retainers carried out armed raids into Brecon. By the laws of the March these two warlords could rule virtually unopposed within their own domains, but Edward I was in no mood to deal leniently with over-mighty subjects while the Welsh were still a potential threat. Because Humphrey had asked for the king's help in the matter, Edward could legitimately meddle in Marcher law and he decided to clip the wings of his subordinates. At first de Bohun abided by the king's command to hold back, but after further raids he too was provoked into armed response against de Clare.

Hearings were convened in 1291 to settle the matter but Gilbert again refused to appear until the arrival of the king at Abergavenny made further procrastination unwise. The two lords were found guilty and summoned to appear at Westminster the following January for sentencing. There they were imprisoned, fined and had their estates confiscated for a time. Gilbert was obviously the more culpable and received a heavier fine. To add to his woes, there was another Welsh uprising in 1294 and his estates in south Wales were targeted by Morgan ap Maredudd of Machen, a local ruler he had dispossessed some years before. Both Morlais and Caerphilly were attacked by the rebels, although the great strength of the latter prevented much damage apart from the destruction of the fledgling town. As a final insult, the rebels eventually submitted to the king rather than the earl. Morgan claimed that he had struck out against Gilbert's harsh rule rather than

The hilltop position of the castle perched above a modern quarry. The mound on the skyline is the remains of the great south keep

The hilltop ruins seen from atop the crumbled remains of the south keep

openly rebelling against the Crown, and this clever move saved his neck and enabled Edward to get another dig at the humbled earl. Morgan was taken into the king's favour and, like so many of his countrymen, later served as a soldier in the French wars.

Gilbert however, died a few months later at the age of 53 and his estates were administered by his widow Joan until her death in 1307. His son and heir (another Gilbert) did not enjoy the vast inheritance for long; a typically brave and enthusiastic warrior, the young Gilbert was one of many unfortunate knights slaughtered at Bannockburn in 1314. The male line of this once great family came to an end, and the estates were carved up among the surviving heiresses.

Morlais Castle therefore had a very short life. It was begun about 1288 and disappears from the records after 1295. There is a lingering tradition that it was never finished, but the evidence of the Buck drawing and the vast heaps of rubble strewn about the site reveal that something major once stood here. The limestone rock on which the castle is situated would have provided an abundant supply of building materials without having to source from further afield and, since the greater part of Caerphilly Castle was built in just four years, the likelihood remains that Morlais was substantially complete by the time the Welsh attacked in the autumn of 1294. Possibly it was so thoroughly ransacked that it was abandoned as a lost cause, but a major factor in its subsequent neglect must be the comparative remoteness of the site; a bleak windswept ridge some 380 metres above sea level was hardly conducive to support a settlement that would bring some measure of economic life to the area. The only town to develop hereabouts was Merthyr Tydfil, and that was due to the growth of the iron industry in the late eighteenth century. Morlais was first and foremost a border stronghold and therefore could not have existed beyond its military *raison d'être*.

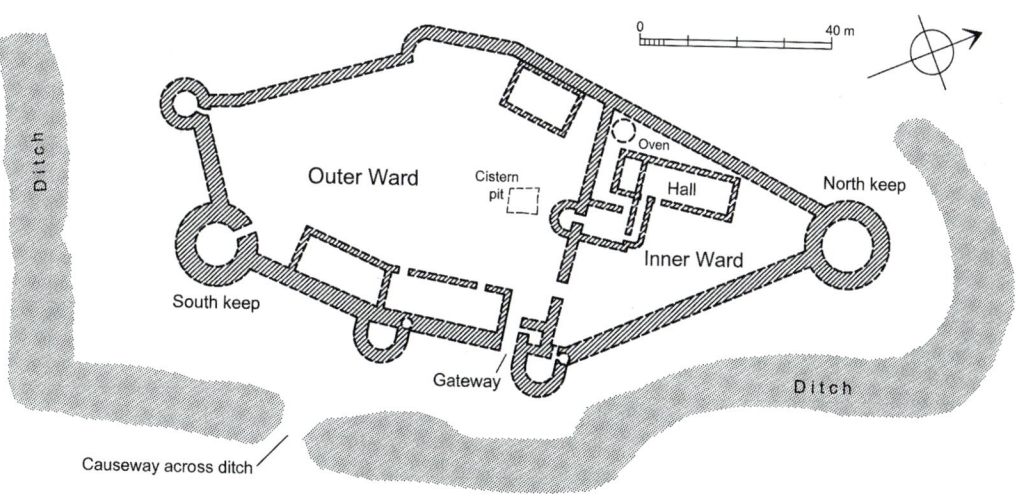

An interpretive plan of the masonry remains with a reconstruction drawing showing how the castle might have looked in 1294. The main defences and rock-cut ditch were massed on the side most vulnerable to attack

The graceful rib-vaulting in the basement of the south keep

Despite the centuries of decay it is easy to recover the basic ground plan of the castle. The heaps of rubble and scree define an impressively large enclosure laid out on the headland like a beached ship. Massive round towers mark the bow and stern, lesser ones guard the vulnerable flanks, and access from the north and east was blocked by sheer-sided ditches cut through the bedrock. Indeed these ditches are a particularly imposing feature of the site and in places reach 15 metres wide and over 5 metres deep. The remaining sides of the castle were protected by steep rocky slopes, but modern quarrying has upgraded these natural defences into precipitous cliffs. On the southern side of the hill there are traces of worn-down rubble ramparts that either formed a lightly defended outer bailey contemporary with the castle, or are the remains of an earlier Iron Age settlement.

The entrance was an arched gate beside one of the flanking towers, a puzzlingly insignificant feature compared to the great gatehouses that were commonly built at this time and feature prominently at Gilbert's other castles. There are footings of a square inner tower, so perhaps the gate was more strongly defended than it now appears; but even so, could it have been this inadequate entrance that enabled the Welsh to overrun the castle? There are signs of another simple gate in the rubble of the southern curtain wall, which must have been reached by a timber bridge spanning the great ditch. A spine of unquarried rock in the ditch is only explicable as a base to support the bridge timbers.

Within the spacious courtyard are the foundations of several rectangular buildings and a deep pit for use as a water cistern. The northern third of the enclosure has been segregated with a cross wall and probably contained the main residential buildings including the hall and kitchen. The northernmost point of the castle is crowned by a massive round tower measuring eleven metres in diameter with four-metre-thick walls. This, presumably, was the hulking ruin shown in the Buck brothers' drawing which came crashing down during a storm at the beginning of the nineteenth century. Only the basement level now remains, but the engraving shows one or two upper floors, possibly with some kind of porch or forebuilding in front. Another similar round tower stood at the opposite end of the courtyard, jutting forward to meet any attacker face-on. A great mound of rubble masks the remains of this second keep, but buried within it is an almost intact basement chamber roofed over with a fine rib-vault springing from a central octagonal pillar. When considering the parlous state of the rest of the castle the survival of this room is truly remarkable, and the quality of the carved stonework reflects what else may have been lost at this shattered site.

Location: *3km north of Merthyr Tydfil off the A465 Heads of the Valleys road at Gurnos. Castle hill lies beyond a golf course beside Pontmorlais road to Vaynor (OS map ref: SO 049 097).*

Access: *on private land, but the castle is on open moorland and can easily be reached by walking up the hillside past the disused quarries. Several gates allow access from the roadside, where there is limited parking.*

References: *RCAHMW (2000).*

Penlle'r Castell, *Ammanford*

Perhaps the oddest thing about this odd site is its location – on the brow of an upland ridge far from any habitation or settlement, a remote outpost seemingly guarding nothing but an expanse of bleak, windswept moorland. Only the mountain road from Morriston to Ammanford crosses the desolation and provides access for modern travellers, but even so, the castle is easy to miss since it lies just out of sight on the crest of the hill. The view to the south is blocked by rising ground, but from west to east the castle oversees a superb panorama across the Amman and Loughor valleys to the ridge of the Black Mountain and beyond. The name says it all – Penlle'r Castell – 'the high place of the castle'; but what is the origin of this strange earthwork, and why was it built in the middle of nowhere?

There are no documents or records that unequivocally provide the answer to this, and the earliest known reference to the site is a brief comment ('Lle'r Castell now in utter ruin') by the Elizabethan antiquarian Rice Merrick around 1585. Since the Welsh word *castell* does not always signify a fortification of medieval date, puzzled antiquarians once thought it was an Iron Age or Roman fort. The superficial resemblance to a motte and bailey led others to the more reasoned conclusion that it was a medieval work, and that its unusual shape and location pointed to a Welsh origin. However, further research has plausibly identified Penlle'r Castell as an English fort established here around the middle of the thirteenth century during a border dispute between William de Braose, lord of Gower,[36] and the Welsh prince Rhys Fychan of Deheubarth. According to one chronicle Rhys attacked and burnt William's 'New Castle in Gower' in the course of the dispute, which might be a reference to this site.

Today Gower is identified as an unspoilt peninsula stretching west from Swansea, but during the medieval period the lordship extended far inland and included a sparsely inhabited upland region abutting the ancient Welsh realm of

How the castle may have looked in the thirteenth century and, opposite, the site today

Deheubarth. Until the middle of the thirteenth century the river Amman formed the northern limits of the lordship, but friction between the Welsh and English kept pushing the boundary back towards Swansea, so that by 1252 King Henry III was forced to intervene and settle the conflict by legal means. The border was eventually fixed at a line just north of the castle (where it acts as the county boundary to this day), but the dispute still rumbled on for years and ownership of this barren waste caused so much strife that the area became known as 'Stryveland'.

This is the historical context in which Penlle'r Castell was built. On the elevated ridge overlooking the contested territory the builders marked out a bullet-shaped area and surrounded it with a deep ditch, using the spoil to create a flattened platform rising only slightly above the level of the moor. The remaining rubble was dumped around the rim of the ditch to form an irregular (and apparently unfinished) counterscarp bank. The upper end of the platform is almost cut through by a separate ditch and forms a sort of *faux* motte, on which can be seen the foundations of a rectangular building or tower. The remainder of the platform is very uneven and bears the outlines of collapsed walls and another tower, all built from drystone and consequently very ruined. Evidently the castle was raised as quickly and cheaply as possible to meet an imminent threat, and the restricted southerly view was considered less important than the northward vista (the direction from which any attack might be expected). The location therefore makes sense if Penlle'r Castell was intended as a short-lived military base to reinforce English authority in this contested corner of the lordship. By the fourteenth century the need for such a remote and inadequate outpost was past and the castle would have been abandoned, perhaps even demolished, to render it unusable by an enemy.

Location: *Penlle'r Castell lies about 5km south-east of Ammanford on the highest point of the ungraded mountain road to Morriston. This road starts from the town centre via Betws, or from the A474 at Pontamman. Keep driving uphill and onto the open moorland, pass under the electricity pylons and, after climbing to the highest part of the hill (limited parking), walk across the moors for about 200m in an easterly direction to the site. The mountain road can also be followed from Morriston Hospital off the M4 at junctions 45 or 46 (OS map ref: SN 665 096).*
Access: *The castle lies on open moorland and is freely accessible.*
References: *RCAHMW (2000).*

Penrice Castle, *Gower*

This is arguably the most substantial 'forgotten' castle in Wales, a spacious ivy-covered enclosure mouldering away in a quiet part of the Gower peninsula. Penrice may not be as large as Morlais or Llangybi, but it still stands up to battlement level and the defensive perimeter is fairly intact. The continued survival of the castle is a testament to the original builders who utilised the rugged local limestone to create a plain, but very durable fortress. Penrice has never been accessible to the public and there are no immediate plans for it to be so, for it lies within the private grounds of

The triple-towered gatehouse as seen from the courtyard

a Georgian mansion. A public footpath crosses the estate, offering an external view of the walls, and it is possible to catch a glimpse from the main road (the ragged ruin next to the gate is an eighteenth-century folly). The lack of recent consolidation work and the absence of proper access are most regrettable, for Penrice is a major historic building on a peninsula already rich in monuments reflecting almost every period of Man's existence in Britain.

The castle originated in the aftermath of the Norman takeover of Gower in 1106, when King Henry I allowed Henry de Beaumont, earl of Warwick, to establish a lordship centred on a new castle and town at Swansea. There is a tradition that de Beaumont himself built the first castle at Penrice, but this evidence is now discredited and it is more likely that it was founded in subsequent years as the peninsula was carved up among his followers. The Penres family probably settled here at an early date and established a castle, church and village in the typical Norman fashion. The massive tree-covered ramparts of the original ringwork can still be seen behind the village today. The seizure of Gower did not pass unchallenged and the main castles were frequently attacked by the Welsh. In 1215 Rhys Gryg of Deheubarth gained supremacy over the region and forcibly evicted all the English settlers from the land. The bloodshed and hardship inflicted upon the civilians by that act has gone unrecorded in the chronicles of the time, but it did not lead to a permanent Welsh victory and Gower was to remain one of the most anglicised parts of the country. By the time the Penres family had regained their lands, the old timber castles were out of date and more efficient masonry defences were needed to repulse attack. Rather than rebuild the existing castle in stone, Robert de Penres decided to relocate to a new site and chose a rocky promontory on the opposite side of the valley.

The first phase of the masonry castle was probably completed by 1250 and comprised an irregular enclosure wall studded with buttresses and linked to a circular keep on the highest part of the site. This tower is one of the castle's many odd features. It is a modestly-sized keep of the type then in vogue throughout the Welsh Marches, containing a basic ground-floor store with one upper room reached by an external stair; but while this chamber has windows and a garderobe, there is no fireplace. If it was intended to be the main apartment here then a portable brazier must have been used for heating. There was also no mural stair to get to the roof, so the only way to reach the battlements would have been by a ladder and trapdoor. Possibly the builders never completed the keep to its intended height. Additional accommodation may have been provided by a long building set against the east curtain wall, but the remains are incomplete and do not display any obvious signs of domestic usage. It is usually considered to have been a barn.

This large but very basic structure served as the home of the Penres family until about 1270 when a series of new works were carried out to improve and strengthen the castle. The threat of Prince Llywelyn's rise to power would have occasioned the need for the elderly Robert to set about upgrading the defences. A new gatehouse was built to replace whatever had stood before and, once again, the Penrice builders opted to create a very odd and unique structure. Most gatehouses

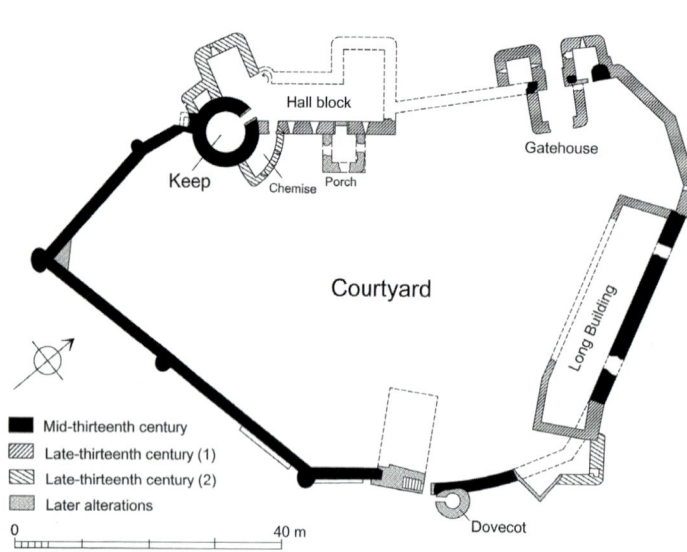

Plan of Penrice Castle and a reconstruction drawing showing how it might have looked in the late-thirteenth century

of the period consist of two elongated towers flanking the entrance passage, but here there are three – two set forward of the gate and a third spanning the passage at the rear. Access into the castle was controlled by a portcullis and wooden doors in the rear tower. The towers are square in plan with rounded external corners, and contain two upper floors of small living rooms with fireplaces, garderobes and windows. There was no glass, just wooden shutters which could be secured with drawbars. The walls in places are still covered with the original smooth plaster. As with the keep, there is no proper stair within the gatehouse and access to the upper floors and roof must have been by way of ladders.

The next improvement to the castle was the building of a hall block adjoining the keep and, since this work involved the demolition of part of the curtain wall, it could only have been carried out after Llywelyn's downfall when the threat of Welsh attack was minimal. Unfortunately this block is now the most ruined part of the castle and the entire north wall has disappeared, so that the internal arrangement is unclear. There was a ground level storeroom with a hall on the floor above, and a square tower jutting into the outer ditch. Shortly afterwards a second tower was added at an awkward angle to the opposite end of the hall, and as this contains fairly comfortable apartments with fireplaces and garderobes on the two upper floors, it very probably functioned as the solar or private chamber of the owners. In order to bring the battlements up to the same level as the rest of the hall block, the keep was then heightened by another storey (although the extra room this created was a useless dark void accessible only by ladder from the chamber beneath). Even more bizarrely, a curving porch or chemise was added to the keep to provide some extra defence for the entrance, but since it only encloses part of the tower, it could hardly have been very effective. All of these additions resulted in a self-contained residential block of haphazard plan, perhaps intended to be defensible even if the rest of the courtyard had been overrun by an enemy.

This phase of building was possibly carried out by William de Penres, who briefly held the castle at the end of the thirteenth century. In 1284, Edward I granted William a seven-year respite from knightly service, perhaps as a concession to the financial burden of castle building. The de Penres family were relatively insignificant landowners and a castle of this size must have been a severe drain on their limited resources. Many of the oddities and imperfections in the design can be accounted for by the lack of funds and the inexperience of local builders. Yet, as previously noted, the strength of the mortar and the durability of the local limestone have at least ensured the survival of Penrice relatively intact, while other more finely constructed castles have not been so lucky.

From 1304 until at least 1341, the castle was the favoured residence of another

Interior view of the round keep

Cutaway view through the gatehouse. The larger inner tower contained guardrooms and the portcullis mechanism, while the two outward-facing towers contained small living rooms on the upper levels

family member named Robert. He was a loyal servant to the Crown and was made keeper of the royal fortress of Haverfordwest as a reward for his services. Yet he was also accused of stealing some of Edward II's treasure left in his care during the closing years of that beleaguered monarch's reign. Although Robert was cleared of the charge in 1331, the recent discovery of a rare jewelled brooch at his nearby manor of Oxwich suggests he was not an entirely innocent bystander in the affair. After his death the castle passed to his brother Richard (d.1356) who built up the family fortunes by marrying the de Camville heiress and acquiring their large coastal fortress of Llansteffan in Carmarthenshire. His son, yet another Robert, was a somewhat disreputable character who apparently neglected the upkeep of his castles, so that by 1367 they were said to be ruinous. Edward III was then at war with France and expected all good knights to do their patriotic duty and ensure their castles were properly fortified in the event of an attack. Robert was ordered on pain of forfeiture to get Penrice and Llansteffan in working order, and the king sent a commissioner to ensure that the necessary works had been carried out. Another impending French attack in 1377 prompted a further royal warning, but in the summer of that year Robert's estates were seized by the Crown when he was convicted of having 'feloniously killed' (i.e. murdered) Joan, daughter of William ap Llywelyn of Llansteffan seven years previously.[37]

A view of the gatehouse from the courtyard

After a hiatus of 14 years his son regained the Penrice estate on payment of a stiff fine, but within a short time he was dead and the castle passed to his cousin John. During the Glyndŵr rebellion Gower was in Welsh control from 1403 until 1408, and the unfortunate John spent some years in captivity. He was released, but died without an heir in 1410 and so the property was conveyed by Isabella de Penres to her husband, Hugh Mansel. The Mansels were another Gower family of no more than local significance until their fortunes rose in the sixteenth century. Sir Rice Mansel (1487-1559) rebuilt Oxwich Castle as a large mansion and acquired the former monastic site at Margam, where another grand house was built. Their Gower estates were leased out to tenants and at Penrice a farmhouse was built below the abandoned castle. The only remaining evidence of the Mansel tenure is a circular stone dovecot adjoining the curtain wall, which is mentioned in a document of 1534. By that time the only real value the castle had was to keep pigeons as a handy source of meat and eggs, and several of the derelict towers were fitted out with stone nesting boxes.

At some point in the next two hundred years the outer front of the hall block and part of the adjacent curtain wall were demolished. This must have been the result of deliberate action rather than natural decay, since the rest of the circuit is so well preserved. The most likely time for this to have happened is during the Civil War, when many reused fortresses were crippled by artillery bombardment, but it is not certain that Penrice ever played a role in that conflict. Perhaps it was rendered indefensible as a precautionary measure. By the time the Buck brothers published their engraving of the ruins in 1741 the castle looked very much as it does today.

A short time after their visit the Mansel estates passed by marriage to the Talbot family of Lacock (Wiltshire). The secluded rural surroundings of Penrice found favour with Thomas Mansel Talbot, who commissioned the architect Anthony Keck to build a neo-classical villa here in 1773. The landscaped gardens and lily ponds were laid out by a student of Capability Brown, and the old castle was pressed into service as an ornamental feature. The walls were repaired and a walkway made around the southern battlements so that the owners could enjoy the vistas over the park to the sparkling expanse of Oxwich Bay. No self-respecting landowner of the time could be without a picturesque gothic ruin and Thomas was fortunate to have a real one in his grounds, but even this wasn't enough; he added the castellated lodge by the gates, which still makes quite an eye-catching feature on the main approach road. Keck's modest villa was greatly extended in Victorian times, but the fickle tastes of the aristocracy changed again and Penrice was abandoned in favour of a vast neo-gothic pile at Margam. In 1910 the estate passed to the Methuen-Campbells, descendants of the last Talbot heiress, who own the house to this day.

Location: *Located within the grounds of Penrice Castle House, Gower. From Swansea city centre follow the signs westward to Gower and Port Eynon via the A4118. About 5km beyond the village of Parkmill there is a sharp left turn to Oxwich bay where a castellated lodge marks the entrance to the estate; carry on along the main road and take the next left to Penrice village, where there is a car park down in the valley (OS map ref: SS 497 886).*
Access: *On private land, but exterior visible from the public footpath that starts from the car park and crosses the estate to the lodge.*
References: *AC (1961); RCAHMW (2000).*

Plas Baglan, *Port Talbot*

There is an enduring tradition that the Norman invaders of Glamorgan allowed the descendants of Iestyn ap Gwrgant to retain possession of part of their ancestral lands and that a castle was built by them at Aberafan from which to rule the truncated territory. There is no doubt that Caradog ap Iestyn and his son Morgan (d.1208) controlled this strip of largely upland territory, but it was through brute force rather than Norman generosity. The Welsh rulers of Afan proved to be a persistent menace to the Anglo-Norman settlers of the Vale; castles, churches and monastic properties were frequently raided, truces periodically made and broken. Aberafan is only mentioned in the *Brut y Tywysogion* in 1153 when it was attacked on Morgan's behalf by the superior forces of Lord Rhys of Deheubarth. The Chronicles boast how the Welsh slew the garrison, burnt the castle and carried away 'immense spoil and wealth beyond telling'. Clearly this was a Norman base designed to guard the coastal route between the fortified enclaves of Neath and Kenfig.

When Gerald of Wales passed through Afan in 1188 his party was accompanied across the hazardous estuary of the river Neath by Morgan 'the leading man of those parts'. What he does not mention is that Morgan had recently built a castle on a crag above the river to control the crossing. The site of this lofty fortress was destroyed a few years ago when the new M4 viaduct was constructed. At least two other castles were built by the Welsh to secure this area; a small motte on the slopes of Mynydd Dinas, and the larger fortification of Plas Baglan opposite the early medieval site of St Baglan's church. This was probably the main stronghold of the belligerent lords of Afan. The site now appears to be nothing more than an overgrown earthwork on a ridge between two small streams, but a few glimpses of masonry suggests that there is a substantial little castle buried here. The remains outline a rectangular hall or keep measuring approximately 17 by 10 metres, with a walled forecourt at the front and an outer ditch. The ditch has been largely filled in, so that the site does not appear as strong as it would once have been. Plas Baglan has been vaguely dated to the twelfth or thirteenth centuries, but only excavation would provide more information about its age and form.

After many years of violence towards their neighbours the Welsh lords of Afan bowed to the inevitable and threw in their lot with the victorious English, even adopting the curious surname 'De Avene'. By the beginning of the fourteenth century Morgan's great-grandson Lleision de Avene had established his seat at Aberafan and probably undertook the rebuilding of that castle in stone (which unfortunately was demolished in the 1890s). The growth of an adjoining borough was encouraged by the grant of a charter to the townsfolk in *c.*1302. The lordship was still owned by Welsh descendants in 1350 when another charter of rights was signed by John de Avene, but sometime before 1373 the last of the family line exchanged the territory with the chief lord of Glamorgan for lands in England. Ownership of Plas Baglan had in the meantime been granted to Lleision's brother Rhys, and it was used by this branch of the family and their descendants for many years as a manor house rather than a fortress. By the fifteenth century Plas Baglan was renowned as a cultural centre for Welsh bards and minstrels and appears to have remained in occupation until the early seventeenth century, when it was abandoned for a new house close by. By the end of the century this one-time stronghold of native independence and cultural aspiration was a decaying shell, known only to the antiquarian Edward Llwyd as *Castell y Wiryones* ('the giantess's castle'). Many stones from the site were later used to build a nearby farmhouse which now, like the castle itself, is just an overgrown ruin.

Location: *on the hillside above Baglan church, Port Talbot (M4 junction 41a). From the A4211 road follow the signposted path at the back of the houses on Smallwood Road, and up over the hill to Cwm Afan. After passing through a gate beside a ruined farm the castle earthworks can be seen at the bottom of the field on the left (OS map ref: SS 736 923).*
Access: *on private farmland, but just visible from a public footpath.*
References: *RCAHMW (1991); Davis (2007).*

Sully Castle, *Barry*

For hundreds of years the ivy-covered walls of Sully Castle had been left to moulder in peace, hardly noted by antiquarians and archaeologists, until housing developers started eying up the potential of the site. Lying between the expanding suburbs of Barry and Cardiff, the coastal village of Sully has become an ideal haven for wealthy commuters. This is not the only rural village in Wales to swell up almost overnight and consume its own green mantle (and it certainly won't be the last), but was the destruction of Sully Castle really necessary to provide upmarket homes? Admittedly, there was not a great deal to see here – no towering walls and battlements, just short, low stretches of crumbling masonry defining a roughly rectangular enclosure beside the parish church – and it might be argued that excavation provided more information than could ever have been gleaned

Sully Castle in the early twelfth century comprised a substantial stone keep and much simpler masonry buildings within the courtyard

from just studying the stonework; but the fact remains that another piece of our heritage has been swept away and replaced by houses that could have been built on any available piece of land.

Excavations were carried out here in Victorian times when G.T. Clark discovered the foundations of a stone keep, but more detailed work was undertaken by archaeologists between 1963 and 1969 in advance of redevelopment. The evidence recovered pointed to a surprisingly complex site that had first been occupied in prehistoric times. Around the beginning of the twelfth century a castle was established on the hilltop next to St John's church, probably by a founder-member of the Sully family, although the name does not appear in records until the end of the century. This first castle was a very large ringwork enclosing a number of crude stone buildings and a substantial rectangular keep. Only the lowest courses of masonry survived, but the remains indicate a substantial building measuring around 20 by 10 metres, with a projecting garderobe turret. The five-metre-thick east wall probably contained the entrance lobby and stairway leading to the upper floors. This keep was positioned on or close to the ringwork bank and probably overlooked the gateway for added security. A very similar layout was adopted at the surviving twelfth-century castles of Bridgend and Coity further west.

*By 1300 the castle had been extended and rebuilt,
with the keep forming a central building within the courtyard*

This Norman stronghold remained in use until the end of the thirteenth century when the whole site was completely rebuilt and extended beyond the limit of the original earthwork defences. A curtain wall was built to enclose a pentagonal courtyard, which had two feeble towers at the north and west corners and a simple gateway. The great keep now occupied a central position within the redesigned castle and was retained as part of a residential complex of buildings. The new works clearly reflected a bias towards domesticity rather than defence, for by 1300 the Welsh threat had receded and the castle's location deep within the Vale of Glamorgan rendered it secure. The archaeologists concluded that the site became uninhabited sometime in the early fourteenth century, probably after the last member of the family, Raymond de Sully, died in 1317. The estate later passed to the lords of Glamorgan and was administered from a new manor site at Middleton nearby. A reference in 1349 to 'a certain messuage [property or holding] enclosed by a stone wall, with a garden ... [and a] stone dovecot' may relate to the castle, suggesting that it was still being utilised, if not occupied at the time. In subsequent years the slow decay was hastened by local people helping themselves to the abundant rubble to construct their houses.

Location: the castle stood behind the church in Sully village, 3km east of Barry on the B4267 to Penarth. The churchyard wall is said to incorporate parts of the castle (OS map ref: ST 152 683).
References: RCAHMW (1991).

Monmouthshire

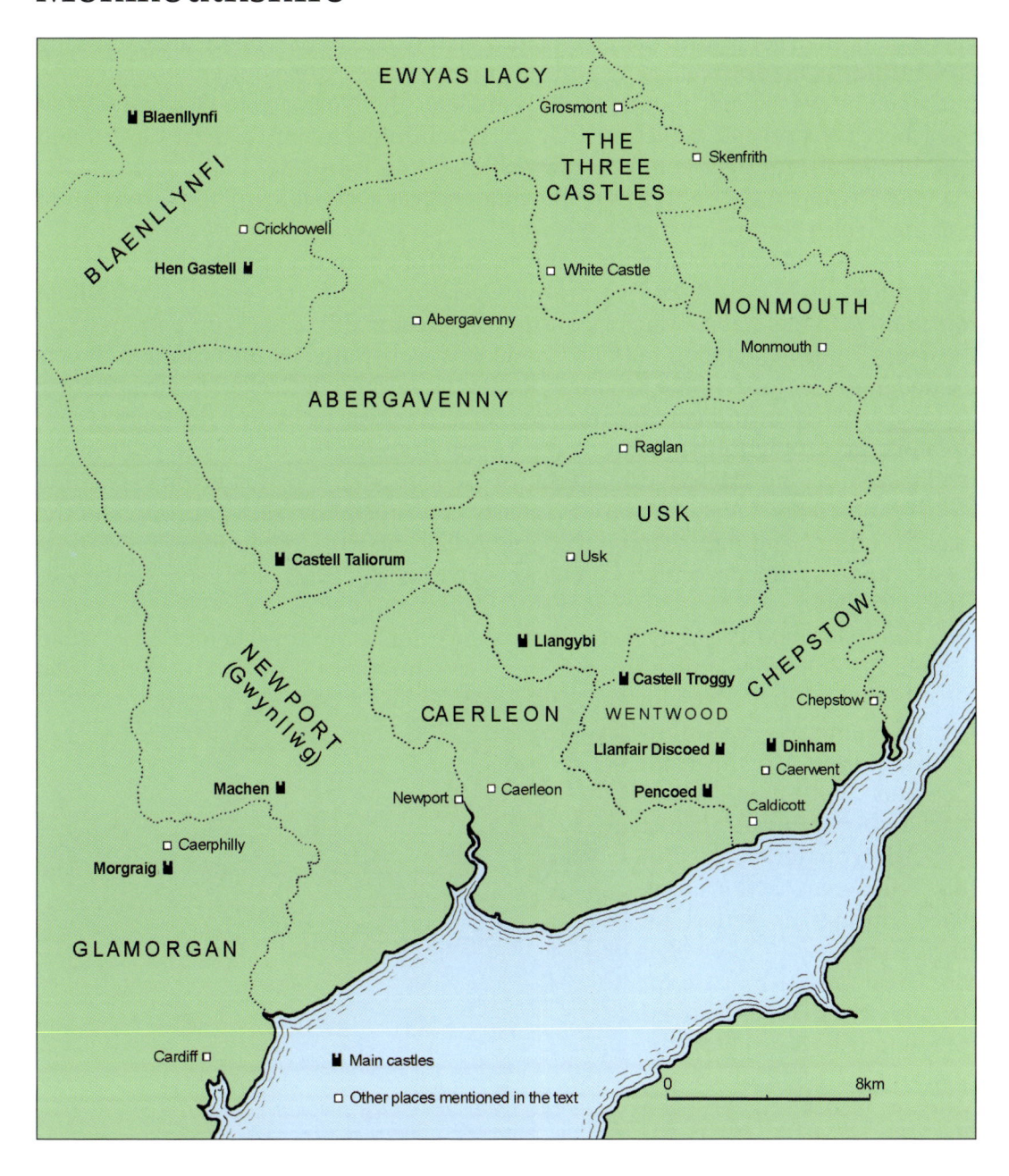

Castell Meredydd (Machen Castle), *Machen*

This fragmentary Welsh castle lay within the *cantref* of Gwynllŵg squeezed in between Glamorganshire to the west and Monmouthshire to the east, and, like many of the early land divisions in this part of south Wales, was made up of a fertile low-lying coastal plain backed by uplands and deep wooded valleys. Norman incursions into this region had taken place soon after William fitz Osbern, earl of Hereford, had established advance bases at Chepstow and Monmouth around 1068. Under the leadership of his son, the Normans penetrated as far west as the river Usk and reached some kind of agreement with the native ruler of the area, Caradog ap Gruffudd. Caradog was using Norman mercenaries against his enemies in 1072, but when he was killed in battle nine years later the Normans took advantage of the power vacuum and moved further west, building a major castle at Cardiff and possibly another at Caerleon. Several smaller castles were later built to control the lowland portion of Gwynllŵg as well, while the less accessible uplands were left in nominal Welsh control.

The descendants of Caradog were successful enough to make their mark on the politics of the region and control of Caerleon Castle was often ceded (albeit reluctantly) to the Welsh. Machen Castle was presumably a back-up base used by the native rulers when their hold on Caerleon was disputed by the Normans. It was located in the foothills of the Rhymney valley, close enough to exert some influence on the coastal plain and yet offering a retreat and escape route into the more secure uplands. According to the historian Sir Joseph Bradney the castle was built in the twelfth century by 'Meredydd Gethin' of Deheubarth, and this erroneous belief still persists today.[38] A strong native dynasty controlled Gwynllŵg throughout the twelfth century and had nothing to do with Deheubarth; the building of Machen Castle can be ascribed to either Hywel ap Iorwerth (d.*c*.1217) or his son Morgan ap Hywel (d.1248).

The castle had certainly been in existence for some time before 1236 when it made its sole appearance in contemporary chronicles. The *Brut y Tywysogion* records that Gilbert Marshal, earl of Pembroke and lord of Usk, ousted Morgan from Caerleon and then seized Machen, fortifying it against a Welsh counterattack. But this belligerent action took place during a period of truce between Llywelyn the Great and King Henry III, and Marshal was forced to relinquish control of the castle to its rightful owner. Morgan must have been pleased to have had his

The two knolls on which the main buildings of Castell Meredydd stood, with remnants of the round keep visible

ancestral stronghold upgraded at someone else's expense. When he died in 1248 Morgan was in possession of Caerleon and had outlived the Marshal dynasty that had caused him so much strife. Lacking a direct heir, the territory passed to his relative Maredudd ap Gruffudd, and then to his son Morgan. The lordships of Usk and Glamorgan were by then under the control of the powerful de Clare family, who made it their business to stamp out any native strongholds in their territories. Gilbert the Red invaded upland Gwynllŵg around 1270 and seized the castle, which then passed into de Clare ownership.[39] However, in 1294-95 there was a general Welsh uprising against the English occupation and the southern insurgents were led by Morgan ap Maredudd, who had his own axe to grind. Gilbert's castles were specifically targeted; Caerphilly was attacked, Llangynwyd and Morlais damaged beyond repair, and perhaps Machen, too, suffered from the rebels' anger. It was listed among the possessions of the last de Clare, who had died in 1314, but such an insignificant little castle could hardly have been of much value and would have been left to decay at an early date.

The few surviving remains represent a very odd and typically unique Welsh castle, set on a natural escarpment above the Rhymney valley. The outcrop has been quarried to form two motte-like mounds of roughly equal height; on the eastern summit there stood a modest round keep, while the other knoll was occupied by either a rectangular building or a small walled bailey. There is much loose stonework scattered about the site and the surviving masonry is now poorly preserved and suffers from erosion and tree root damage. Enough remains to indicate that the keep had an internal diameter of about 3.8 metres with at least one upper residential chamber, since a garderobe drain can be seen discharging over the cliff edge.

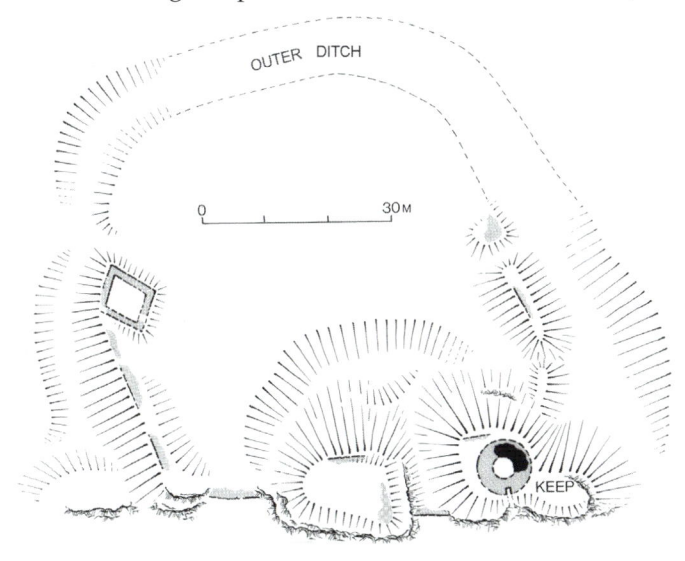

A plan of the castle with a surviving remnant of the round keep (below)

How Castell Meredydd may have appeared after rebuilding work in 1236

The escarpment provided sufficient protection for the southern flank, while the more vulnerable northern approach was defended by a walled bailey with a broad outer ditch. This was the 'great fortification around [the castle]' specifically referred to in the chronicles as having been built by the earl of Pembroke in 1236. The other structures were presumably already in existence. The outer gate may have been on the west side next to what appears to be the base of a square tower (but the walls are very thin and it may be a later building). Most of the courtyard has long been occupied by a cottage garden and any early features seem to have been obliterated; it is now very overgrown. Excavation is needed to establish the full layout and expose the walls hidden by debris; but a far more desirable course of action would be to clear away the trees and consolidate the few remains of this strange Welsh castle.

Location: *8km east of Caerphilly on the A468 road to Newport. Pass through Machen village and after a sharp bend in the road there is a left turning (marked Hanson Quarry). Follow this under the railway bridge, then continue on foot (public right of way) up the hillside to where the castle site will be seen in the trees behind the first house (OS map ref: ST 225 887).*
Access: *On private land and no public access, but visible from the path.*
References: *Brut; BBCS (1979); Bradney (ed.1993); GCH (2008).*

Castell Taliorum, *Llanhilleth*

On a mountaintop overlooking the mining valley of Abertillery stands the redundant church of St Illtyd, a small forlorn edifice with a saddleback tower, accompanied in its isolation by just a few farms and the prominent mound of a Welsh or Norman castle. Far less obvious than either the mound or the church is a hummocky field and a scatter of stones behind the pub, which mark the site of a remarkable archaeological discovery made in 1924. The earthworks had long been known to antiquarians and William Coxe described them *c*.1804 as 'a small tumulus and circular entrenchment … [with] vestiges of subterraneous walls'; but it was not until excavations took place that the site was identified as a medieval castle. The partial foundations of two freestanding towers were uncovered; one was a substantial round keep with an external diameter of about 18 metres, and the base of a central pillar to support the upper floors; a few metres away stood a slightly larger tower of a unique cruciform plan. Very few dressed stones were recovered from the round keep but a large number were found in the other tower, including pieces of a newel stair and round-headed doorway and windows from the vanished upper floors. The only dateable finds were some late Roman coins, fourteenth to fifteenth century potsherds, and various pieces of refuse from the seventeenth century onwards. No sign of an enclosing curtain wall was revealed in the limited excavation trenches. After two seasons the dig was concluded and since that time no further exploratory work has been carried out. The site remains a puzzle.

Was it a Welsh castle? The peculiar shape, arrangement, and location of the towers would suggest so; but the archaeologists believed that the dressed stones were imported from the Forest of Dean, which makes a native origin unlikely. Also, the abundance and quality of the ashlar points to a wealthy aristocrat rather than an impoverished upland princeling. It has been suggested that the towers were built by Gilbert de Clare while

The possible appearance of the unique cruciform tower of which the partial foundations were unearthed in 1924

suppressing the independent territory of Gwynllŵg in the 1260s. The circular keep is very similar to the ones he built at Castell Coch and Morlais, yet the round arches of the cruciform tower are characteristically Norman and imply an origin no later than the beginning of the thirteenth century. Furthermore, Llanhilleth is not in Gwynllŵg at all, but over the border in the lordship of Abergavenny.

Another suggestion is that the castle was a fourteenth-century hunting lodge. Such a late date might explain the cruciform keep, since many oddly-shaped towers appeared in the later Middle Ages, but it would not explain the presence of round arches (unless one assumes that the openings were deliberately styled in an archaic fashion just for decorative effect). And why have two towers standing so close together with no curtain walls? One possibility is that they are not contemporary and relate to separate phases of occupation. From these scraps of evidence and theories a plausible scenario might be offered; around 1200 the lords of Abergavenny established a fortified settlement in this remote area, and built a cruciform keep within an earthwork enclosure beside the pre-existing church of St Illtyd. Later in the thirteenth century work began on the round tower as the first stage of a planned new castle on site, but the lack of ashlar might imply that it was never completed. For years afterwards the rubble would have been plundered for enlarging the church and building all the nearby farmhouses and field walls that criss-cross the uplands. But this is all conjecture – answers to the mystery may only be obtained by a more thorough and meticulous excavation than that carried out in the 1920s.

One puzzle that can be resolved is the claim (repeated in many publications and websites) that Llanhilleth was the 'Castell Hithell' mentioned in the *Brut y Tywysogion* as having been destroyed by Llywelyn the Great in 1233. In fact, no such castle is mentioned in the chronicles. The *Brut* survives as a number of manuscript copies with slight textual variations and all agree that Llywelyn ravaged an impressive number of English strongholds that year. Two versions of the text list *Castell Hychoet* (or *Hithoet*) among Llywelyn's victims, but this lay somewhere near Clun and Oswestry in the middle Marches. In the standard versions of the *Brut* this unknown site is named as Castell Coch – i.e. Powis Castle at Welshpool – which is a more likely setting for the attack than distant Llanhilleth.

Location: *Llanhilleth lies about 2km south of Abertillery town centre on the mountain road from the Ebbw Valley to Abersychan. There is a signposted turning to St Illtyd's church off the main valley road (A467) at Aberbeeg; follow this up through a housing estate and onto the open mountaintop. The motte is prominently sited next to a farm, while the site of Castell Taliorum is in the field behind the Carpenter's Arms (OS map ref: ST 217 019).*

Access: *There is no public access although the earthworks can easily be seen from the roadside.*

References: *Brut; AC (1924-25, 1961).*

Castell Troggy, *Newchurch*

In summer the most that can be seen of this neglected site is an overgrown copse in a field, and even when the undergrowth has died back in winter the view is not much better; a few gaping openings and wall fragments so wreathed in mature trees that it is hard to see where the roots begin and the masonry ends. The centuries of neglect and complete lack of consolidation work has brought this small fortress to a deplorable state. The accompanying photographs were taken in the spring of 2009 and show that the arched window heads cannot remain intact for very much longer. Much of the fabric lies buried in its own rubble. This was a sizeable building in its day, sporting the advanced, luxurious details that typify late medieval castle architecture, yet it was little more than a glorified hunting lodge for the wealthy lords of Chepstow.

The odd place-name (usually abbreviated to Cas Troggy) has never been convincingly explained, but derives from the Troggy brook which breaks out beside the ruin. In medieval records it appears as 'Tarogi' or 'Toroggy'. The sixteenth-century antiquarian William Camden misidentified this site as the castle of Striguil, which is actually the old name for Chepstow, in which lordship it lies. A near-contemporary, Thomas Churchyard, made a marginal note in his rambling poem *The Worthiness of Wales* (1587) in which the main castles of Monmouthshire are mentioned: 'Castle Stroge doth yet remain three mile from Usk, but the Castle is almost clean down'. Leland had seen 'very notable ruins' fifty-odd years earlier. Clearly it had long been ruinous and played no part in history.

A few scant records link the origin of the castle to one of the richest and most

The massive arched entrance to the garderobe pit

powerful men in the thirteenth century, Roger Bigod, fifth earl of Norfolk and Lord Marshal of England. Roger was the last of a dynasty that had held sway in East Anglia since the time of William the Conqueror. The already sizeable Bigod estates were increased with the acquisition of the lordship of Chepstow in 1245. When the fifth earl succeeded to the title in 1270 he took a great interest in his Welsh properties and transformed the old Norman stronghold of Chepstow into a palatial residence worthy of his standing. He practically financed the wholesale reconstruction of nearby Tintern Abbey, thereby leaving to posterity one of the grandest monastic sites in Britain, as well as carrying out building work at his other estates in England. Not surprisingly, these costly schemes helped to plunge the earl into debt, and by the end of the century Roger's financial problems were as bad as his relationship with the king. In a celebrated encounter at parliament in 1297 Roger refused to fight in France on the king's behalf, considering it to be outside his feudal obligations; 'By God earl you shall either go or hang' roared the king, to which Roger replied 'by the same oath O king, I shall neither go nor hang'. He stood his ground against the formidable Edward I, but by 1302 the earl was an elderly widower with no direct heirs and, rather than allow his hated brother to claim the estate on his death, he made everything over to the king in return for an annuity. In his few remaining years Roger embarked on another building spree at the monastic grange of *Plateland*, which he acquired from the monks of Tintern. Expense accounts for the year 1303-4 mention the 'New Castle' and a 'Master William the Mason', and so he had lost no time in starting work on Castell Troggy, despite his dwindling wealth. Two years later Roger died and the inventory of his estates mentions 'a certain tower newly built which is worth nothing after its maintenance per annum'. Royal accounts for 1308-10 record wages paid to a keeper, but the lack of subsequent entries suggest that the castle might have been neglected and abandoned thereafter.

Being located in a marshy hollow of negligible defensive strength and of little strategic value, the castle's real purpose was to provide quality accommodation for the earl and his aristocratic guests whilst hunting in the surrounding forest of Wentwood. This vast expanse of upland heath and oak woodlands stretched between the Usk and the Wye and in ancient times separated the region in two; Gwent Uwchcoed and Gwent Iscoed (literally, 'above' and 'below' the woods). From the sixteenth century onwards gradual enclosure reduced the area to its present extent of about a thousand acres, although it is still the largest ancient woodland remaining in Wales. A number of small castles had been established along the edge of the forest, including Dinham, Llanfair and Pencoed, in order to control the resources of the area. Wentwood was a jealously guarded hunting preserve where the Norman aristocracy could indulge in the time-honoured pastime of decimating the local wildlife.

The rights and laws of the Forest were laid down in statutes that lasted well beyond the medieval period. The fortuitous survival of a survey dating to 1271 lists the owners of neighbouring estates who held certain liberties within the forest;

these included *housbote* (the right to gather wood to repair and maintain a house), *heybote* (collecting underwood to repair fences and hedges) and *pannage* (allowing swine to feed on acorns and beechmast). Those who were caught poaching game and fish, stealing beehives, robbing hawks' nests or cutting down trees without authorisation, faced a swift and severe punishment. A court met twice a year at an ancient copse of trees known as the Forester's Oaks, and any convicted thief would be strung up from the sturdy branches. Tenants had to pay a yearly rent

How Castell Troggy might have looked after the hall block was finished

to the lord and provide an annual meal for the forest ranger in order to retain their rights. A record of 1664 states that on one occasion the ranger demanded from Mr Lawrence of Wilcrick a meal comprising boiled beef, leg of pork, double rib of roast beef, roast goose, a loaf of bread and four gallons of ale. Presumably this feast was for several officers, rather than one gluttonous ranger. The forest is still a nature reserve today, cared for by the Woodland Trust and the Forestry Commission, although most of the great oaks have been replaced by conifers.

Castell Troggy lies on the northern side of the Forest, on a slight plateau (the *Plateland* of the monks?) above a steep drop to the Usk valley. If the undergrowth allows, the outlines of a small rectangular courtyard can be seen in the middle of the field, outlined by a low earth rampart (which may conceal the remains of a buried wall) and a silted-up ditch. The proximity of the Troggy spring makes it likely that the ditch was once flooded, or at least formed a boggy hindrance to any potential attacker. Within the enclosure several terraces and foundations indicate the position of vanished buildings. The more obvious part of the site consists of a tree-covered mass of rubble and upstanding walls, representing a substantial two-storey rectangular hall block capped at either end by large towers.

This layout appears in a number of late thirteenth-century castles and can be better appreciated at more intact sites such as Carew, Castell Coch, Narberth and Shrewsbury. Because of the very ruined nature of the stonework it is now difficult to confirm the outward shape of the towers, but from surviving fragments and antiquarian plans they may have been octagonal (as indicated in the accompanying drawing). If so, they would have contrasted with the more traditional rounded plan of Earl Roger's buildings at Chepstow, and also Gilbert de Clare's contemporary work at Llangybi Castle not far away; but multangular towers had appeared before – most notably at Caernarfon and Denbigh in the 1280s, and Stokesay (Shropshire) around 1290 – and they achieved a certain vogue as the fourteenth century progressed. Quite possibly Earl Roger wanted something a bit more fanciful for his country retreat.

Regardless of their shape, these massive towers would have contained a basement store and at least two upper floors of high quality accommodation, with stairs and ample garderobes in adjoining turrets. The eastern tower retains an enormous vaulted cesspit almost identical to those at Llangybi, with an entrance so large that it would have accommodated a cart for workers to shovel out the effluent. That such a dangerously vulnerable opening should be built at all says much about the attitude to defence at this time and the growing importance of domestic comfort over military needs. The adjoining hall block is now very ruined, and only the outer wall still stands, in which the ragged openings of two large windows and a central fireplace can be seen.

The hall block may not have been intended to stand alone and probably represents the first stage of an ambitious unfinished scheme in which further ranges and towers would have extended to the north.[40] The moat is impressively broad and deep on the southern flank but absent on the remaining sides, and the

Earl Roger Bigod's tower at Chepstow (left) and an octagonal tower at Stokesay (right). The ruinous towers at Castell Troggy could have resembled either of these late-thirteenth century examples

east tower awkwardly juts out far beyond the line of the courtyard. This suggests that the relatively insignificant courtyard buildings are the remains of an older structure (perhaps the monastic manor acquired by the earl in 1302) which would have been swept away as work progressed, had death not intervened and brought the project to an abrupt halt.

Location: *Marked on maps as Cas Troggy, the ruin lies approximately 3km north-west of Llanfair Discoed, which is signposted off the A48 Chepstow to Newport road at Caerwent. Follow the road through Llanfair village and up into Wentwood Forest. After clearing the plantations the road begins to descend towards the Usk valley. At the next junction, take the sharp right turn and the overgrown castle site can be seen in a field on the left (OS map ref: ST 414 953).*

Access: *On private land, but visible from the roadside and from a signposted footpath which crosses the adjoining field.*

References: *Morgan & Wakeman (1863); GCH (2008); for a detailed survey of Castell Troggy and Roger Bigod's works see: R. Turner & A. Johnson* Chepstow Castle, its history and buildings *(Logaston Press 2006).*

Dinham, *Caerwent*

Long before Roger Bigod's masons began work on his abortive fortress, numerous manors on the fringes of Wentwood had already been provided with small castles for defence. A few, like Penhow, Pencoed and Llanfair (p.157) remained in use for many years and underwent considerable extensions and rebuilding; Dinham was an unlucky one, abandoned long before the medieval period passed and now little more than a chaotic jumble of rubble in dense woodland. The site consists of a rather weakly defended escarpment overlooking a little valley winding down from the hilltop village of Shirenewton to the Caerwent plain. Scattered about are several stony earthworks and ruined foundations, the most obvious being a small rectangular building set within a walled enclosure of roughly oval plan. At the west end of the site one wall survives of a square building (or tower) that has otherwise collapsed down the slope. The abundant rubble clearly indicates that *something* once stood here, but the layout is rather confusing and none of the walls appear to be thick enough for defensive purposes.

The few known historical facts about Dinham were collated by Octavius Morgan and Thomas Wakeman in their *Notes on the ecclesiastical remains at Runston, Sudbrook, Dinham and Llanbedr* (1856). As the title suggests, they were more interested in the ruined church that stood at nearby Dinham Farm (since swallowed up by the Caerwent army base) but they did provide a sketch and plan of the castle that differs little to what remains here today. Dinham was one of three *hardwicks* (farmsteads belonging to herdsmen) recorded in the Domesday survey of 1086. In 1128 it is again mentioned in connection with disputes over the ownership of church lands, and in the 1271 Survey of Wentwood, Adam Walens de Dynam is mentioned as holding rights in the forest. Further genealogical information gathered by Morgan and Wakeman does not concern us here, but it is significant that they too were puzzled by the remains. The antiquarians noted that the site was known locally as 'the old church', the implication being that it was not a castle at all but an ecclesiastical building, perhaps a forerunner to a later replacement church that survived for many years as a patched-up barn at Dinham Farm.

The records suggest there was a castle at Dinham in medieval times, but was it an insignificant earthwork here, or at a hitherto unidentified site nearby? Are the remains in the wood those of a church, or a manor house with nominal

Some of the remnant walling at Dinham

defences? An archaeological evaluation of the site has recently been carried out, and the suggestion has been mooted that the remains are those of a demolished medieval castle with a later church built on top.[41] An excavation may hopefully be carried out in the near future which will reveal what lies buried here and solve the mystery of Dinham.

Location: *Dinham is situated in Golden Valley approximately 1.5km south of Shirenewton village, which lies just off the B4235 road from Chepstow to Usk (OS map ref: ST 481 924).*
Access: *The site is on private land and there is no access, although a public footpath passes through the valley below. The path starts from the roadside just before the entrance to the golf course.*
References: *Morgan and Wakeman (1863).*

Llanfair Discoed, Caerwent

A few kilometres west of Dinham is another neglected castle that once guarded the upland hunting preserve of Wentwood, but unlike the scanty remains of the former site, a substantial amount of Llanfair Castle still survives, albeit in a shockingly neglected state. Mature trees sprout from the high walls and the interior is choked with nettles and brambles. A modern house occupies part of the site, and the owner opposes any visits to the castle. No attempt has been made to consolidate the masonry; all that CADW inspectors can do is periodically record the deteriorating condition.

The place-name (commonly anglicised to Llanvair) means 'the church of St Mary below the woods', a reference to the great forest that played such an important role in the history of this area. In the Domesday Book Llanfair appears as *'Lamecare'*, one of the three hardwicks established in the eastern reaches of the great lordship of Chepstow by 1086. The estate was valued at a knight's fee, and so was probably defended by a castle, although the only documentary reference to one occurs much later. The historian Sir Joseph Bradney collated

The south-east tower at Llanfair Discoed

some information relating to Llanfair and provided a detailed genealogy of the twelfth-century owners of the manor, starting with Payne fitz John of Painscastle (d.1137). The fitz Paynes were in possession of Llanfair until the end of the thirteenth century, by which time most of the primary masonry castle must have been constructed. Robert fitz Payne and his 'house' at Llanfair is mentioned in the 1271 Survey of Wentwood.

The family line continued into the fourteenth century, but for some unclear reason by about 1290 the castle had passed into the ownership of Ralph de Monthermer (d.1325), erstwhile earl of Gloucester during the minority of the de Clare heir. Monthermer (who presumably came from Monthermé in the Champagne region of France) rose from obscure origins to a position of some standing by secretly marrying Joan of Acre, daughter of Edward I and widow to the Red Earl, Gilbert de Clare. Surprisingly for the time, this seems to have been a genuine love match rather than just ladder-climbing. When the king found out about his daughter's clandestine marriage to a mere squire, he flew into a rage, confiscated her property and imprisoned Ralph in Bristol Castle. Joan bravely faced up to her father and begged for his release, saying that it was no disgrace when a great earl married a lowly girl, therefore why should a great woman not marry a promising young man? Several noblemen added their pleas for clemency, and the king was swayed to release Ralph, who was thereafter allowed to hold the late earl's titles until Joan died in 1307. The estates then reverted to the young Gilbert de Clare, and Ralph was ennobled with the title of Baron Monthermer. Both lords later fought in the royal army against the Scots, but while Gilbert fell in the mêlée at Bannockburn, Ralph was captured alive. Fortunately for him, he had a more convivial time than most prisoners, being entertained at table by the victorious Robert Bruce and then released without ransom. This chivalrous gesture was supposedly in return for a previous favour. When Bruce was at the English court several years earlier Ralph overheard a plot to arrest the Scottish leader and sent him a gift of coins (bearing the king's head) and a set of spurs. Bruce took the subtle hint and galloped off back to Scotland and safety.

Llanfair Discoed remained with the Monthermers for the duration of their short-lived dynasty. Ralph's sons Edward and Thomas both died in 1340 and the estate passed to Thomas's daughter Margaret, who conveyed it by marriage to John Montacute, earl of Salisbury. It is hardly conceivable that a small castle in the increasingly settled Welsh countryside should thereafter have been considered of much importance to such a powerful family. Ownership passed through various members of the Montacute-Salisbury line until the estates were seized by the Crown in 1541 when the elderly Countess Margaret Pole, having incurred the displeasure of the tyrannical Henry VIII, was savagely executed. Llanfair was granted in succession to a number of local magnates before ending up with the Kemeys of Cefn Mably (whose descendants still own the property to this day). In 1635 Rhys Kemeys built a large house down in the village and so by that date the castle was probably unfit for occupation and little more than a handy quarry for building materials. It is not known if it played any role in the Civil War, but since substantial parts of the walls are missing, there may have been some punitive or preventative slighting. Antiquarian drawings depict a ruinous structure much as it appears today, with only the south curtain wall and corner tower dominating the view. In 1801, William Coxe published his *Historical Tour of Monmouthshire*, noting that the overgrown site was used as a kitchen garden by the occupants of an adjoining cottage. A modern house was built within the outer bailey in the 1970s.

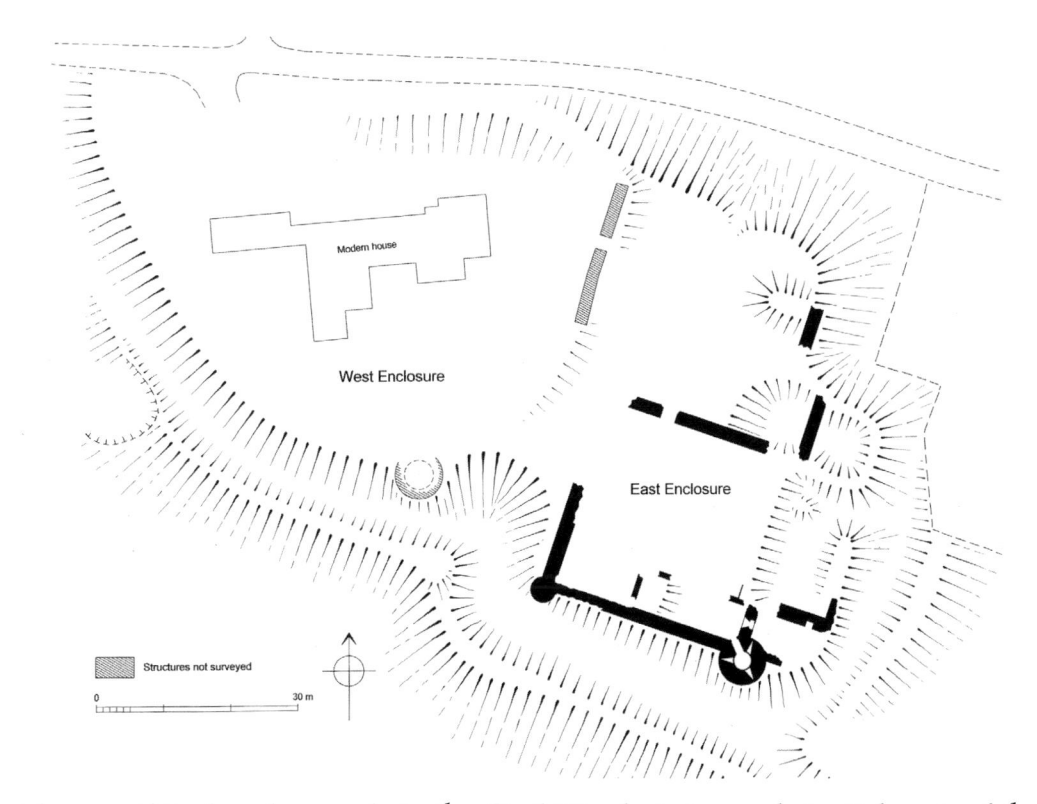

The castle consists of two clearly defined parts: a rectangular masonry stronghold overlooking the church and village, and a large earthwork enclosure guarding the western flank. This western enclosure is presumably the remains of an outer bailey, but its shape and elevation is rather unusual and it is not at all unlikely that it is the remains of the primary castle, a large ringwork built on the highest part of the ridge. There are slight remains of a small round tower on the rampart but the thin ragged walls prompt the suspicion that it is a later structure, perhaps a dovecot. Excavation would be needed to clarify the function of this enclosure, but as it is now occupied by the house and gardens, the archaeological potential is not very promising.

The best preserved section of the castle is the southern front, which is defined by a straight length of curtain wall with a rounded bastion on the west angle and a cylindrical tower on the corresponding east corner. This tower survives up to battlement level (indeed it is amazingly intact considering the state of the remainder) and contains three floors, each under three metres in diameter and provided with plain arrow slits covering practically every approach. There are no fireplaces or garderobes within the tower, so it was intended purely for military needs. A surviving section of the battlements reveals the holes for a projecting timber hourd. The hall adjoined this tower and occupied the first floor above a dark basement. Perhaps the most surprising feature here is the odd arrangement of the garderobes, which were reached by a mural passage from the hall and were housed in a timber lean-to structure jutting out from the castle and supported on stone brackets (this type of feature survives intact at Stokesay Castle in Shropshire). Such an arrangement hardly makes much military sense and would have been a particularly vulnerable target during a siege, and yet it appears to be original and not an alteration of less war-like days.

Stone robbers have been particularly busy at Llanfair, and one of the few dateable pieces of ashlar remaining is a fragment of an arrow slit with a square hole at its base. This detail also appears at Caerleon, Chepstow and Usk castles and is believed to date from the first quarter of the thirteenth century. The round tower bears a marked similarity to the larger Garrison Tower of Usk, which was raised by William Marshal between 1210 and 1220.

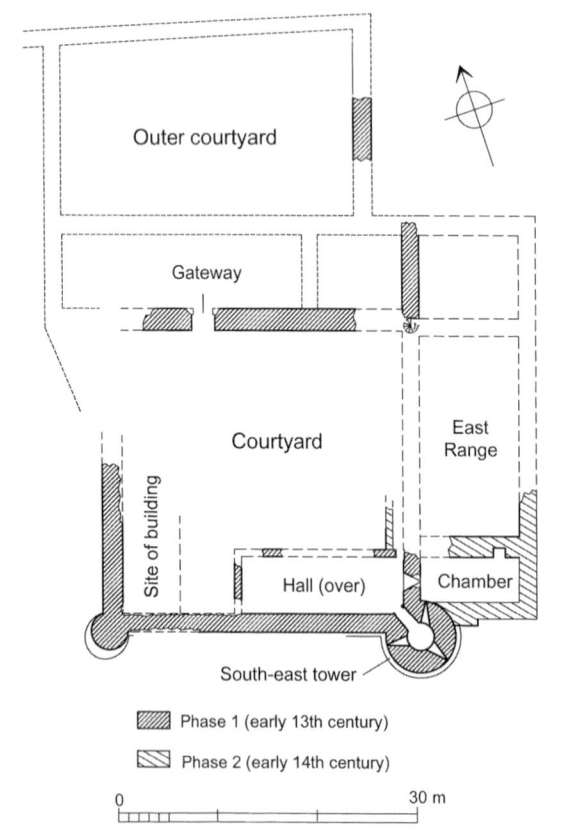

Ground-floor plan of the surviving masonry remains at Llanfair Discoed with a reconstruction drawing of the south front

The spiral stairway in the south-east tower

On this analogy, the likely builder of the stone castle was Roger fitz Payne (d.1239). The simple details and unsophisticated design accord well with an early thirteenth century date, and we might envisage a four-square enclosure with round towers on the corners.

Regrettably the rest of the castle is not as complete or informative as the southern side. There is no sign of a gatehouse, and the complex of rectangular buildings and courtyards only serve to confuse, rather than clarify, the plan. The castle was evidently extended beyond the confines of the early circuit, and a large range was built out into the east ditch to increase the accommodation. Although appearing to be more of a domestic character, these additions have walls thick enough to withstand most siege machines and therefore must have been built when attack was still a possibility. The tenure of the Monthermers would be a likely period for these additional works. Clearly a fuller understanding of the history and evolution of this castle will only be unravelled by geophysical survey and excavation, followed by essential conservation work to preserve the fabric from further decay.

Location: *The village of Llanfair lies about 2.5km north-west of Caerwent and is signposted off the A48 Chepstow to Newport Road. Pass through the village and the castle site will be seen in the trees behind the church (OS map ref: ST 446 924).*
Access: *On private land and no access allowed. Parts of the ruins can be seen from the churchyard and the roadside.*
References: *Morgan & Wakeman (1863); Bradney (1932); Pevsner (2000).*

Llangybi Castle, Usk

The castle built on a hilltop overlooking the Usk valley at Llangybi was one of the largest and grandest medieval fortifications in Wales, yet it is now one of least known. Long hidden by a dense forestry plantation, it comes as a shock to stray from the footpath and see towering walls shrouded in trees and creepers, like a forgotten jungle ruin. Some of the encroaching undergrowth was cut back for small-scale excavations carried out by the Time Team in 2009, but Llangybi is still an overgrown and unconsolidated ruin with no official public access. The decay

The vegetation-covered walls of Llangybi

and subsequent neglect of this castle is due to a combination of factors, but its location within the private grounds of a country house (a situation comparable to Penrice) is the main reason. The house has now gone, but the ruin is still owned by a descendant of the family that has lived here since the sixteenth century. Apart from a few brief antiquarian accounts, the first proper study of the building was carried out by David Cathcart King and Clifford Perks in 1956. Their survey has since been augmented by a re-examination of the structural and documentary evidence by Stephen Priestley and Rick Turner in 2003, and the following account is based on these sources.[42]

The history of the castle begins with the building of a ringwork and bailey some distance away from the old Welsh church of St Cybi. Probably this was a Norman outpost designed to control the lands lying between the main strongholds of Usk and Caerleon, and throughout the medieval period it was known as the manor of Tregrug. Usk was extensively rebuilt by the powerful Marshal dynasty in the early thirteenth century, but there does not seem to have been any interest shown in Tregrug until the lordship passed to another influential castle-building family, the de Clares. Sometime in the 1280s Gilbert de Clare, the 'Red Earl', granted Tregrug to his brother Bevis,[43] who often stayed here prior to his death in 1294. The earl himself died in 1295 and his widow Joan and her new husband, Ralph de Monthermer, controlled the lordship before the young heir, Gilbert, succeeded to his inheritance in 1307.

At some point the ringwork was abandoned in favour of a large new site on the adjacent hilltop, although when that happened is a matter of debate. Building accounts relating to the lordship of Usk fortunately survive and give some clues as to what went on here, but they are not a complete record and do not provide a conclusive answer to the origin of this castle. The accounts mention repairs to a tower and part of the curtain wall in 1301-3, then in 1305-6 a tower was roofed with lead and the hall, kitchen, bakehouse and stables repaired. These works were necessitated by war damage and if, as might be supposed, this was caused by the uprising of Madog ap Llywelyn in 1294-95, then there must have been a masonry castle here in either Bevis's or the Red Earl's time – but was it the old ringwork or the new hilltop site? The ringwork shows no sign of being anything other than an earth and timber fort (although it is not impossible that masonry buildings did exist but have since been robbed away). The new castle may be ambitious in scale, but apart from the unusual buildings on the western façade (which will be described below) the bulk of the structure is typical of the late thirteenth century and might well have been started by either Bevis or the Red Earl. The references to the 1301-06 repairs could therefore be to the 'new' castle.

King and Perks were dismissive of this two-phase theory and believed that the castle was built in one go, but the results of the Time Team investigation indicated that the western façade was a secondary development. Priestley and Turner consider that Gilbert ordered the construction of the castle soon after 1307, but that work was brought to a temporary halt by his unexpectedly early death in 1314 and was then continued by his widow Matilda, who was allowed to hold the lordship in dower right. Building accounts dating to 1315-16 refer to a gate and portcullis, and in 1319-20 a 'little hall' and stable are mentioned. More significantly, work was already underway on a major tower which was roofed with 2,000 tiles the following year.

By that time Matilda had died and the vast inheritance had been split up among Gilbert's three surviving sisters. The lordship of Usk (including the manor of Tregrug) passed to Elizabeth and her husband Roger Damory. One of their first acts was to strengthen Tregrug with timber defence works[44] – evidently they were expecting trouble. At that time the country was nominally ruled by Edward II, but the real power behind the throne was the ruthless and grasping Hugh Despenser, who had acceded to the lordship of Glamorgan through his marriage to another of de Clare's sisters. The sudden acquisition of the Gloucester estates pushed the ambitious Hugh into the limelight and onto a path that ultimately led to disaster. Hugh inveigled himself into the confidence of the weak and pliable king and with his father's help built up a power base in south Wales using whatever unscrupulous means possible. The rapid rise of Despenser created many enemies amongst the aristocracy, including Damory, who was ousted from his own favoured position with the king. Finally in 1321 Damory and a group of Marcher lords rose in rebellion against the new favourite, sacked his castles and forced the king to concede to his banishment. But the setback was only temporary, and in 1322

Despenser turned the tables on his enemies. Royalist opposition was crushed at the battle of Boroughbridge, and Damory was condemned as a traitor, dying of his wounds whilst besieged at Tutbury. Elizabeth and her children were imprisoned, and she was coerced into handing over Usk. With such blatant abuses of power going on, there were few people who shed any tears for Despenser's eventual downfall and savage execution, least of all Elizabeth, who regained her rightful inheritance with the accession of Edward III. Although her favourite residence was Usk, she often stayed at Tregrug with her household during the summer months and commissioned additional residential buildings there in 1341-42. The castle makes fewer subsequent appearances in the records and it is safe to assume that all the main works had been carried out by the time of her death in 1360.

The immense fortification that the de Clares built on Tregrug hill was a fairly simple enclosure of roughly rectangular plan, with at least three rounded flanking towers and two gateways. But in scale and detail it is truly remarkable. The courtyard alone encompasses almost three acres, making it one of the largest single-enclosure medieval castles in Britain. The flanking towers are now poorly preserved; so too is the south gate, which seems to have been a typical twin-towered structure of the type the de Clares had built at Llangynwyd and Caerphilly.

However, this pales into insignificance when compared to the monumental buildings on the western front of the castle. Principal of these is the Great Gatehouse, a hugely ambitious structure with a host of features that make it doubtful it served a purely military purpose. Anyone entering the castle would have approached the gate along a raised ramp and drawbridge crossing the deep outer ditch. The entrance was rather weakly defended by a set of wooden doors and at least one portcullis, although the passage had a raised wooden floor that could have been fitted with trapdoors to hinder any attacker.[45] The two elongated D-shaped towers on either side of the entry passage might be expected to contain basic guardrooms or stores, but instead are residential chambers with stairs,

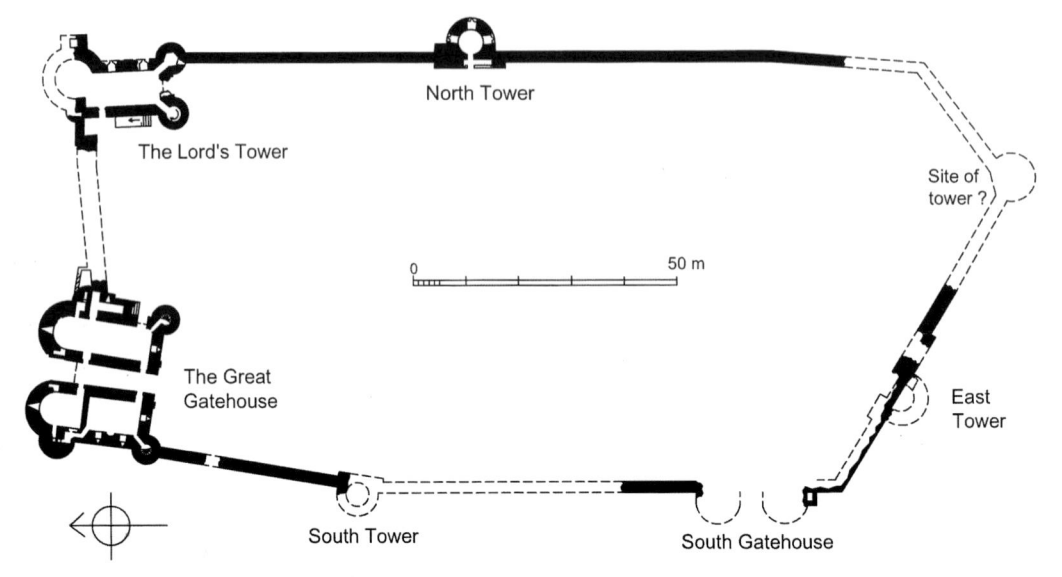

Reconstruction drawing based on the plan of the castle opposite. Many of the features are conjectural, particularly the internal buildings and ornamental gardens

fireplaces and ample garderobes. In fact the quality of the sanitary arrangements here is most surprising considering the norm at medieval castles. There was a large cesspit on the south side of the gatehouse with stone arches to support multiple privies at different levels of the building. One compartment even has a carved stone basin beside the seat for necessary ablutions. The disappearance of the upper floors is most regrettable. Gatehouses of this period usually had a chamber at first floor level above the entrance passage containing the drawbridge and portcullis mechanism. There would be smaller rooms for the garrison, perhaps even a small chapel, with a larger residential apartment on the top floor for the constable and his family; but given the ambitions of the builder, we cannot be sure what the upper levels were like.[46]

From the gatehouse a spacious walkway along the top of the western curtain wall led to another surprising feature here, a keep-like structure now known as the Lord's Tower. The building has an unusual asymmetrical plan, a conjoined round tower and rectangular block bristling with flanking turrets; one turret contains garderobes, another a spiral stair and the third seems to have been an elaborately decorated closet or oriel. In places the finely dressed stonework looks as sharp as it did when it was carved seven centuries ago. The ground floor entrance to the tower was defended with a portcullis to bar access from the courtyard. Few details survive to indicate the layout of the upper level, and it is not certain if there were any further floors above. A third storey would be expected in a 'normal' castle, but Llangybi is anything but, and the scale and quality of the accommodation may have been sufficient for just two levels, as it seems to have been in the Great

Reconstruction drawing of the Lord's Tower, seen from the north. It is possible that the battlements were originally topped with ornamental heads (as at Chepstow, see photo on p.155)

Gatehouse. Perhaps the intended scheme was curtailed, but since the Lord's Tower may be identified with the building roofed over in 1320-21 then it must have been completed.

There is nothing quite like this elsewhere in Wales. During the later Middle Ages, bizarrely-shaped towers appeared in England, probably inspired by examples from the Continent, including Caesar's Tower (at Warwick), Dudley, Nunney, Pontefract and Warkworth. Tower-houses of the Scottish borders display a similar mishmash of round and square plans, although these date from a much later period. If any building inspired the design of the Lord's Tower, it may have been Marten's Tower at Chepstow, which had been built by Roger Bigod around 1290 (see photograph on p.155). This massive three-storeyed residential keep incorporates some of the elements noted at Llangybi, particularly the portcullis-barred entrance and the flanking turrets, yet retains a more traditional D-shaped plan.

There appears to be a very strong decorative element to Llangybi, as if it were really a grand house dressed up like a castle; and perhaps it was, for the de Clares did not need another stronghold midway between the older fortresses of Usk and Caerleon. Priestley and Turner consider that this huge edifice was a showpiece hunting lodge and rural retreat for one of the richest families in medieval England. Significantly, the Great Gatehouse and Lord's Tower are not positioned on the flank most exposed to attack, but overlook the deer park stretching out to the west. There was also a rabbit warren here, and there were fishponds in the valley below. Anyone crossing the park would hardly fail to be impressed by the gleaming whitewashed walls of the elaborate western façade, which would have crowned the summit of the hill like the ornate castles depicted in contemporary illuminated manuscripts. The broad walkway between the tower and gatehouse seems to have functioned as a viewing platform for the residents (it even has its own garderobe).

A strategic military base it may not have been, but it would be wrong to conclude that Llangybi was merely a 'pleasure palace' for the elite. Strong defences were still essential for a nobleman's residence in the barely quiescent Welsh Marches, and the young Gilbert may have embarked on this costly scheme to show off his ambitions and to live up to his father's castle-building reputation. Gilbert rebuilt Llanbleddian Castle near Cowbridge around the same time and, although on a smaller

Detail from a ceiling vault

scale, Llanbleddian shares certain similarities with Llangybi, and might even be considered a dry-run. As for the persistent tradition that Llangybi was left unfinished at Gilbert's untimely death, the existence of all the building accounts spread over a 25-year period should undermine that belief.[47] Further proof is provided by the north curtain wall, which extends for over 120 metres along the steepest part of the hill and still stands up to battlement level. As this wall was finished to full height on the most secure part of the site, it follows that the defensive circuit on the weaker flanks had to have been completed to the equivalent standard. It may be, as mentioned above, that the Great Gatehouse and Lord's Tower were not built to their intended height, but they were almost certainly roofed over and habitable. In any case, Countess Elizabeth would hardly have spent so much time here if the place was a building site!

After Elizabeth's death in 1360 Llangybi was probably neglected, although it was not completely abandoned since modest sums were later paid to caretakers to look after the buildings. The estate passed to her granddaughter and down through the Mortimer line by marriage. Whether the castle was used in the Glyndŵr rebellion is uncertain. Usk was prepared for the worst when the revolt spread south in 1402 and in the following year Newport and Abergavenny were besieged. In 1405 the rebel army suffered a major defeat first at Grosmont and then at Usk, which marked the turning point in the revolt. But there are no records of any involvement of Llangybi. Was it garrisoned as a precaution, or had it decayed in the intervening years to such an extent that it was considered incapable of defence? The absence of the castle from the lists of Mortimer assets in 1398 and 1424 might be taken as evidence of this. The lordship became Crown property in 1461 when the Mortimer heir Edward, earl of March, became King Edward IV during the Wars of the Roses.

John Leland was here in around 1539 but he does not comment on the condition of the castle, only that the name-change from Tregrug to Llangybi was taking hold. In fact the lack of any specific reference to this huge structure prompts the suspicion that he never saw the castle up close. In 1555 Roger Williams of Usk purchased the estate and either refurbished some existing buildings or constructed a new house here before his death in 1585. The evidence for this supposition is provided by the Elizabethan poet Thomas Churchyard, whose long rambling prose poem *The Worthiness of Wales* (1587) contains many references to the local castles; 'Upon a mighty hill Langibby stands, a castle once of state: where well you may the country view at will, and where there is some buildings new of late'. This implies that something notable had happened to the castle in recent years. The historian Sir Joseph Bradney did not believe Williams ever occupied the old castle and thought that his dwelling was on the same site as the later mansion at the foot of the hill to the east. But during the Civil War Sir Trevor Williams garrisoned Llangybi for the king with 60 men, and in 1645 the place was described as 'strong and inhabited and fortified'. The Time Team excavations indicated that both gatehouses were being used at this period to get into the castle, which implies that the line of the curtain walls must still have been intact. The outer ditch appears to have been substantially modified and additional earthworks constructed to serve as artillery bastions.

Oliver Cromwell distrusted Williams immensely (and with good reason, for he had changed sides twice) and ordered his arrest in 1648; 'he is a man (as I am informed) full of craft and subtlety, has a house, Langebie, well stored with arms and very strong ... if you seize his person, disarm his house'. This must surely be a reference to the old castle. Presumably there was a Tudor building standing in the vast courtyard, a similar arrangement to Montgomery, Pencoed and St Fagans. Unfortunately no internal buildings can be seen today, and no convincing trace was revealed by the Time Team excavations. The courtyard has suffered considerable damage from ploughing and tree root growth over the years, and it must be supposed that the foundations of what were probably timber-framed buildings have been thoroughly obliterated.

The parlous state of the castle today suggests that Cromwell's orders to disarm the 'house' were carried out with gusto. The systematic demolition was exacerbated by stone robbing for the construction of a new mansion at the foot of the hill once Williams had been restored to his lands. It is significant that the worse preserved sections of the castle are along the eastern side facing the house, where it would have been easiest to cart the stonework away. All the outlying earthworks have been filled in on this side too. New gardens were laid out to suit the refined sensibilities of the time, and trees were planted in a splendid avenue stretching down to the river 1.6km away. The old castle became a picturesque ruin in the deer park and the Norman ringwork was utilised for quite a different purpose (it is still known as the 'Bowling Green'). But the fate of many country estates befell Llangybi, and after years of declining fortunes and neglect, the derelict house was demolished in 1951. Only the stable block and a few ruined outbuildings remain.

But one other relic of the castle may be preserved in an old building down by the Usk road. Tregrug Barn dates from the seventeenth century and has recently been converted into a private dwelling, but it has reused roof timbers taken from a high-status late medieval building. The arch-braced trusses would have supported a panelled or plastered ceiling curving above a grand chamber measuring at least 18.6m by 5.6m. It is thought that this roof was brought from the castle, and if so, may have formed part of the Tudor buildings dismantled after the chaos of the Civil War.

Location: *Within the grounds of Llangybi Castle estate, 1km north-west of Llangybi village on the road between Usk and Caerleon. A whitewashed lodge marks the beginning of a public footpath along the drive and up through the wooded hillside on which the castle stands (OS map ref: ST 364 974).*
Access: *The overgrown ruin is not accessible although a public footpath passes close by.*
References: *Fox & Raglan (1951); AC (1952, 2003); GCH (2008); Knight & Johnson (2008); Time Team excavation report (2009) will be available on the Wessex Archaeology website.*

Pencoed Castle, *Llanmartin*

Although this is the largest and most impressive of the Wentwood castles, what survives at Pencoed today is the echoing shell of a Tudor mansion dressed up with turrets and battlements to reflect its feudal past. A small portion of the medieval fabric does remain and so it is justifiably included here – as indeed it should be in any book highlighting the plight of neglected buildings. This is one of the major casualties of the changing status of the country house in twentieth-century Wales, a massive building still substantially intact and offering potential for rescue and reuse, but teetering on the edge of a downwards spiral of neglect.

    The documented early history of Pencoed is meagre. It was one of the fortified manors established in the vicinity of the great forest and was associated with a local family, the de la Mores. Richard de la More's 'house at Pencoyde' is mentioned in the 1271 Survey of Wentwood, but only some truncated curtain walls and a small round tower survive of this. The tower occupies the south-west corner of a rectangular enclosure and has three floors with a corbelled parapet. The square-headed dressed stone windows are later insertions. The few details can only broadly hint at a thirteenth- or fourteenth-century date. The formidable-looking gatehouse contains a vaulted ground-floor passageway and two upper chambers with stairs and privies housed in polygonal flanking turrets. This was once thought

The crumbling remains of the Tudor gatehouse with the medieval round tower beyond

to be medieval, but is now considered to be a Tudor addition when mock-military features were all the rage. Similar gatehouses survive at the inhabited mansions of Moynes Court and St Pierre not far away. Probably the original castle was a simple square enclosure with corner towers and an outer moat, a layout reflected by the arrangement of the later buildings that now dominate the site.

The transformation from medieval castle to Tudor mansion began in the 1480s when Thomas Morgan (d.1510) was rewarded by Henry Tudor for his services on the battlefield of Bosworth. Thomas was not the only local magnate to benefit from the accession of a monarch of Welsh descent. He was knighted in 1495 and undertook the rebuilding of Pencoed to reflect his new-found wealth and status. Only part of the north range survives of his work, but probably more of the earlier buildings were absorbed into the ongoing reconstruction by his descendants. The main part of the house is a stunning three-storeyed range containing vast kitchens, a central hall and a tower-like chamber block. The abundance of apartments, fireplaces, stairways, windows and privies clearly reveals what mattered most to the Tudor gentry, and the few remaining medieval military features were retained just for show. Surrounding the house there were extensive gardens, ponds and outbuildings.

John Newman, author of the 'Pevsner' guide to Monmouthshire, ascribes the main hall block to Thomas's grandson (another Thomas) between 1542 and his

A close-up of the medieval corner tower, with part of the Tudor mansion in the background

death in 1565. However, there is a striking similarity between Pencoed and the smaller mansion of Llancaiach Fawr in the hills near Caerphilly. Since Llancaiach is dated to the early part of the century, the hall block could be a generation earlier and be the work of Thomas's son, William Morgan, between 1510 and 1542. John Leland's comment about a 'fair manor place' (c.1539) would therefore refer to the building more or less as it stands today.

Ownership of Pencoed subsequently changed hands with alarming frequency and by the end of the eighteenth century it was little more than a tenanted farm. When the antiquarian William Coxe paid a visit around 1800 it was semi-ruinous, with broken windows and sagging roofs. Another century of neglect passed before a valiant rescue effort was undertaken by David Alfred Thomas, Viscount Rhondda, who acquired the estate and used some of his vast wealth accrued from the coal industry to restore the ailing house. The architect G.H. Kitchen drew up the plans and began work, notably adding huge new windows to the hall and a very fine timber ceiling to the Great Chamber. Far less praiseworthy was his transformation of the roofscape, replacing the original high pitched dormers and tiled gables with flat lead roofs bristling with battlements.

But the rescue came too late. The year was 1914, and within a short space of time a World War transformed the social order of the British Empire forever. The work was halted and Viscount Rhondda died in 1918. His wife resumed the restoration the following year and employed another architect, Eric Francis, to continue with the scheme. Francis also built an attractive Arts and Crafts house beside the great hall, but this second phase of restoration also came to an abrupt end and the estate was eventually sold in 1931. The unfinished buildings were left to moulder, and the interior suffered from being used to house chickens. Further schemes have been mooted to restore Pencoed to life by converting it into a 200-bed luxury hotel with golf-course, or into offices or upmarket flats. The most ambitious project (and the one that raised the most hackles) was for it to be restored as part of a £750 million 'Legend Court' theme park. All the schemes have so far fallen flat, the sheer size of the undertaking being a most daunting challenge for any entrepreneur.

Location: *Pencoed Castle lies just off the A48 Newport to Chepstow road, approximately 5km east of M4 junction 24. Take the turning off the A48 south to Llandevaud, pass through the village and at a sharp bend continue straight on along a narrow lane leading to the castle (OS map ref: ST 406 895).*
Access: *There is no access to the derelict building but the exterior can adequately be viewed from the public footpath crossing the grounds.*
References: *Coxe (1801); Pevsner (2000); Tree & Baker (2008).*

Appendix: Lesser Sites

Aside from the castles looked at in detail in the preceding pages, a number of other neglected sites almost qualified for inclusion, but since they are either undergoing restoration work or are now open to the public, these sites have been demoted to this appendix where, for the sake of completeness, they are briefly described below.

Aberlleiniog, *Anglesey* (SH 616 793)
This motte was built by the earl of Chester in the period 1088-1093 as part of an abortive invasion of Gwynedd. Like many of the early Norman castles it is an impressively large structure with a deep encircling ditch, although the original summit has probably been truncated for the construction of a rectangular stone fort with corner turrets. While appearing to be medieval, the masonry defences were probably added during the Civil War by Thomas Cheadle, constable of Beaumaris. After years of neglect the site was restored by Menter Môn and made fully accessible to the public in 2009. The timber bridge spanning the ditch and the stair climbing the side of the mound give a good impression of the original access arrangements to these wooden castles.

Cardigan, *Ceredigion* (SN 178 459)
This strategic military base was originally founded by Roger of Montgomery in 1093 and shuffled back and forth between the Welsh and English before Edward I established it as the administrative centre of Cardiganshire. Historic highlights include its rebuilding in stone by the Lord Rhys in 1171 (the first recorded Welsh masonry castle) and the setting for Rhys' cultural contest in 1176 (the first recorded Eisteddfod). A considerable amount of money was expended by various owners to repair and improve the defences, but all that can be seen today are the propped-up walls around the river frontage. Besieged and damaged in the Civil War, whatever remained of the castle was incorporated into an elegant Georgian mansion within landscaped grounds. Part of a rounded mural tower still survives, and embedded within the house is a D-shaped structure (possibly a keep or part of the gatehouse). The whole site has been in an appalling state of neglect and decay for many years, but following the death of its eccentric owner the castle was acquired by the County Council and is now in the hands of the Cadwgan Building Preservation Trust. The Trust is currently (August 2010) seeking financial aid to turn the site into a heritage centre and Welsh language school.

Hawarden, *Flintshire* (SJ 319 653)

A substantial motte and bailey castle with massive outer defence works served as a springboard for Norman advance into north Wales in the late eleventh century. In 1265 Llywelyn ap Gruffudd destroyed the castle, and after 1277 work began on bringing the defences up to scratch. In March 1282 Llywelyn's brother Dafydd launched a night attack on the castle, but the builders subsequently completed the masonry defences, their course partly dictated by the pre-existing earthworks. On the summit of the motte was built a two-storey round keep, very much like the one at nearby Flint, and perhaps the work of the same royal designer. The small bailey was enclosed with a curtain wall and later works include a barbican and a square tower jutting out from the east flank. The castle was refortified and garrisoned for the king during the Civil War, and subsequently slighted in 1647. Around 1810 nearby Broadlane Hall was transformed into a gothic mansion and renamed Hawarden Castle, the remains of the old castle then preserved as a landscape feature. The mansion is still privately owned, although the ruins are open to the public on weekends in the summer.

Hay-on-Wye, *Powys* (SO 230 424)

The imposing ruins of Hay Castle dominate the market place of this famous book town, although not a great deal of the medieval fabric remains apart from the patched-up keep and gateway, now very overgrown and in a poor state of repair. The prominent multi-windowed edifice (part ruin, part inhabited) is a private mansion built in around 1660 and gutted by devastating fires in 1939 and 1977. As a major border stronghold Hay suffered many attacks by the Welsh. The first castle here was probably the small motte beside the church, built by one of Bernard de Neufmarché's followers, and subsequently passing to Earl Miles of Hereford. A new and larger ringwork castle was then established on a stronger hilltop site nearby and either Miles or the next owner, William de Braose, added the square keep and walled courtyard. Further works were carried out to strengthen the modest gateway, but since so much of the castle was removed to convert the grounds into a formal garden in the seventeenth century, only excavation will reveal the extent of the defensive perimeter. The castle is in private ownership, although the second-hand bookshop within the mansion is open to the public.

Knucklas, *Powys* (SO 250 746)

Massive earthworks on a steep hill above the village mark the collapsed remains of a stone castle established here in the second quarter of the thirteenth century by Ralph Mortimer to secure his claim to the territory of Maelienydd. In 1262 the castle was captured and destroyed by Llywelyn ap Gruffudd after besieging nearby Cefnllys. It was rebuilt, for the castle was garrisoned in the war of 1282-83, but was probably soon left to decay. The original appearance of Knucklas Castle has become obscured by debris, although a few vestiges of walling suggest it might have been a rectangular enclosure with round towers on the corners, rather like Aberedw. The hill is leased to a community land trust and accessed by footpaths from the village and the B4355 Knighton road.

Llanddew, *Powys (SO 055 308)*

CADW has recently carried out some restoration work on the meagre remains of the Bishop's castle at Llanddew near Brecon. From the roadside a long stretch of curtain wall with an added half-round tower can be seen, along with a recess housing a well and an attractive stone archway beside the village green. However, a coherent plan of the site is hampered by later buildings and the disappearance of most early features. Within the vicarage garden is a large rectangular block containing a first-floor hall with a garderobe turret. Llanddew was a fortified residence of the Bishops of St Davids, and when Gerald of Wales was appointed archdeacon of Brecon between 1175 and 1203 he often stayed here, describing it as 'a tiny dwelling house ... convenient enough for my studies and work'. However, the building standing here today is thought to have been the work of Bishop Henry de Gower in the fourteenth century. By Leland's time it was an 'unseemly ruin'.

Newport, *Pembrokeshire (SN 057 388)*

Stronghold of the Marcher lordship of Cemais in north Pembrokeshire. It was established by William fitz Martin around 1200 to replace the older castle of Nevern (see below), but was destroyed by Llywelyn the Great in 1215 and again by Llywelyn ap Gruffudd in 1257. The defences of the ringwork were later replaced with masonry walls, a twin-towered gatehouse and three flanking towers. Two of the towers are now very fragmentary, but the third is a fairly well preserved D-shaped structure boldly jutting out of the south flank. An adjoining chamber has an intact rib-vaulted undercroft. The castle may have been in decay from the time of the Glyndŵr rebellion, but around 1860 the gatehouse was rebuilt as a mansion and is still occupied today. The site is privately owned but just visible from the road alongside the parish church.

Nevern, *Pembrokeshire (SN 082 402)*

This complex twelfth-century Norman castle is owned by the Nevern Community Council and is freely accessible to the public. It is currently undergoing excavation by a team of archaeologists from Durham University. The remains of timber and stone-based buildings have been detected within the bailey and the foundations of a round tower exposed on the motte summit. Founded by Robert fitz Martin around 1108 the castle is more strongly associated with Lord Rhys who seized Nevern from his son-in-law William fitz Martin in 1191, and was later imprisoned there for a brief time by his rebellious sons. The castle was believed destroyed in 1195 to prevent it being reclaimed by the Fitz Martins, and the site was then abandoned in favour of nearby Newport. The defences comprise a triangular enclosure on the edge of a rocky gorge, with a motte at the forward point, and additional outer ramparts on the more vulnerable northern flank. There is a walled enclosure beyond a deep rock-cut ditch containing the collapsed remains of a stone tower. How much of the masonry is Welsh or English may be clarified by the ongoing excavations.

Ruthin, *Denbighshire* (SJ 121 580)

Along with Flint and Rhuddlan, Edward I began the construction of Ruthin in 1277 but work was interrupted by the outbreak of war in 1282. The king later rewarded Reginald de Grey with the territory and work was resumed at his expense. Edward's master masons probably gave advice on the development of the castle in its early stages. Building continued to the end of the century and resulted in a large and strong fortress of red sandstone surrounded by deep rock-cut ditches. The plan comprised a rectangular outer ward with a pentagonal inner ward, the corners capped by round or D-shaped towers. In 1400 the unscrupulous actions of another de Grey provoked Owain Glyndŵr into rebellion, and Ruthin town was the first target to suffer in the uprising. In the early seventeenth century the estate was sold to the Myddletons of Chirk and the decaying castle was patched up for use in the Civil War. After the inevitable slighting the remains were left to moulder until 1826 when a large part of the site was incorporated into a new mansion, which was extended in 1848-53 with some interiors by William Burges of Castell Coch fame. The surviving medieval remains were extensively altered and utilised as garden features. The mansion is now a hotel and guests can explore the old ruins in the grounds.

Usk, *Monmouthshire* (SO 377 011)

A large and substantial hilltop castle that cries out to be properly excavated and adequately restored. The castle, which overlooks the town of Usk and the site of a Roman fort, may have been founded by the earl of Hereford in the 1070s, but is not mentioned in the chronicles until 1138 when the lordship was in the hands of the de Clares. Later in the century a small square gatehouse-keep was added to the inner bailey (which may have been walled in stone). When William Marshal, earl of Pembroke, married the de Clare heiress, he rebuilt the castle on a grand scale around 1216-20, utilising the latest defensive features of geometrically planned enclosures with boldly projecting round towers. Subsequent works have obscured Marshal's design, but the keep-like Garrison Tower and modest inner gateway reflects his work elsewhere at Chepstow and Pembroke. Usk was subsequently regained by the de Clares and greatly enlarged and improved by Elizabeth (see the entry on Llangybi). It fell into gradual decay after the Glyndŵr rebellion although the outer gate was later converted into a house. The Humphreys family, who have lived here from 1908 onwards, have carried out some excavations and turned the courtyards into formal gardens. The castle is now run by a local charity and there is public access most days of the week.

Select bibliography, references & further reading

Aside from the publications specifically quoted as references at the end of the individual entries (and detailed below), there are a number of excellent books providing general information on castles and medieval Welsh history, including:

Castellarium Anglicanum, an Index and Bibliography of the Castles in England, Wales and the Islands D.J. Cathcart King (New York 1983).
Castle M. Morris (Pan 2004).
Castles in Wales and the Marches, Essays in honour of D.J. Cathcart King (ed.) R. Avent & J. Kenyon (University of Wales Press 1987).
Conquest, Co-existence and Change 1063-1415 R.R. Davies (Clarendon Press / University of Wales Press 1987).
The Decline of the Castle M.W. Thompson (Cambridge University Press 1987).
Destruction in the English Civil War S. Porter (Sutton 1994).
The Medieval Castle in England and Wales, a social and political history N.J.G. Pounds (Cambridge University Press 1990).
The Rise of the Castle M.W. Thompson (Cambridge University Press 1991).
Ruins, their Preservation and Display M.W. Thompson (British Museum Publications 1981)
The Revolt of Owain Glyndŵr R.R. Davies (Oxford University Press 1995).

There are many internet sites dealing with the subject of medieval castles, but the most useful for anyone interested in the Principality is *The Castles of Wales* (www.castleswales.com).

Abbreviations used
AC	*Archaeologia Cambrensis*, journal of the Cambrian Archaeological Association.
Austin	David Austin, *Carew Castle Archaeological Project (1994 interim report)*.
AW	*Archaeology in Wales*, journal of the Council for British Archaeology.
BBCS	*Bulletin of the Board of Celtic Studies*
Bradney	Joseph Bradney *History of Monmouthshire* (Vol 1-4 1904-33; Vol 5 ed. Madeleine Gray 1993).
Brut	*Brut y Tywysogion* (Chronicles of the Princes), Peniarth MS 20 version, trans by Thomas Jones (University of Wales Press 1952)
Brycheiniog	*Brycheiniog*, journal of the Brecknock Society.
CADW	CADW Welsh Historic Monuments guidebooks: *A Nation under siege*, Peter Gaunt (1991) *Dyfed*, Sian Rees (1992) *Glamorgan & Gwent* Elizabeth Whittle (1992) *Clwyd & Powys*, Helen Burnham (1995) *Gwynedd*, Francis Lynch (1995) *Dolwyddelan Castle*, Richard Avent (2004).

Coxe	William Coxe, *An Historical Tour of Monmouthshire* (1801).
Charles	B.G. Charles *Place-names of Pembrokeshire* (National Library of Wales 1992).
Davis	Paul Davis, *A Company of Forts* (Gwasg Gomer 2001); *Castles of the Welsh Princes* (Y Lolfa 2007).
Davies	John Davies, *A History of Wales* (Penguin Press 1990).
DAT	Dyfed Archaeological Trust (sites & monuments record & website).
Fox & Raglan	Cyril Fox & Lord Raglan, *Monmouthshire Houses* (volume 1, 1951).
Gerald	Gerald of Wales, *The journey through Wales & the Description of Wales* trans. Lewis Thorpe (Penguin 1978).
GCH	*Gwent County History* volume 2, ed. Ralph Griffiths (University of Wales Press 2008).
HKW	*History of the King's Works*, ed. H.M. Colvin (HMSO 1963).
Homfrey	Jeston Homfrey, *Castles of the Lordship of Glamorgan* (Cardiff 1828).
Jones (1996)	Francis Jones, *Historic Houses of Pembrokeshire* (Brawdy Books 1996).
Jones (1805)	Theophilus Jones, *History of the County of Brecknock* (1805-09).
Knight & Johnson	Jeremy Knight & Andy Johnson (eds.), *Usk Castle, Priory and Town* (Logaston Press 2008).
Leland	John Leland *Leland's itinerary in Wales 1536-39*, (ed. Lucy Smith London 1906).
Merioneth	Journal of the Merioneth Historical Record Society.
Morgan & Wakeman	Octavius Morgan & Thomas Wakeman, *Notes on Wentwood, Castle Troggy and Llanfair* (Newport 1863); *Notes on the Ecclesiastical Remains at Runston, Sudbrook, Dinham and Llanbedr* (Newport 1856).
Pevsner	The 'Pevsner' guides to the Buildings of Wales: Edward Hubbard, *Clwyd* (Penguin 1986). John Newman, *Monmouthshire* (Penguin 2000). Thomas Lloyd, John Orbach, Robert Scourfield, *Pembrokeshire* (Yale University Press 2004).
Porter	Stephen Porter, *Destruction in the English Civil War* (Sutton Publishing 1994).
Radnor	Transactions of the Radnorshire Society.
Remfry	Paul Remfry, *Castles of Radnorshire* (Logaston Press 1996); *Castles of Breconshire* (Logaston Press 1999).
RCAHMW	Royal Commission on Ancient and Historical Monuments (Wales); *Caernarfonshire* inventory volume 1 (HMSO 1956). *Glamorgan* inventory volume 3 part I (HMSO 1991) part II (HMSO 2000). *Cefnllys Castle*, David Browne & Alastair Pearson.
J.B. Smith	J. Beverley Smith, *Llywelyn ap Gruffudd, Prince of Wales* (University of Wales Press 1998).
Smith	Peter Smith, *Houses of the Welsh Countryside* (HMSO 1988).
TCNS	*Transactions of the Cardiff Naturalists Society.*
Thompson	Michael Thompson, *The Decline of the Castle* (Cambridge University Press 1987).
Tree & Baker	Michael Tree and Mark Baker, *Forgotten Welsh Houses* (Hendre 2008).

References

1. Traditionally Welsh surnames were taken from the father's forename, therefore Gruffudd ap Cynan means simply Gruffudd, son of ('ap') Cynan; this method enabled families to trace their line back many generations.
2. The process had been started by Edward I who created a number of English-style shires out of the Crown lands seized from the Welsh princes.
3. These were Carew, Picton and Stackpole; only Picton now remains, making it one of the oldest continually inhabited buildings in Wales.
4. Castles Studies Group newsletter (1999-2000).
5. Quoted in Richard Avent's essay *'The restoration of castles in Wales; philosophy and practice'* in *Archaeologia Cambrensis* (2007), an overview of the perils and pitfalls of restoration work.
6. The flooding of the moats, now a particularly impressive feature of Caerphilly, did not take place until the 1950s.
7. Cardigan is a classic example; built 'in stone and mortar' by Lord Rhys of Deheubarth in 1171 but later reconstructed by the English so that we now have no idea of what it originally looked like.
8. The form of the tower is uncertain. A twelfth-century keep might be expected to be square, but the conical shape of the knoll would naturally lend itself to one of circular plan, as suggested in the reconstruction drawing.
9. Adapted from R.R. Davies *Conquest, Co-existence and Change* (Clarendon Press / University of Wales Press 1987).
10. Orderic Vitalis (c.1075-1142) *Historia Ecclesiastica*.
11. Historians are uncertain about the exact year this took place; it may even have been 1093.
12. Prehistoric and Roman finds have been made here and some of the rock-cut ditches may be pre-medieval. Also it seems that the builders commenced work at a nearby location, but Lestrange was ordered to start again at the present site.
13. Some accounts suggest it was rectangular, but there is a local tradition of it being semicircular (AC 1927).
14. See *Castles in Wales and the Marches - essays in honour of D J C King* ed. R. Avent & J. Kenyon (University of Wales Press 1987)
15. Discussed briefly further on.
16. David Sweetman's *The Medieval Castles of Ireland* (Boydell Press 1999) is an excellent source of further information on tower-houses and similar fortified buildings.
17. Since there is now only one fireplace in the tower, there must have been more in the lost hall, or perhaps in adjoining buildings that have since disappeared.
18. A reeve was usually elected by the lord on a yearly basis to manage his estate, and the name of David Hychyn appears twice in the records. Records relating to the Slebech estate (incorporating Newhouse) are available online at isys.llgc.org.uk
19. Alternatively (as Rick Turner of CADW suggests), some timbered floors in medieval buildings could have been surfaced with flagstones to create a fireproof surface.
20. This building stands in a field behind the old post office and should not be confused with the well-known 'Old Rectory' tower-house.
21. The square moat is particularly well preserved, but is too small for domestic use and must have surrounded a dovecot or some other ornamental garden feature.
22. Only a handful of stone castles were built in Britain before 1100. Comparison of Castell Dinas to the early masonry of Chepstow (traditionally ascribed to William around 1068) is no longer viable, since recent re-evaluation suggests it belongs to a later generation.
23. King first believed that Blaencamlais (p.ADD) was Llywelyn's castle.
24. Jones claimed that Einion built Penpont castle in the fourteenth century after retiring from a long period of military service in France (History of the County of Brecknock, 1805-09).

25. Antiquarians have suggested that there were flanking towers as well. There are low mounds on each angle of the wall, too small for towers, but possibly the remains of semicircular buttresses.
26. Maud is the vernacular of Matilda, and in medieval times the two names were often interchangeable. The suggestion that it was named after Robert Tibetot, one of Edward I's ministers, is less likely. There may also be some confusion with another formidable Matilda (d.1210), wife of William de Braose II, who rebuilt Painscastle in Elfael in 1195 and which was renamed Maud's Castle in her honour.
27. A claim that Tinboeth was destroyed by Llywelyn in 1260 is now considered unreliable.
28. Some authorities think that Mortimer rebuilt a pre-existing castle here. The *Brut y Tywysogion* merely states that the 'castle of Maelienydd' was fortified, but later references always refer to it as the 'new castle', making it more likely that it was a new foundation.
29. After translations by A.E. Brown, *Transactions of the Radnorshire Society* 1972.
30. Incidentally, it was this family name, along with local legends about a ghostly hound, which inspired Sir Arthur Conan Doyle's most famous literary work.
31. It may be due to their less than perfect draughtsmanship that the keep appears to stand in front of the house, rather than behind it. They probably also exaggerated its height.
32. This is the usual descent, but it is also claimed that Pencelli was owned by the Vaughans of Tretower from the fourteenth century and was left by Maud Vaughan in 1597 to her nephew Sir Richard Herbert (*Brycheiniog* 1978-9).
33. There are said to be medieval arches in the cellar of the house, and yet the chapel is also supposed to have been in the attic! Unfortunately, I was not allowed to carry out a survey of the house so cannot confirm the veracity of these claims.
34. This fabricated history was originated by Sir Edward Stradling (d.1609) of St Donats, who was desirous to push his family ancestry back to Norman times.
35. It was long assumed that the tower was the original building here, to which all the other structures were appended in less war-like times; but the RCAHMW survey revealed that it was a secondary addition to a range of domestic buildings.
36. This is not the same William de Braose as the one mentioned in previous entries on Breconshire castles. The name was very popular and this William belonged to a minor branch of the family who had settled in Swansea and Gower.
37. Unfortunately I have not been able to find out any further details of this intriguing episode, which is mentioned in John Lloyd's *History of Carmarthenshire* (1935).
38. It is repeated in certain castle websites and even in the 'Pevsner' guide to Monmouthshire (Penguin 2000).
39. There is some uncertainty whether it was Maredudd or his son Morgan who was dispossessed by Gilbert.
40. Rick Turner of CADW disagrees with my hypothesis and considers that the hall block was a freestanding completed structure.
41. Personal information from Dr Neil Phillips of A.P.A.C. Ltd (a report on the preliminary survey will be published in *Archaeology in Wales* in due course).
42. Both accounts can be found in *Archaeologia Cambrensis* 1956 and 2003.
43. His name also appears in history as the rather unfortunate variant Bogo.
44. Accounts mention hourds and targes – literally 'shields', perhaps a type of shutter or flap attached to the battlements to provide extra cover for the defenders.
45. The lower walls of the passage have now been recognised as part of an older and smaller entrance that stood here before the gatehouse was built.
46. Rick Turner has pointed out that the number of garderobe shutes suggests there was only one upper floor in the gatehouse (per comm.).
47. A recent volume of the *Gwent County History* (2008) contains the statement that the great castle was 'left unfinished and empty, a monument to the over-ambitiousness of the Clare family'.

Index

Numbers in bold refer to the main entry for the castle; in italics to illustrations

Abbey Cwmhir 31, 72
Aber Iâ, Castell **52-53**, 54
Aberafan Castle 37, 140
Aberconwy, Treaty of 21
Aberdyfi 9
Aberedw Castles 38, **71-74**, *73*, 174
Abergavenny Castle 79
Aberlleniog Castle, Anglesey 7, 173
Aberthaw 107
Abertillery 149
Aberyscir, Brecon **74-76**
    Court 75-76
Aberystwyth Castle 20, 24, 32
Afan 22, 140-142; *see also* de Avene
Ancient Monuments Protection Act 35, 36
Angharad 93
Angle 69
    Old Rectory 60, *62*, 63
Anglesey 21
ap Thomas, Sir Rhys 118
archaeological work 35, 37, 38-39, 42, 53, 116, 124, 143, 149, 157, 161-162, 175
Arthurian myths 54
Ashby de la Zouch Castle 25
Avent, Richard 35

Bach, Ifor 101
Bangor Cathedral 71
Barlows of Slebech 70
    Roger 30, 70
    William 70
Barnwell, Edward Lowry 65
Bankes, Lady Mary 32
bastle 26
Battle Abbey Chronicle 87
Bayeux tapestry 7
Beauchamp earls of Warwick 73, 96
Beaufort, duke of 33, 36
Beaumaris Castle 20, 32
Beeston Castle, Cheshire *17*, 18, *19*, 124
Bigod, Roger 152, 154
'black-and-white' houses 60
Blaenllynfi Castle **78-80**, *78*, *79*, 99
Blaencamlais Castle **76-77**, *76*, *77*
Blaenllynfi Castle 38, 84
Bodiam Castle, Sussex 24-25
Bolingbroke Castle, Lincolnshire 56, 124
Bonville's Court, near Saundersfoot 65, *65*
Boulston 62
Bovehill Castle, *see* Landimôr
Bradney, Sir Joseph 146, 157-158, 168
Brecon Castle 16, 84, 99
Breconshire 99
Bridgend Castle 13, *13*, 143
Bristol 113
Bronllys Castle 16, *17*

Bruce, Robert 158
Brut y Tywysogion 14, 44, 45, 46, 90, 99, 141, 146, 150
Brycheiniog 8, 74, 75
Buck, Samuel and Nathaniel 33-34, 58, 63, 80, 97-98, 126, 140
Builth 9
    Castle 77
Burges, William 36, 176
Bute, third marquis of 36
Butler, Lawrence 57
Bwlchyddinas 82

CADW 35, 36, 42, 110
Cadoxton 107
Caerlaverock, Scotland 56
Caerleon Castle 99, 146, 160
Caernarfon Castle 32, 52, 154
Caerphilly Castle 19, *19*, 20, 32, 36, 119, 123, 126, 128, 147, 164
Caerwent Castle 8, 82
Caldicot Castle 16, 36
Cambrian Archaeological Association 35, 36
Camden, William 96, 151
Candleston Castle, Glamorgan 37, 65, **108-110**, *108*, *109*
cantref, definition 6
Caradog ap Gruffudd 146
Cardiff Castle 6, 8, 13, *13*, 29, 36, 82, 101, 102, 146
Cardiff, Shire Hall 30
Cardigan Castle 9, 16, 30, 37, 173
Carew Castle 29, 154
Carn Fadryn **53**
Carreg Cennen 24, 36
Carswell, near Tenby 60-61, 62
castell, meaning 132
Castell Carndochan 38, **41-43**, *41*, 124
Castell Coch, Cardiff 36, 102
Castell Coch, Newhouse 67
Castell Coch, Ystradfellte (Mellte Castle) 29, 77, **81-82**, *81*, 150, 154
Castell Dinas, Talgarth 13, 38, **82-86**, *83*, *84*, *85*, 99
Castell Du, Sennybridge **86-87**, *87*, 125
Castell Meredydd 16, 38, **146-148**, *146*, *147*, *148*
Castell Prysor **43-44**, *43*, 53
Castell Taliorum **149-150**, *149*
Castell Tinboeth 38, **88-90**, *88*, *89*
Castell Troggy 38, **151-155**, *151*, *153*, *155*
castles, 'concentric' 19
    cost 10, 23, 27, 73, 85
    damage 37, 38, 50, 110, 112
    decay 27-28, 57, 62, 74, 80, 121
    defences 19, 20, 23, 49, 64, 113, 133, 148, 160, 164, 175
    definition 2-3
    destruction 37, 142, 175
    development
        early 6-8, 45

Norman 6-8
    thirteenth century 15-20
    later Middle Ages 23-26
    fourteenth/fifteenth centuries 24-26
    post-Reformation 27-30
domesticity 24-25, 56-57, 70, 109, 144
features
    brattices 12
    brick 25
    curtain walls 15, 48, 109
    defensive 20, 49
        mock-military features 171
        'murder-hole' slots 20
    donjon 11, 16, 25, 48
    dovecot 139, 144
    drawbridge 11
    earthworks 8
    fighting galleries 12
    garderobes 11-12, 20, 117, 147, *151*, 160, 165, 167
    gatehouse 18, *18, 19*, 20, 47, *134,* 135-136, *138*, 164-165, 170-171, *170*
    great hall 7, 93, 117, 154
    guardroom 18, *18*
    heating 11, 47
    hourd *12*, 160
    interior decor 11
    keep 12, *17, 18*, 49, 135
        apsidal 124
        cylindrical 17
        D-shape 17
        miniature 26
        rectangular 17, 123, 124
        round 16, 30, 77, 147 *147*
    loop-holes 15
    masonry 9-13, 78
        construction 10
    medieval hall 69, 70
    motte and bailey 6-7, 43, 53
    pentagonal layout 56, 123
    portcullis 11
        position *18*
    putlog holes 12
    residential chambers 11
    rib-vaulting *130*
    ringwork 8, 102, 159
    sanitary arrangements 11-12
    shell-keep 13, *13*
    stairs 12, 68, *161*
    stockades 13
    strongpoint 6, 16
    tower 18, 49, 57, 64, 85, 154-155, *155, 171*
        D-shape *87*, 89, 123
        multangular 51, 52, 154
        round 15, 76, 170, *170*
        twin-towered structure 164
    windows 11, 68, 136, 170
forgotten 38-39
functions 3
'hermit crab' 82
illustrations 33-34, 36, 55, 65

livestock within 85-86
preservation 37, 60
restoration work 36, 37, 38, 172, 173
role 4, 23, 25-26
shoddy workmanship 78
'show castles' 25-26, 55, 167
slighting 32-33, 48, 58, 140, 159, 174, 176
stone-robbing 53, 76, 95, 112, 121, 144
surveys 28-30, 33, 57, 80, 85, 162
usefulness in war 23-24, 27
castle guard 4
Castlemartin peninsula 62
Cathcart King, David 2, 4, 77, 87, 162
Cefn Mably 158
Cefnllys Castle 26, 38, **90-93**, *91, 92*
Cemais 175
Ceredigion 9
Charles I 30-31
Cheadle, Thomas 173
Chepstow 8, 151
    Castle 12, 16, 18, *19, 155*, 160, 167
Chester, earls of 5, 173
Chilham Castle, Kent 13
Chirk Castle 29, 33, 55
church buildings, decline 28
Churchyard, Thomas 151, 168
Cilmery 72
Civil War 30, 31-32, 57-58, 140, 168-169, 173, 174, 176
Clare, House of 9
Clark, G.T. 101, 106, 143
Clifford Castle, Herefordshire 124
coastal erosion 108, 114, 116
Cobb, Joseph 36
Coity Castle 13, 29, 143
commote, definition 6
Conisbrough Castle, Yorkshire 13
Continent, the 27
Conwy Castle 20, 24, 49
Corbet, William 5
Corfe Castle, Dorset 32, 52
Cosmeston 107
Coxe, William 149, 159, 172
Cradock, Sir Mathew 109
Cresswell Castle, Pembrokeshire 29-30
Criccieth Castle 19, 42, 124
Cromwell, Oliver 169
    Thomas 28
Cwm Aran Castle 88

Dafydd ap Gruffudd (d.1283) 21, 174
Dafydd ap Llywelyn 20, 46
Damory, Elizabeth 163, 164
    Roger 163, 164
Davies, John 21
de Avene family 142
    John 142
    Lleision 142
de Baskerville, Ralph 98
de Beaumont, Henry, earl of Warwick 9, 135
de Bohun, Humphrey 77, 91, 119, 126

de Braose family 78-80, 99
   Giles 79
   Matilda 89, 95, 99
   Philip 9, 75
   Reginald 79-80, 98
   William I 78-79
   William II 79, 84
   William III 79, 95, 174
   William IV 81-82
de Burgh, Hubert 16, 95
de Camville family 139
de Cantilupe family 108
   Nicholas 108
   Robert 108
de Clare family 121, 123, 126-127, 147, 163, 167, 176
   Bevis 162
   Elizabeth 168, 176
   Gilbert 'the Red', earl of Gloucester and Glamorgan 19, 22, 77, 119, 123, 125, 127, 128, 147, 149, 154, 158, 162, 163, 167
   Gilbert II 128, 162
   Joan 128, 162
   Matilda 163
   Richard 19, 105, 123
   Walter 75
de Grey, Reginald 55, 176
de Lacy, Henry 55
de la More family 170
   Richard 170
de Montfort, Eleanor 21
   Simon 20, 89
de Monthermer family 158
   Edward 158
   Margaret 158
   Ralph 158, 162
   Thomas 158
de Mortimer, Ralph 75
de Neufmarché, Bernard 75, 78, 84, 98, 174
   Sybil 78
de Penres family 135, 137, 139
   Isabella 139
   John 139
   Richard 139
   Robert 23, 135
   Robert II 139
   Robert III 139
   William 137
de Somery, Roger 110
de Sully family 143
   Raymond 144
de Tosny family 71, 96
   Ralph 73, 96
de Umfraville, Gilbert 102
de Warenne, John, earl of Surrey 55
Deganwy Castle **44-49**, *47*, 50
   town 48
Deheubarth 6, 8
Denbigh Castle 33, 52, 55, 154
Despenser, Hugh 106, 114, 163, 164
Deudraeth Castle, *see* Aber Iâ

Dinas Brân, Llangollen 55, 124
Dinas Emrys **54**
Dinas Powys 38, **110-112**, *111, 112*
Dinefwr Castle 9, 16, 37
Dineley, Thomas 33
Dinham Castle 39, **156-157**, *156*
Dolbadarn Castle 16, 42
Dolforwyn Castle 37, 42, 124
Dolwyddelan Castle 12, *12*, 36, 42, 54, 124
Domesday Book 45, 156, 157
Donnington Castle, Berkshire 57
'double-pile' house 100
Dover Castle 52
Dudley Castle 167
Dugdale, William 33
Dyserth Castle 46, 48, **50-52**, *50, 51*

Eastington manor, Rhoscrowther 63, **64-66**, *65*, 109
Edward I 19-20, 21, 22, 32, 44, 49, 51, 54, 55, 71, 87, 89, 127, 137, 152, 158, 173, 176
   building of new castles 21
Edward II 90, 92, 99, 114, 139, 163
Edward III 23, 139
Edward IV 92
Eisteddfod 9
Ewloe Castle 17, *18*, 42, 124

fief, definition 4-5
Fitzhamon, Robert 101, 104
fitz Herbert, Peter 79, 80
fitz John, Payne 95, 158
fitz Martin, Robert 175
   William 175
fitz Osbern, Roger 74, 84
   William 74, 84, 146
fitz Payne family 158
   Robert 158
   Roger 161
fitz Richard, Gilbert 9
fitz Unspac, Bernard 75
Fitzalans of Arundel 56
Flimston 62, 63, 109
Flint Castle 20, 77
Fonmon Castle 102
forest rights 152-154
Forester's Oaks 153
fortified houses 55, 59-63, 94, 118, 167, 170
   decay 62
   purpose for building 62-63
Francis, Eric 172
   George Grant 36

Gerald of Wales 14, 44, 52-53, 141, 175
Glamorgan, south 8
   Vale of 101-108
Glyndŵr, Owain 23, 24, 56, 60, 86, 92, 104, 139, 168, 176
Goodrich Castle 113
Gower peninsula 9, 29, 117, 132-133, 134
Grey, Lord, of Ruthin 24
Grosmont Castle 16, 96, 124

Grosvenor, Sir Thomas 58
Gruffudd ap Cynan 8, 53
Gruffudd ap Rhys 123, 125
Gruffudd of Powys 21, 22
Gwenllian ferch Llywelyn 21
Gwladys Du 80, 88, 98-99
Gwynedd 6, 15, 21-22, 41, 44, 45-46, 48
    House of 21, 46, 50
Gwynllŵg 22

Hackelutel, Walter 73-74
hardwicks 156
Harlech Castle 20, 24, 57
Haroldston 62
Hastings 7
Hawarden Castle 77, 174
Hay-on-Wye Castle 99, 174
Hen Gastell Castle **93-95**, *94*
Henry I 8-9, 60, 101, 135
Henry II 9, 10, 14
Henry III 16, 20, 46, 50, 79, 80, 91, 95, 105, 133, 146
Henry IV 24
Henry V 24
Henry VII 60, 118
Henry VIII 27, 28, 158, 171
Herbert family 25, 32, 99
Hereford, earls of 5
'hermit crab castle' 82
Herstmonceux Castle 25
heybote 153
Holt Castle 29, **54-58**, *55, 57, 58*
Homfray, Jeston 104
Hopton Castle, Shropshire 31
housbote 153
housing development 142
Hugh of Avranches, earl of Chester 45, 46
Humphreys family of Usk 176
hunting lodge 63, 86, 106, 151, 152, 167
Hywel ap Iorwerth 146

Iestyn ap Gwrgant 101, 110, 140
Ieuan ap Philip 26, 92
Iorwerth ap Owain 15, 54
Ireland, 'ten-pound towers' 62
Iron Age hillforts 50, 53, 82, 89, 120
Isabella, Queen 92

James of St George, Master 19
Joan of Acre 158
John, King 15, 79, 95, 98
Johnys, Sir Hugh 118
Jones, Theophilus 87, 100

Kemey family of Cefn Mably 158
    Rhys 158
Kenfig Castle 38, 108, **112-116**, *115, 116*
    town 114
Kingston Farm, near Pembroke 61, *61*, 62, 63
Kip, Johannes 33
Kirby Muxloe Castle 25

Kitchen, G.H. 172
knight's fee, definition 4
Knucklas Castle 174-175

Lamphey
    Bishop's Palace 62, 63, 69-70
Landimôr Castle, Gower **117-118**, *117, 118*
Laugharne, siege of 31
Laugharne Castle 37
Launceston Castle, Devon 13
le Sore family 104
    Peter 104
    Robert 104
Le Wafre family 98
Leland, John 28-29, 33, 56, 80, 86, 93, 104, 106, 107, 112, 151, 172, 175
Lestrange, John 46, 50
Lewys Glyn Cothi 92, 93
Llanbleddian Castle 34, 37, 167-168
Llancaiach Fawr mansion 172
Llanddew Castle 175
Llandough Castle 102
Llandrindod 92
Llanfair Discoed Castle 38, 156, **157-161**, *157, 159, 160, 161*
Llangybi Castle 20, 32, 38, *38*, 39, 154, **161-169**, *162, 164, 165, 166, 167*
Llangynwyd Castle 35, **119-121**, *119, 120*, 147, 164
Llanhilleth Castle 38; *see also* Taliorum, Castell
Llanquian Castle **106-107**, *106, 107*, 108
Llanstephan Castle 23, 139
Llanthony Priory 86
Llantrithyd 5
Llwyd, Edward 33, 142
Llywelyn ap Gruffudd 20-21, 42, 51, 71-72, 76, 82, 87, 91, 96, 99, 119, 123, 125, 126, 174, 175
Llywelyn ap Iorwerth, 'the Great' 15, 19, 20, 37, 42, 44, 48, 49, 54, 80, 84, 88, 92, 95, 98, 99, 146, 150, 175
Llywelyn Bren 22, 123
London, Tower of 52
Longtown Castle 16
Loughor Castle 8, 82
Louvre, Paris 16, *16*
Lulworth Castle, Dorset 29
Lydstep 62

Machen Castle, *see* Meredydd, Castell
Madog ap Iorwerth 42
Madog ap Llywelyn 22, 163
Madog ap Maredudd 9
Madryn Castle 53
Maelienydd 88, 90, 174
Maesglas Castle, Newport 37
Manorbier Castle 12, 36
Mansel, Hugh 139
    Sir Rice 139
Mansell, John 46
maps *5, 22*, 30, *40, 59*, 67, *145*
Marcher lords 5, 14, 21, 27, 54, 60, 72, 75, 95, 111, 163
Marcross **103-104**, 107

Maredudd ap Cynan 53
    ap Gruffudd 147
Margam 139
Marsh House, Aberthaw 107
Marshal family 162
    Gilbert 146
    William 16, *16*, 18, 160, 176
Meares family 66
Meldrum, Sir John 27, 30
Mellte Castle 38; *see also* Coch, Castell, Ystradfellte
Merrick, Rice 30, 101, 114-115, 132
Merthyr Mawr 109
Mertyr Tydfil 128
Miles of Gloucester, earl of Hereford 78, 174
military needs 23-24, 27
    artillery forts 27
    cannons 27
    gunpowder 27
Minwear 62
Mirehouse, John 66
Môn, Menter 173
Monknash 103
Monmouth Castle 12, 16, 30
Monmouthshire 145-172
Montacute, John, earl of Salisbury 158
Montgomery Castle 16, 18, 29, 32, 52, 96, 169
    Treaty of 21, 91
Morgan ap Caradog 140, 141
    ap Hywel 146, 147
    ap Maredudd 22, 127, 147
    Octavius 156
    Sir Thomas 30, 171
    William 172
Morgannwg 8, 110
Morganwg, Iolo 110
Morgraig Castle 35, 38, 56, **121-125**, *122*
Morlais Castle 38, 77, **125-131**, *126, 127, 128, 129, 130*, 147, 150
Mortimer family of Wigmore 80, 88-92, 168
    Edmund 72, 92
    Edmund IV 92
    Edward (King Edward IV) 92, 168
    Ralph I 88
    Ralph II 90, 99, 174
    Richard 92
    Roger 55, 66
    Roger II 91
    Roger III 88, 89-90, 92, 99
    Roger IV 90, 92, 99
Moynes Court 171
Myddleton family of Chirk 176
    Sir Thomas 33

Narberth Castle 29, 154
National Monument Record 35
Neath Abbey 103
Neath Castle *121*
Nerber Castle, *see* Llanquian
Nerber family 106
Nevern Castle 9, 175-176

Newcastle Emlyn Castle 29
Newhouse manor 38, **66-70**, *67, 69*
Newman, John 171
Newport Castle, Pembrokeshire 175
Newton House, Brecon 100
Nicholl, Sir John 109
Norden, John 57
Norman invasion 3, 4, 60, 71, 74, 98, 101, 135, 146
Nunney Castle 25, *25*, 167

Odiham Castle 52
Ogmore Castle 12
Old Wardour Castle, Wiltshire 25
Orford Castle, Suffolk 10, 13
Owain de la Pole 22
Owain Gwynedd 9, 15, 44, 53, 54
Owen, George of Henllys 30, 60
Oxwich Castle 29, 117, 139
Oystermouth Castle 36, 37, 117

Paincastle Castle 38, **95-97**, *96*
pannage 153
pele-tower 26, *26*, 59; *see also* tower-house
Pembroke Castle 16, 30, 36
Pembrokeshire 8
    castles 60
    fortified houses 59-63
Pen y Castell **53**, 54
Pen y Garn **53**, 54
Penally 62
Pencelli Castle 84, **97-100**, *97, 99, 100*
Pencoed Castle 29, 156, 169, **170-172**, *170, 171*
Penhow Castle 156
Penlle'r Castell **132-134**
Penmaen Castle 117
Penmark Castle 4, **102-103**, *103*, 107
Pennard Castle 117
Penpont church 87
Penrice Castle 23, 32, 117, **134-140**, *134, 136, 137, 138, 139*
Perfeddwlad (cantref) 46, 48, 51
Perks, Clifford 162
Perrot family 62, 65
Peterston-super-Ely Castle **104**, *104*, 107-108
Pevsner 65
Philipps family 65-66
Picton Castle 32, 66
picturesque ruins 169
Philip Augustus, King of France 16
plague 114
Plas Baglan 38, 94, **140-142**
Pole, Countess Margaret 158
Pontefract Castle 167
Portmeirion 53
Powell, Thomas 99
Powis Castle 29, 150
Powys 6, 15
Priestley, Stephen 162
Pyle 114

Radnor 9, 99
Raglan Castle 25-26, *25*, 32
Rennes, Normandy 7
Rhaeadr 9
Rhodri ap Gruffudd 22
Rhoose Castle 37, 107
Rhuddlan 8
    Castle 20, 45, 50, 51
Rhys ap Gruffudd, Lord, of Deheubarth 9, 14
    ap Maredudd 22, 126
    ap Tewdwr 8, 75, 101
    ap Thomas, Sir 29
    Lord 173
Rhys Fychan 132
Rhys Gryg of Deheubarth 135
Richard I 14
Richard III 118
Robert, earl of Gloucester 101, 113, 119
Robert of Rhuddlan 45
Roger of Montgomery 173
Roman period 54, 75, 82, 176
Royal Commission on Ancient and Historical Monuments in Wales (RCAHMW) 35, 39, 111, 125
Rumney Castle 37
Ruperra Castle 29, 30
Ruthin Castle 55, 176

St Davids, bishops 175
    Cathedral 8
    Palace 62
St Donats Castle 102
St Fagans Castle 29, 102, 169
St John family 103
St Pierre mansion 171
St Quintin family 105
    John 105
Sais, Einion 87
Scotland 26, 158
Scotsborough, near Tenby 62, 63, 64
Senghenydd 123
Shrewsbury 21
    Castle 154
    earls of 5
Siward, Richard 105
Skenfrith Castle 16, *17*, 96
Speed, John 30, 67
Stephen, King 9
Stokesay Castle, Shropshire 154, *155*, 160
Striguil 151
strong-house 59
Sully Castle 37, **142-144**, *143, 144*
Sully family, *see* de Sully
Surdwal, Hugh 75
surveys, *see under* castles
Swansea Castle 117

Talyvan Castle **104-106**, *105*, 108
Tattershall Castle 25
Thomas, David Alfred 172
Time Team *38*, 161, 163, 168
Tintern Abbey 152
Tomen Castell **54**
Tonbridge Castle, Kent 19
Tosny, *see* de Tosny
Totnes Castle, Devon 13
tower-house 26, *26*, 59, 60, 61, *61*, 64, 109, *109*, 110, 167; *see also* pele-tower
    and piracy 60
Tregrug Barn 169
    Castle, *see* Llangybi
Tretower Castle 16
Turner, Rick 162
Tythegston Court 110

Upper Lamphey Park 63
Usk Castle 12, 16, *17*, 160, 162, 163-164, 176

Vaughans of Tretower 26

Wakeman, Thomas 156
Wales, Prince of, title 20, 21
    territorial divisions *22*; *see also under* each name
Warkworth Castle 167
Wars of the Roses 24, 92, 168
Warwick Castle 167
Welsh Assembly 44
Welsh castles
    distinctive features 42
    early development 42
    new building by Edward I 21
    number 3
    signs that a castle is or is not Welsh 124-125, 149-150
Welsh princes 6, 8, 9, 14, 23, 42, 54, 71
Welshpool 22
Wentwood forest 152, 157, 170
Wenvoe 107
Weobley Castle, Gower 118
West Tarr Farm 61, *61*, 63
White Castle 13
Whittington Castle, Shropshire 124
Wigmore Castle 88, 89
William I (the Conqueror) 3, 5, 8, 74, 101
William of Gloucester 101
William Rufus 79
Williams, Roger of Usk 168
    Sir Trevor 168-169
Williams-Ellis, Sir Clough 53
Willoughby de Eresby, Lord 36
Wiston Castle 13
Wrinstone 107

y Bere, Castell 42, 44, 124
York Castle 10
Ystrad Tywi 22
Ystradfellte 81